Paul's Corporate Christophany

Paul's Corporate Christophany

An Evaluation of Paul's Christophanic References
in Their Epistolary Contexts

Rob A. Fringer

PICKWICK *Publications* · Eugene, Oregon

PAUL'S CORPORATE CHRISTOPHANY
An Evaluation of Paul's Christophanic References in Their Epistolary Contexts

Pickwick Publications
An Imprint of Wipf and Stock Publishers
199 W. 8th Ave., Suite 3
Eugene, OR 97401

www.wipfandstock.com

PAPERBACK ISBN: 978-1-5326-4528-0
HARDCOVER ISBN: 978-1-5326-4529-7
EBOOK ISBN: 978-1-5326-4530-3

Cataloguing-in-Publication data:

Names: Fringer, Rob A., author.

Title: Paul's corporate christophany : an evaluation of Paul's christophanic references in their epistolary contexts / Rob A. Fringer.

Description: Eugene, OR: Pickwick Publications, 2019. | Includes bibliographical references and index.

Identifiers: ISBN 978-1-5326-4528-0 (paperback). | ISBN 978-1-5326-4529-7 (hardcover). | ISBN 978-1-5326-4530-3 (ebook).

Subjects: LCSH: Paul—Apostle, Saint—Conversion. | Bible—Epistles of Paul—Theology.

Classification: BS2651 F78 2019 (print). | BS2651 (ebook).

Manufactured in the U.S.A.   02/20/19

In loving memory of my father,
Virgil Lee Fringer
(1935–2015)

Contents

Acknowledgments

THE CURRENT BOOK REPRESENTS a slight revision of my PhD Thesis, which was completed through the University of Manchester and carried out at Nazarene Theological College, Manchester. I want to give a special thanks to those who walked with me in my PhD journey and to Pickwick Publications for helping me bring it to its present book form.

First and foremost, I give thanks to God—Father, Son, and Holy Spirit. God's sustaining presence has enabled me to move forward in all areas of my life in both times of feast and times of famine.

I give thanks to my family for their constant love and support. My wife Vanessa has been a deep source of strength and encouragement, and she has sacrificed as much and more than I have over these years of study. My two children, Sierra and Brenden, have been a source of joy and motivation, extending love and patience.

My primary supervisor, Dr. Kent Brower, has challenged me intellectually, vocationally, and spiritually. I count him both a mentor and a friend. I thank God for Kent's example; he is one who evidences the ability to operate at the highest levels of academia while still being passionately involved in the local and global church and living out the grace and compassion of Christ to all. I am thankful for Dr. Dean Flemming, my secondary supervisor, who has exemplified these same characteristics and who has helped me immensely through his editorial comments and through conversation. I also want to thank my two examiners, Dr. Sarah Whittle and Prof. Markus Bockmuehl, for their time, commitment, and feedback, which made this work stronger.

I am grateful to multiple lecturers and fellow students who read or heard portions of my thesis and who have asked difficult questions and given helpful critiques along the way. While I cannot mention all of them here, I want to give a special thanks to Dr. James Romano and Dr. Jim Moretz who are among my closest friends. It has been a great pleasure to walk this journey with them and to challenge one another in our thinking and writing.

Finally, I am indebted to the following institutions and their leaders: Community Chapel Church of the Nazarene in Nashua, NH; Redlands Church of the Nazarene in Ormiston, QLD; Nazarene Theological College in Brisbane, Australia; Nazarene Theological College in Manchester, England; the University of Manchester; and Pickwick Publications.

Abbreviations

Primary Sources

1–4 Macc	*1–4 Maccabees*
1 En	*1 Enoch*
1QH	*Hodayot/Thanksgiving Hymns*
1QM	*Milhamah/War Scroll*
1QpHab	*Pesher Habakkuk*
1QS	*Serek Hayahad/Rule of the Community*
1QSa	*Rule of the Congregation*
2 Bar.	*2 Baruch (Syriac Apocalypse)*
4Q369	*Prayer of Enosh*
4Q374	*4QDiscourse on the Exodus/Conquest Tradition*
4Q377	*Apocryphal Pentateuch B*
4QFlor	*Florilegium/Midrash on Eschatologya (4Q174)*
4QMMT	*Miqṣat Maʿaśê ha-Torah*
4QpPsa	*Pesher Psalm 37*
11QMelch	*Melchizedek*
Abr.	*De Abrahamo* (Philo)
Ant.	*Antonius* (Plutarch)
As. Mos.	*Assumption of Moses*
Bar	Baruch
Inst.	*Institutio oratoria* (Quintilian)
Jos. Asen.	*Joseph and Aseneth*
Jub.	*Jubilees*

Jdt	Judith
L.A.B.	*Liber antiquitatum biblicarum* (Pseudo-Philo)
Mor.	*Moralia* (Plutarch)
Mos.	*De vita Mosis* (Philo)
Mut.	*De mutatione nominum* (Philo)
Pesiq. Rab	*Pesiqta Rabbati*
Pol. Phil	Polycarp, *To the Philippians*
Pss. Sol.	*Psalms of Solomon*
QE	*Quaestiones et solutions in Exodum* (Philo)
RomAnt	*Roman Antiquities* (Dionysius)
RomHist	*History of Rome* (Livy)
Sacr.	*De sacrificiis Abelis et Caini* (Philo)
S. Eli Rab.	*Seder Eliyahu Rabbah*
Sib. Or.	*Sibylline Oracles*
Sir	Sirach
Soph.	*In sophistas* (Isocrates)
Tg. Onq.	*Targum Onqelos*
T. Jud.	*Testament of Judah*
T. Levi	*Testament of Levi*
Tob	Tobit
Virt.	*De virtutibus* (Philo)
Wis	Wisdom of Solomon

Secondary Sources

AB	The Anchor Bible
ABR	*Australian Biblical Review*
ACNT	Augsburg Commentaries on the New Testament
AGJU	Arbeiten zur Geschichte des Antiken Judentums und des Urchristentums
AnBib	Analecta biblica
ANTC	Abingdon New Testament Commentaries
AP	*Aldersgate Papers*
AYBRL	Anchor Yale Bible
BBR	*Bulletin for Biblical Research*
BECNT	Baker Exegetical Commentary on the New Testament

BETL	Bibliotheca ephemeridum theologicarum lovaniensium
BEvT	Beiträge zur evangelischen Theologie
BHGNT	Baylor Handbook on the Greek New Testament
BHT	Beiträge zur historischen Theologie
Bib	*Biblica*
BibInt	*Biblical Interpretation*
BibRec	*Biblical Reception*
BIS	Biblical Interpretation Series
BJRL	*Bulletin of the John Rylands University Library of Manchester*
BNTC	Black's New Testament Commentaries
BRS	The Biblical Resource Series
BSac	*Bibliotheca sacra*
BTB	*Biblical Theology Bulletin*
BZ	*Biblische Zeitschrift*
BZAW	Beihefte zur Zeitschrift für die alttestamentliche Wissenschaft
BZNW	Beihefte zur Zeitschrift für die neutestamentliche Wissenschaft
CBQ	*Catholic Biblical Quarterly*
CBQMS	The Catholic Biblical Quarterly Monograph Series
CBR	*Currents in Biblical Research*
ConBNT	Coniectanea biblica: New Testament Series
COQG	Christian Origins and the Question of God
CTaM	*Crucible: Theology and Mission*
DSD	*Dead Sea Discoveries*
ECCA	Early Christianity in the Context of Antiquity
EDNT	*Exegetical Dictionary of the New Testament*
ESEC	Emory Studies in Early Christianity
ETL	*Ephemerides theologicae lovanienses*
ExpTim	*Expository Times*
FRLANT	Forschungen zur Religion und Literatur des Alten und Neuen Testaments
GBS	Guides to Biblical Scholarship
GCT	Gender, Culture and Theology
GHAT	Göttinger Handkommentar zum Alten Testament
GNS	*Good News Studies*
HCOT	Historical Commentary on the Old Testament

HNT	Handbuch zum Neuen Testament
HNTC	Harper's New Testament Commentaries
HTR	*Harvard Theological Review*
IBC	Interpretation: A Bible Commentary for Teaching and Preaching
ICC	The International Critical Commentary
JBL	*Journal of Biblical Literature*
JBQ	*Jewish Bible Quarterly*
JETS	*Journal of the Evangelical Theological Society*
JHC	*Journal of Higher Criticism*
JSNT	*Journal for the Study of the New Testament*
JSNTSup	Journal for the Study of the New Testament: Supplement Series
JSOT	*Journal for the Study of the Old Testament*
JSOTSup	Journal for the Study of the Old Testament Supplement Series
JSP	*Journal for the Study of the Pseudepigrapha*
JTS	*Journal of Theological Studies*
KEK	Kritisch-exegetischer Kommentar über das Neue Testament (Meyer-Kommentar)
LCL	Loeb Classical Library
LEC	Library of Early Christianity
LNTS	Library of New Testament Studies
LPS	Library of Pauline Studies
NAB	New American Commentary
NBBC	New Beacon Bible Commentary
NCB	New Century Bible
NCBC	New Cambridge Bible Commentary
NEzT	Neutestamentliche Entwürfe zur Theologie
NIB	*The New Interpreter's Bible*
NIBCNT	New International Biblical Commentary on the New Testament
NIBCOT	New International Biblical Commentary on the Old Testament
NICNT	The New International Commentary of the New Testament
NICOT	The New International Commentary of the Old Testament
NIDNTT	*New International Dictionary of New Testament Theology*

NIGTC	The New International Greek Testament Commentary
NIVAC	The NIV Application Commentary
NovT	*Novum Testamentum*
NovTSup	Supplements to Novum Testamentum
NSBT	New Studies in Biblical Theology
NTL	New Testament Library
NTS	*New Testament Studies*
NTSI	The New Testament and the Scriptures of Israel
NTT	New Testament Theology
OTL	Old Testament Library
PBM	Paternoster Biblical Monographs
PCNT	Paideia: Commentaries on the New Testament
PCS	Pentecostal Commentary Series
PNTC	The Pillar New Testament Commentary
PRSt	*Perspectives in Religious Studies*
RB	*Revue biblique*
RNBC	Readings: A New Biblical Commentary
RRev	*Rhetoric Review*
RSR	*Recherches de science religieuse*
RTNT	Reading the New Testament
SacPag	Sacra Pagina
SANT	Studien zum Alten und Neuen Testament
SBLDS	Society of Biblical Literature Dissertation Series
SBLMS	Society of Biblical Literature Monograph Series
SBLSymS	Society of Biblical Literature Symposium Series
SBT	Studies in Biblical Theology
SHBC	Smyth & Helwys Bible Commentary
SNTSMS	Society for New Testament Studies Monograph Series
SNTW	Studies of the New Testament and its World
SP	Sacra Pagina
ST	*Studia theologica*
StBL	Studies in Biblical Literature
STDJ	*Studies on the Texts of the Desert of Judah*
STJ	Scottish Journal of Theology
SwJT	*Southwestern Journal of Theology*
TANZ	Texte und Arbeiten zum neutestamentlichen Zeitalter

TBNJCT	*Themes in Biblical Narrative Jewish and Christian Traditions*
TDNT	*Theological Dictionary of the New Testament.*
THKNT	Theologischer Handkommentar zum Neuen Testament
THNTC	The Two Horizons New Testament Commentary
TJ	*Trinity Journal*
TNTC	Tyndale New Testament Commentaries
TynBul	*Tyndale Bulletin*
VEE	*Verbum Et Ecclesia*
VT	*Vetus Testamentum*
VTP	Veteris Testamenti Pseudepigrapha
WBC	Word Biblical Commentary
WTJ	*Westminster Theological Journal*
WUNT	Wissenschaftliche Untersuchungen zum Neuen Testament
ZAW	*Zeitschrift für die alttestamentliche Wissenschaft*
ZECNT	Zondervan Exegetical Commentary on the New Testament
ZNW	*Zeitschrift für die neutestamentliche Wissenschaft und die Kunde der älteren Kirche*
ZTK	*Zeitschrift für Theologie und Kirche*
ZWB	*Zürcher Werkkommentare zur Bibel*

Other

CCAA	Corinthian Challenge and Apostolic Apologia
CEV	Contemporary English Version
DRE	Damascus Road Experience
DSS	Dead Sea Scrolls
DSSSE	*The Dead Sea Scrolls Study Edition*
ESV	English Standard Version
fpp	First Person Plural/s
HCSB	Holman Christian Standard Bible
ISV	International Standard Version
KJV	King James Version
LEB	Lexham English Bible
LXX	Septuagint
MMT	Maccabean Martyr Theology
MT	Masoretic Text

NA28	Nestle-Aland Greek New Testament, 28th edition
NASB	New American Standard Bible
NETS	New English Translation of the Septuagint
NIV	New International Version
NKJV	New King James Version
NRSV	New Revised Standard Version
NT	New Testament
OT	Old Testament
RSV	Revised Standard Version
STJL	Second Temple Jewish Literature

1

Introduction

ANY STUDENT OF THE Apostle Paul and his letters will eventually engage, no matter how shallowly, with the subject of his "Damascus Road Experience" (DRE). As one does, a multitude of questions will quickly surface. The difficulty in answering any such questions is quickly deduced as one surveys the copious pages of literature on the subject and comes to recognize there is much more said about this event than is actually known. The legendary status of Paul's DRE is as much fabricated as it is factual. Much of what is reconstructed comes from the three accounts in Acts (9:1–19; 22:1–21; 26:4–18) and not directly from the Pauline epistles. This is not a statement about the historicity of one or the other.[1] Each writer employs these references for particular purposes unique to his various situations and audiences.[2]

This book will not evaluate Luke's accounts in Acts or compare and contrast them to Paul's own references.[3] It is enough to acknowledge that both authors write about an event in Paul's life where Christ is manifested, in some form, to Paul. Thus, this event can be called a Christophany (Χριστός + φανερόω). Since this work relies exclusively on Paul's accounts of this event, it will employ the language of "Christophany" and its cognates rather than DRE, even where others refer to this event with DRE language.

---

1. See Thompson, "Paul in the Book of Acts," 425–36; Porter, *Paul in Acts*; Jervell, *The Unknown Paul*, 68–76. Contra Vielhauer, "On the 'Paulinism' of Acts," 33–50; Phillips, *Paul, His Letters, and Acts*.

2. See esp. Gaventa, *From Darkness to Light*.

3. So Kim, *Origin of Paul's Gospel*, 28–31; Dietzfelbinger, *Die Berufung des Paulus*, 43–89; Fredriksen, "Paul and Augustine," 3–34; Barrett, *Acts of the Apostle*, vol. 1, 437–45; Hengel and Schwemer, *Paul between Damascus and Antioch*, 38–43; Wright, *Resurrection of the Son of God*, 388–98; Churchill, *Divine Initiative and Christology*, 98–249; Keener, *Acts*, Vol. 2, 1597–697.

A Review of the Relevant Literature

The literature addressing Paul's Christophanic references can be broadly grouped into three approaches: (1) those seeking to reconstruct that which precipitated the event, the specifics of the event itself, or the particularities of Paul's subsequent mission to the Gentiles; (2) those seeking to discover the foundations for Paul's Christology and/or to reconstruct Paul's Christology; and (3) those focusing on conversion and/or call in general.[4] These broad categories overlap both in content and in scholarship. Therefore, those scholars who are most relevant to the discussion are highlighted showing their foci, methodologies, strengths, and weaknesses. This is followed by a brief comparison of these works and concluded with explanation of how the current study both differs from and augments these works.

Seyoon Kim

Seyoon Kim's published doctoral thesis is perhaps the most ambitious attempt to locate not only Paul's apostleship, but moreover, the whole of Paul's gospel within his Christophany.[5] Against the scholarly tide of his day, which effectively dismissed Paul's Christophany arguing Paul spoke "surprisingly seldom"[6] about it, Kim insists that references and allusions to this event abound in the Pauline corpus.[7] Conflating the Pauline accounts and Acts, Kim seeks a historical re/construction[8] of the event from whence to derive and subsequently construct Paul's Christology and soteriology. He begins by denying any psychological pre-conversion preparation saying, "[Paul] was rather satisfied with his achievement in Judaism."[9] Kim argues adamantly for an "objective, external event" wherein "Christ appeared to Paul

---

4. These studies often use a sociological or psychological methodology, which is not the focus of this study.

5. Kim, *Origin of Paul's Gospel*, 31, 99, 334–35. Kim does allow for a greater span of time for development of Paul's Christology while still arguing it is grounded in his Christophany in: Kim, *Paul and the New Perspective*, 14.

6. Bornkamm, *Paul*, 16; so also Wilckens, "Die Bekehrung des Paulus," 11–32.

7. Kim, *Origin of Paul's Gospel*, 3–31. For Kim, this includes both undisputed and disputed Pauline letters.

8. The use of "re/construct" is meant to illustrate that these various attempts to reconstruct Paul's Christophany are usually better understood as construction by these later interpreters, which may or may not be accurate. Cf. Nanos, *The Galatians Debate*, xii n1.

9. Kim, *Origin of Paul's Gospel*, 54.

accompanied by the radiance of glory (2 Cor 4.6; Acts 9.3; 22.6; 26.13)"[10]
and whereby Paul was both converted and commissioned. The physical act
of seeing God's glory stands at the center of Kim's thesis, which relies heavily
on 2 Cor 3:4—4:6. Kim believes Paul saw Christ as the εἰκὼν τοῦ θεοῦ (2 Cor
4:4; Col 1:15), a concept nearly synonymous with Christ as the Son of God
(Gal 1:16)—"Paul saw the risen Christ as the Son of God and as the Image of
God at the same time, namely at the Damascus Christophany."[11] This εἰκών-
Christology,[12] as Kim calls it, forms the basis for Paul's Wisdom-Christology
and Adam-Christology. From the former derives Paul's understanding of
Christ as pre-existent (divine), as agent of divine revelation and salvation,
and as one who supersedes the Torah.[13] From the latter derives his understanding of the humanity of Christ, as the one who restores the divine glory
enabling believers to be justified in Christ and thus bear the image and glory
of Christ as part of the new creation.[14]

Kim's work has several strengths. It takes seriously Paul's Christophany
as a major source of Paul's gospel. In so doing, it also attempts to show Paul
as a shaper rather than an inheritor of early church theology. However,
Kim's attempt to explain the complexities of Paul's Christology and soteriology as solely rooted in his Christophany is not convincing.[15] If he is wrong
about 2 Cor 3:4—4:6, either about it being a Christophanic reference or
about it giving concrete descriptions concerning this event, then his thesis is seriously weakened. Moreover, his overconfidence in 2 Cor 3:4—4:6,
read in consultation with the Acts accounts, and through the lens of various throne-theophany visions (e.g., Dan 7; Ezek 1),[16] is too dependent on
strained philological connections. In his attempt to re/construct the historical foundations of Paul's thought and then to explicate his Christology
and soteriology, Kim often ignores the literary contexts of Paul's various
Christophanic references.

---

10. Kim, *Origin of Paul's Gospel*, 56.

11. Kim, *Origin of Paul's Gospel*, 257.

12. Kim, *Origin of Paul's Gospel*, 104–257.

13. Kim, *Origin of Paul's Gospel*, 258–60.

14. Kim, *Origin of Paul's Gospel*, 260–68.

15. Kim, *Paul and the New Perspective*, 213, 296, slightly alters his initial thesis.

16. Kim, *Origin of Paul's Gospel*, 205–52; Kim, *Paul and the New Perspective*,
194–208, where Kim stresses the importance of understanding Paul's Christophany as
a *merkabah* vision.

James D. G. Dunn

James Dunn has not written a full monograph on Paul's Christophany but has published many essays around this topic and has addressed it in appropriate sections of his various commentaries and books. His writings on the subject span decades and evidence minor shifts in thinking on the matter.[17] Like Kim, Dunn's work in mostly an attempt at historical re/construction. Unlike Kim, Dunn focuses more on the aftermath of this experience than on the event itself. In regard to what Paul actually "saw" in the Christophany, Dunn concludes "[t]he only answer that Paul allows us to give is 'Jesus'";[18] beyond this Paul gives no further information, most likely because there is no further information to give. In Dunn's reading of 2 Cor 4:4, 6, which he believes is a Christophanic reference, Paul's seeing of Jesus was likely in the form of a physical "blinding light," which for Paul was "the visible manifestation of God . . . it was all that could be seen by the human eye of the risen Jesus."[19] In critique of Kim, Dunn warns that 2 Cor 4:4, 6 speaks of "the impact of the event on Paul rather than a description of the event itself."[20]

Dunn stresses calling over conversion[21] and argues that from the beginning "God's purpose in revealing his Son in Paul (that is, on the Damascus road) was to commission Paul as apostle to the Gentiles."[22] This point is made clear in Paul's writings (esp. Gal 1:15–16) and confirmed in the Acts accounts (esp. 26:13–18). Furthermore, it is not necessarily an auditory appeal[23] (or command), but a derivative of Paul's first-hand experience

---

17. Kim, *Paul and the New Perspective*, 1–84, accuses Dunn of multiple "self-contradictions." On some of these points, Kim's argument is valid (esp. 14–15). However, most of Dunn's so-called contradictions can be explained as slight shifts in thinking, mostly as a result of addressing different aspects of Paul's Christophany. Dunn's constant element remains the focus on Paul's calling to the Gentiles. Kim's frustrations are mostly targeted at Dunn's disagreements with Kim's work and at Dunn's "New Perspective" reading. Kim's critique is not entirely fair, since Dunn's treatment of the Christophany is usually incidental within a larger discussion.

18. Dunn, *Jesus and the Spirit*, 106.

19. Dunn, *Jesus and the Spirit*, 107; cf. Dunn, *Theology of Paul*, 290.

20. Dunn, *Jesus, Paul and the Law*, 95.

21. Dunn does not shy away from the language of conversion in relation to this experience but usually still means "commission." See esp. Dunn, *Jesus and the Spirit*, 97–114; Dunn, "Paul and Justification," 86–87.

He does speak of conversion in the traditional sense in: Dunn, *New Perspective on Paul*, 357–64; and Dunn, *Theology of Paul*, 178–79, 346–53, where he argues that it is not a conversion away from his Jewish faith but a conversion from Pharisaic Judaism and from the "zealot" tradition of Phinehas and the Maccabees.

22. Dunn, *Jesus, Paul and the Law*, 89, also 99–100.

23. Dunn, *Jesus, Paul and the Law*, 102 n. 8; cf. Dunn, *Spirit*, 113–14.

with the cursed Christ (Deut 21:23; cf. Gal 3:13).[24] Paul came to understand God had "accepted and vindicated this one precisely as the crucified" and this meant "God must therefore favour the cursed one, the sinner outside the covenant, the Gentile."[25] This revelation transformed Paul's identity, his self-understanding as a Jew.[26]

In his earlier works, Dunn makes a clear distinction between Paul's commission, which was the "chief content" of the Christophany, and Paul's Christology and soteriology, i.e., the content of his gospel.[27] Dunn argues it is from this calling that Paul eventually formed his understanding of the antithesis between the law and Christ,[28] and the related issue of God's righteousness vis-à-vis one's own righteousness, mostly as a result of the Antioch incident (Gal 2:11–21).[29] This view slightly shifts in Dunn's later works where he writes: "It would be more accurate to say that the principle [Gal 2:16] was implicit in the 'revelation' made to him on the Damascus road."[30] Likewise, of Paul's gospel, Dunn later writes: "But however Paul achieved the conscious expression of his gospel, the point for us to note is that in Paul's mind the gospel was already contained within that appearance outside Damascus; his gospel was simply an 'unpacking' of 'the revelation of Jesus Christ.'"[31] In regard to Christology, Dunn supports an Adam-Christology[32] based on Paul's εἰκών language in 2 Cor 4:4, 6, which may be traced back to his Christophany, but argues Paul's Wisdom-Christology would have taken longer to develop.[33]

One of the greatest strengths of Dunn's work is his recognition of the limitations of Paul's Christophanic references in providing the exact details of this event. While seeing the Christophany as a "fulcrum point" of Paul's life and theology,[34] he, nevertheless, is cautious about attributing specifics to this experience. Dunn places a higher value than does

---

24. Dunn, *Jesus, Paul and the Law*, 99–100. Dunn, *New Perspective on Paul*, 351–53, slightly amends this position.

25. Dunn, *Jesus, Paul and the Law*, 100.

26. Dunn, *Jesus, Paul and the Law*, 99; Dunn, "Paul and Justification," 86.

27. Dunn, *Jesus, Paul and the Law*, 90–92.

28. Similarly, Räisänen, "Paul's Conversion," 404–19.

29. Dunn, *Jesus, Paul and the Law*, 98–99; 162–63; Dunn, "Paul and Justification," 99.

30. Dunn, "Paul and Justification," 99; cf. Dunn, *New Perspective on Paul*, 356.

31. Dunn, *Jesus and the Spirit*, 111, cf. 108; cf. Dunn, *Theology of Paul*, 179.

32. For fuller discussion see, Dunn, *Christology in the Making*, 98–128; Dunn, *Theology of Paul*, 90–101.

33. Dunn, *Jesus, Paul and the Law*, 97–98; Dunn, *Theology of Paul*, 267–77, 290; Dunn, *Christology in the Making*, 176–94.

34. Dunn, *Theology of Paul*, 722–29.

Kim on Paul's pre-conversion knowledge, which derives from his Jewish background, and how this comes to shape his understanding of the Christophany. Rather than stressing the singular source of Paul's thought and its immediacy in this single event, Dunn allows for extended contemplation on Paul's part and takes seriously various other sources for Paul's thought, including his Jewish upbringing, Jewish literature,[35] and the Jesus tradition[36] handed down to him from the other apostles (Gal 1:18;[37] cf. 1 Cor 15:3). Finally, Dunn's exegesis of the various references, especially Gal 1, better engages the literary and historic contexts in which they are found. Nevertheless, Dunn's work focuses on his "New Perspective" reading, for which the topic of Paul's Christophany is largely tangential. Therefore, several questions remain unanswered.

Timothy Churchill

Timothy Churchill's published thesis[38] is the latest attempt to explore Paul's Christophany in order to define his Christology. Churchill acknowledges the broad similarities between his work and Kim's with two main distinctions.[39] First, Churchill says he is more concerned with the event itself than with the outcome of this event. To some extent, this is a splitting of hairs as both Churchill and Kim seek to re/construct Paul's Christology. While Kim's approach is to understand how Paul's Christology (and soteriology) derives from his Christophany and the particular details therein, Churchill's approach is more literary; he seeks to read the Christophany within the genre of ancient Jewish epiphanies. Based on Churchill's understanding of how this literary genre functions, the Christophany (or epiphany) itself reveals the Christology. Second, while both Churchill and Kim include the accounts of Paul and Acts, Churchill evaluates these two separately, allowing them their own voices before comparing and contrasting the results, whereas Kim merges the two.

Churchill evaluates a selection of Jewish Epiphany narratives from the OT, Apocrypha, OT Pseudepigrapha, DSS, Philo, Josephus, and Rabbinic writings. Besides defining the basic narrative structure (introduction,

---

35. Dunn, *Theology of Paul*, 716–22.

36. Dunn, *New Perspective on Paul*, 352.

37. Dunn, *Jesus, Paul and the Law*, 108–28.

38. Churchill, *Divine Initiative and Christology*.

39. Churchill, *Divine Initiative and Christology*, 7. Two additional differences are Churchill's evaluation of only undisputed Pauline letter references and his move beyond only an evaluation of Christological titles in his construction of Paul's Christology.

appearance, message, departure, and conclusion[40]), he also categorizes these various epiphanies into two broad patterns and two characterization types. The two categories are 1) Divine Initiative epiphanies: "those involving the appearance of heavenly beings without the prior knowledge or expectation of their human counterparts, in order to deliver a message or perform an action that is entirely unanticipated" and 2) Divine Response epiphanies: "those involving the appearance of heavenly beings in response to a human request for a vision or appearance, or in answer to a human question or desire for knowledge."[41] The two characterization types are Type-I, which depict God in "angelomorphic or anthropomorphic forms," and Type-II, which depict God "in neither human nor angelic form."[42]

Churchill's evaluation of the undisputed Pauline Christophanic references is in general agreement with Kim's. However, Churchill argues 2 Cor 3:4—4:6 is not a Christophanic reference but "involves pre-Pauline creation-incarnation imagery" and if it is a reference to an actual vision, then it is more likely speaking of 2 Cor 12:1–4.[43] His analysis of Paul's accounts under the genre of epiphany narrative is strained as he himself admits they are *not* presented in narrative form and are missing common structural elements.[44] His solution is the amalgamation of the various references with greatest reliance on Gal 1. Churchill is forced to "construct a comprehensive narrative summary of the event."[45] The main elements of Churchill's construction are as follows:

1. *Introduction* (usually includes summary title and setting[46])—Churchill believes that Gal 1:11–12—"the gospel preached by me is . . . by the revelation of Jesus Christ"—serves as Paul's given title for his epiphany narrative. Concerning setting, Churchill argues that Paul does not give these details, because they are insignificant. Instead, his past life and past identity function as the setting.[47]

2. *Appearance* (usually includes transition from introduction, identity of epiphanic figure, and imagery of revelation and sight)—Churchill argues that the transition is abrupt, showing the appearance was an

40. Churchill, *Divine Initiative and Christology*, 36–41.

41. Churchill, *Divine Initiative and Christology*, 41.

42. Churchill, *Divine Initiative and Christology*, 88.

43. Churchill, *Divine Initiative and Christology*, 252, for full argument see 130–35.

44. Churchill, *Divine Initiative and Christology*, 149

45. Churchill, *Divine Initiative and Christology*, 150.

46. Bracketed descriptions are taken from Churchill, *Divine Initiative and Christology*, 37–38.

47. Churchill, *Divine Initiative and Christology*, 150–51.

"unexpected interruption in Paul's life, which occurred at the time of God's choosing."[48] Jesus is clearly identified as the epiphanic figure, although with a variety of terms. Paul's references to revelation (Gal 1:12, 16) and seeing (1 Cor 9:1; 15:8) are clear. Churchill believes that this event was likely both an external encounter and a vision.[49]

3. *Message* (usually includes central message either by words, actions, or images, recipient's reaction, recipient's questions and epiphanic figure's response)—Paul does not give the direct words or actions of Jesus, nor does he tell of his immediate reaction or response. Churchill argues that the content of the message is clearly and consistently seen in many of Paul's Christophanic references: "first, that Jesus called Paul to be his messenger; second, that Jesus gave Paul his message, the gospel; third, that Jesus gave Paul his audience, the Gentile nation."[50]

4. *Departure* (this element is often omitted; when included it describes departure and gives recipient's response)—This element is omitted in Paul's retellings.

5. *Conclusion* (usually resolves the epiphany by stating the effects on the recipient)—While there is little information given by way of conclusion, Churchill sees Gal 1:16–17 (Paul's going to Damascus and Arabia and not to Jerusalem) as serving this function.[51]

Churchill then evaluates the category and type of Paul's epiphanic narrative. Churchill sees little evidence that Paul initiated this encounter, either by way of an internal struggle or by external actions or words. Therefore, it is categorized as a Divine Initiative epiphany. Furthermore, because it was an unexpected event which Paul did not initiate, Churchill argues that it cannot be taken as a *merkabah*-like experience.[52] With regard to type, Churchill evaluates the direct and indirect characterizations of Jesus given by Paul in his Christophanic references. He concludes that Paul presents Jesus as having a "unique relationship to God the Father, and as divine."[53] However, this is atypical of both Type-I and Type-II categories of characterization. "This represents a significant innovation from other ancient Jewish epiphanies, since the characterization of a human in divine form either breaches the boundary between God and other beings, or implies a presumption of

48. Churchill, *Divine Initiative and Christology*, 151.

49. Churchill, *Divine Initiative and Christology*, 152.

50. Churchill, *Divine Initiative and Christology*, 153.

51. Churchill, *Divine Initiative and Christology*, 154.

52. Churchill, *Divine Initiative and Christology*, 154–65.

53. Churchill, *Divine Initiative and Christology*, 186.

Jesus's pre-existence."[54] The last section of Churchill's work evaluates the accounts in Acts and comes to the same conclusions concerning category and type. Furthermore, Churchill argues Acts also recounts the same basic message about Paul's calling to the Gentiles and presents the same picture of Jesus as being in a unique relationship with God and as divine.[55]

Churchill's work has several strengths. First, its approach offers the potential for bringing greater clarity to Paul's Christophany while avoiding reliance on minute details for the re/construction of Christology. Churchill's findings are cautious and measured. Second, he is not primarily concerned with historical re/construction of the event and attempts to take seriously the literature and its context. Churchill's analysis is strongest when evaluating the many Jewish epiphanies and the Acts accounts, which fall within the broader genre of narrative. But Churchill's melding of the various Pauline Christophanic references in order to form his own narrative epiphany exposes the weaknesses of his chosen methodology.

Beverly Roberts Gaventa

Beverly Roberts Gaventa has done extensive work on the subject of Paul's Christophany. Her unpublished PhD dissertation[56] is her most comprehensive treatment[57] and investigates the full scope of Paul's experience including cause, event, and result, through a comprehensive literary evaluation of Paul's accounts apart from Acts.[58] Her evaluation includes Gal 1:11–17; 1 Cor 9:1–2; 15:8–10; 2 Cor 4:6; 12:1–4; Phil 3:2–11; and Rom 7. Through this evaluation, she dismisses 2 Cor 4:6; 12:1–4; and Rom 7 arguing they do not directly pertain to Paul's Christophany.[59] Of the remaining references, Gaventa finds little information which would enable a re/construction of the cause or the event itself, believing such an attempt would be "fruitless."[60]

---

54. Churchill, *Divine Initiative and Christology*, 254. Churchill doesn't believe the Christophanic references evidence a belief in the pre-existence of Christ, but does see this belief in other sections of Paul's letters.

55. Churchill, *Divine Initiative and Christology*, 191–249.

56. Gaventa, "Paul's Conversion."

57. See also Gaventa, *From Darkness to Light*, 17–51, which is mostly a reduction of chapter 3 of Gaventa's dissertation. This work will be referenced when it differs from Gaventa's earlier work or when its addition is significant.

58. Gaventa, "Paul's Conversion," 113, notes this omission is largely based on space. However, in *From Darkness to Light* she devotes the largest portion of her attention to Acts (52–129), treating it separately from Paul's letters.

59. Gaventa, "Paul's Conversion," 186–88, 190–92, 336–37.

60. Gaventa, "Paul's Conversion," 281.

From 1 Cor 9:1–2 and 15:8–10, she concludes this event was "a call to apostolic office," which included the preaching of the gospel to the Gentiles, and "a call from unworthiness to faithfulness."[61] These points are confirmed and augmented in the final two references, which Gaventa believes are the most significant in understanding Paul's conversion. Galatians 1:11–17 adds an understanding of this call as aligning with the OT prophets[62] and together with Phil 3:2–11 the following is deduced:

> (1) While Paul speaks of his past, he does so with neither guilt nor remorse; (2) he characterizes the change which took place in his life as one of cognition; (3) the identity of the Messiah was central to this change in Paul's understanding; and (4) Paul implicitly connects his own personal change in understanding with the cosmic change which has come about in the Christ-event and draws upon both in order to persuade his audiences that they must also change their own perceptions.[63]

Gaventa's reference to Paul's conversion as a cognitive shift is easily misconstrued. Here, it appears Gaventa is making a distinction between conversion and call[64] as she goes on to articulate Paul's self-understanding as one who continued to stand within the traditions of his Jewish heritage. In explanation, Gaventa writes: "Paul underwent a radical change in his understanding of what made his own life worthwhile."[65] However, in a later article, Gaventa appears to alter or at least supplement her views on what took place. She writes: "Paul does not construct his theology out of the content or experience of his conversion. Indeed, the reverse is true. It is Paul's understanding of the gospel that brings about a re-construction or re-imagining of his past."[66] These words give the impression that the event itself could have been largely imagination.

A further conclusion is reached regarding the purpose of Paul's Christophanic references within their literary context. Gaventa argues Paul includes these references "for the purpose of theological persuasion, and in each case the goal of that persuasion is to encourage Christians to imitate Paul

---

61. Gaventa, "Paul's Conversion," 194.

62. Gaventa, "Paul's Conversion," 236.

63. Gaventa, "Paul's Conversion," 341.

64. Gaventa concludes that neither word is adequate and that this event combines elements of both conversion and call (Gaventa, "Paul's Conversion," 353–54; Gaventa, *From Darkness to Light*, 40).

65. Gaventa, "Paul's Conversion," 344.

66. Gaventa, "Galatians 1 and 2," 313.

himself."[67] This is an intriguing proposal that needs to be fleshed out further in Gaventa's exegetical analysis, which only includes a few passing mentions of this idea.[68] Furthermore, in *From Darkness to Light*, this aspect is almost completely absent,[69] which is unfortunate as Gaventa devotes a section to "The Transformation of Believers,"[70] which would have benefited from a discussion on imitation. One notable exception to this lacuna comes in an article on Galatians[71] where Gaventa articulates the dangers of reading Gal 1–2 merely for historical re/construction[72] and as a result viewing these chapters as having a distinct purpose and focus from the rest of the epistle.[73]

In Galatians as a whole, Gaventa proposes, Paul has constructed his autobiographical narrative as a "biography of reversal" whereby he "juxtaposes his former way of life with his response to revelation."[74] In Gal 3, Paul transitions from his situation to the Galatians' as he invites them to "reflect on their own experience of the gospel,"[75] which culminates in what Gaventa believes is a call to imitation in 4:12.[76] This argument has merit but will require further substantiating if it is to have wider scholarly acceptance.

Gaventa's work, which is ultimately an attempt at historical re/construction of the cause, event, and the result of Paul's Christophany, is safeguarded by her literary methodology. In the end, she contributes little to historical re/construction, and her work is stronger for it. Her grounding of the various references in their literary context positions her to answer the more accessible, and arguably, more significant, question of why Paul included these references in their particular socio-historical and literary contexts. In so doing, she is able to postulate a paradigmatic purpose behind Paul's use of these references, especially in relation to Galatians. However, because her focus has largely been on a historical re/construction of Paul's Christophany, Galatians being the exception, Gaventa's conclusions concerning the literary purpose have been tangential and as a result have not received the attention due them.

67. Gaventa, "Paul's Conversion," 346.

68. Gaventa, "Paul's Conversion," 129, 166, 245, 280.

69. Gaventa, *From Darkness to Light*, 33, does have one statement related to imitation.

70. Gaventa, *From Darkness to Light*, 40–46.

71. Gaventa, "Galatians 1 and 2," 309–26.

72. Gaventa, "Galatians 1 and 2," 311–13.

73. For her singular theological reading see, Gaventa, "Singularity of the Gospel," 147–59.

74. Gaventa, "Galatians 1 and 2," 315.

75. Gaventa, "Galatians 1 and 2," 318–19.

76. Gaventa, "Galatians 1 and 2," 321–22.

Paula Fredriksen

Paula Fredriksen has done limited work on Paul's Christophany, mainly because she views it as relatively unimportant in understanding Paul who makes "brief" and "infrequent" references to this experience.[77] Her only substantial engagement on the subject comes in one article.[78] Nevertheless, the challenges she raises must be addressed by those seeking a historical re/construction of Paul's Christophany and its impact. Fredriksen's historical evaluation is cautious, arguing the historian is unable to know "[w]hat *actually* happened, what the convert actually thought or experienced at the time of his conversion."[79] Instead, Fredriksen seeks to free Paul from multiple anachronistic readings. Primarily, she is convinced that most of the work done on Paul's Christophany is built upon either intentional or "back door" readings of Acts. Of particular disturbance to Fredriksen is "[n]ot the narrative details of Luke's portrayal, but the situation it presupposes of two clearly perceived and sharply contrasting religious options,"[80] namely, between Judaism and Christianity.[81]

Once the Lukan influence is removed, Fredriksen argues, there is very little concrete detail concerning the Christophany itself. First, it should not be designated a conversion. Instead, Paul speaks of this event in terms of a prophetic call similar to those found in Isaiah and Jeremiah and fully within acceptable and known Jewish boundaries.[82] Second, Paul "did indeed experience a radical change in his religious consciousness,"[83] which for Fredriksen was probably an internal or intellectual struggle after having been introduced to the early Jesus movement through a Jewish community in Damascus.[84] Therein, Paul became convinced Jesus was God's son and/or the messiah and he should stop persecuting these Jewish Christ-followers[85] and begin preach-

77. Fredriksen, "Paul and Augustine," 15 and n. 38.

78. Although see, Fredriksen, "Judaism, the Circumcision of Gentiles," 533–64; Fredriksen, *From Jesus to Christ*, 52–61, 133–76.

79. Fredriksen, "Paul and Augustine," 34, emphasis hers.

80. Fredriksen, "Paul and Augustine," 5.

81. This is an area of significant interest for Fredriksen. E.g., Fredriksen, "The Birth of Christianity," 8–30; Fredriksen, "What 'Parting of the Ways'?," 35–63.

82. Fredriksen, "Paul and Augustine," 15–17, 30.

83. Fredriksen, "Paul and Augustine," 16.

84. Fredriksen's stance on the historicity of this event is unclear. Using Paul's language, she sometimes speaks of a revelation of Jesus Christ (*From Jesus to Christ*, 52, 154, 174) but speaks more often of his interaction with Jewish Christians in Damascus, which she believes to have been his home base (so "Paul and Augustine," 9–14; *From Jesus to Christ*, 55, 154–57).

85. For Fredriksen's view of Paul's persecution see "Judaism," 548–58; Fredriksen,

ing this Christ and his imminent return to the Gentiles.[86] Here, Fredriksen is on speculative historical ground as she attempts to re/construct the cause of Paul's "radical change" based purely on conjecture from particular data points, which ironically are strongest in Acts.

Fredriksen's most intriguing proposal concerns the "retrospective self" and her treatment of retrospective conversion narratives. She uses Augustine as a model and compares his earlier reflections on his conversion, as well as on the conversion of the apostle Paul, to those written some fourteen years later in his *Confessions*.[87] She notes a dramatic change saying of Augustine: "His view of his conversion, continually contoured by his circumstances, maximizes its theological and polemical value."[88] She finds similarities between how Augustine and Paul both retrospectively shape their conversion narratives to meet current circumstances. Fredriksen sees Paul's Christophanic references as rhetorical arguments used to persuade his various audiences (and possibly himself) toward recognition and affirmation of his apostolic authority and his message.[89] In Fredriksen's words: "To see a content-filled moment of conversion is to have constructed a narrative whereby the moment emerges retrospectively as the origin of (and justification for) one's present."[90]

Fredriksen's restrained reading of Paul's Christophanic references is both a strength and a weakness. Her willingness to allow for a historical event such as Paul's Christophany, while being unwilling to re/construct the particulars, allows her to focus on other more defined (and definable) data points. It is a welcome reminder to the modern reader that Paul has his own agenda in writing, and details and differences within his Christophanic references may be more reflective of the historic situation necessitating the particular letter than the historic Christophanic event itself.[91] Nevertheless, this restrained reading does not engage the literary context of Paul's Christophanic references enough; her reading of Paul is too historically focused and allows outside data almost fully to govern Paul's past and

---

From Jesus to Christ, 142–57.

86. Fredriksen, "Paul and Augustine," 19; cf. Fredriksen, *From Jesus to Christ*, 157–76; Fredriksen, "Judaism, the Circumcision of Gentiles," 558–64.

87. Fredriksen, "Paul and Augustine," 20–26.

88. Fredriksen, "Paul and Augustine," 26.

89. Fredriksen, "Paul and Augustine," 29; Fredriksen, *From Jesus to Christ*, 158–59.

90. Fredriksen, "Paul and Augustine," 33.

91. Ladd, *Theology of the New Testament*, 415. Ladd writes: "The fact that Paul's letters are *ad hoc* correspondence, usually called forth by specific situations in the Pauline churches, places certain limitations upon our study of his thought, the chief of which is that we do not have Paul's *complete* thought" (emphasis his).

present thought. An additional critique of Fredriksen's work concerns the correlation between Augustine's and Paul's "conversion" experiences. She adamantly claims Paul's Christophanic experience to be a call and not a conversion and yet is content to compare it to Augustine's experience, which is undoubtedly a conversion. While it may be viable to speak of Paul modifying or emphasizing different aspects of his Christophany to meet specific aims, it does not necessitate these aims always being polemical. There is a variety of possibilities for why one might reference such an event; for example, Gaventa's suggestion of imitation.

Comparison of the Various Works

The Pauline scholars who comment upon Paul's Christophanic experience are many, but those considered above are significant voices in the ongoing discussion concerning the importance and complexity of Paul's Christophanic references and are representative of the diversity of literature surrounding this debate. Kim, Dunn, Gaventa, and Fredriksen all have as their goal (whether stated or implied) historical re/construction, but they approach this goal from very different angles. Kim is the most optimistic, believing that the Pauline accounts together with the Acts accounts contain all the information necessary for unlocking the mystery of this event and its results. This optimism brings Kim and Churchill nearer, even though Churchill's stated goal is Christological re/construction and his methodology is literary-form critical, rather than historico-philological. Closer still, it is nearly impossible to separate Kim's Christological conclusions from his re/construction of this event. For Churchill, the event and Paul's Christology are so interconnected as to make them one and the same. Dunn places far less value on re/construction of the actual event but his later works show an increased emphasis on the impact of this event on Paul's Christology, although allowing for extended contemplation. In this respect, Dunn, Kim and Churchill are not far apart in both historical re/constructions and the belief Paul's description of this event provides significant evidence for unlocking his Christology.

This (over)confidence is balanced by the realism of Gaventa and Fredriksen, who evidence varying degrees of skepticism about the re/constructive value of Paul's words. Gaventa arrives at this conclusion through a literary critical approach whereas Fredriksen's approach is more strictly historical, at least as it pertains to Paul. Together their work goes a long way in closing the door on subsequent attempts at historical re/construction of the details of the event itself or of the causes behind this event; indeed, they show past attempts to be construction rather than re-construction. This conclusion should not, however, negate the possibility of employing these Christophanic references toward an understanding of Paul's Christology or of his self-understanding. This is confirmed in Dunn's work on how Paul's Jewish background shapes his understanding of the Christophany, in Churchill's correlation between Paul's accounts and Jewish epiphany, and in Gaventa's and Fredriksen's recognition of pro-phetic call in Paul's language. These explorations have immense value as do most attempts that seek to understand the impact of the Christophany. However, unlike Kim's view, this impact must not be overly reliant upon an accurate re/construction of the event itself.

Another significant connection and contribution of Gaventa's and Fredriksen's work is their desire to take seriously the purpose behind Paul's employment of these references in their current state and current locations. Fredriksen's heuristic comparison between Augustine and Paul leads to the conclusion Paul's purpose is apologetic. This apologetic purpose, along with statements Fredriksen makes concerning the cause of Paul's transformation, may lead readers to the conclusion that Paul's Christophanic accounts are fictitious productions, maybe not in their entirety but at least in many of their details. However, Fredriksen would likely agree that since the historic-ity of this event is neither provable nor disprovable, such a conclusion is neither warranted nor helpful. Gaventa's more literary approach concludes that Paul's purpose is to provide a paradigm for believers to emulate. This conclusion exposes the value Paul places in this personal experience and simultaneously reveals Paul's understanding that this experience is not for him alone. This reading seems both plausible and helpful and will receive further exploration as this current study unfolds.

The Differences, Similarities, and Uniquenesses of this Study

These significant scholarly works provide helpful illumination to Paul's Christophanic experience. But there are gaps that this study will address. These differences can broadly be grouped into the categories of *focus* and *methodology*.

First, unlike Kim, Dunn, and Churchill, this study is not concerned with re/construction of the event or what precipitated it. Like Gaventa and Fredriksen, this author is skeptical regarding the possibility and the results of such an endeavor based on the evidence available. In a similar vein, this study is neither seeking to re/construct Paul's Christology nor to argue how or if it derived from his Christophany. While there is value in the former, Paul's Christophanic references are too sparse to accomplish the latter. Generally speaking, Kim, Dunn, and Churchill are primarily focused on the event itself. Thus, their hermeneutical methodologies are fixated on getting behind the text. Even when evaluating the text, their "behind the text" focus limits their engagement and the literary context is not given due attention. This study differs both in focus and methodology from these scholars.

Although Fredriksen does engage in some re/construction of the event itself, her primary concern is to discover why Paul employs his Christophanic references. This could lead to a text-centered approach. But her chosen methodology is a mixture of "behind the text" historical evaluation and "in front of the text" social-psychological evaluation. While this study is in general agreement with Fredriksen's focus, it will differ significantly from her methodology. As such, the conclusions reached will also differ. While differences in methodology do not automatically lead to differing conclusions, just as similarities in methodology do not automatically lead to like conclusions, some foci lend themselves more readily to particular methodologies, which then have the potential for more fruitful results. The question "Why does Paul employ his Christophanic references?" lends itself to an "in the text" approach which takes seriously the literary context as well as the socio-historical context connected to the various letter that include these references. This does not negate the use of either "behind the text" or "in front of the text" methodologies; they are, however, secondary.

Gaventa's stated focus is a re/construction of the cause, event, and results of Paul's conversion, which is closest to Kim and Dunn. However, her methodology, which significantly engages the text in its literary and socio-historical context, moves her away from her stated focus. Instead, what inevitably emerges is a secondary, less articulated, and more tangential focus, which is similar to Fredriksen's. While the methodological approach taken in this thesis is similar to Gaventa's, it is augmented by evaluation of the various citations, allusions, and echoes to OT Scripture both in and around Paul's Christophanic references. This will aid in understanding Paul's aim in employing these Christophanic references and may also illuminate Paul's underlying theological convictions concerning his conversion/call and/or believers' conversion/call within the eschatological Kingdom.

Unlike Gaventa, the primary focus of this study is on answering the question, "Why does Paul employ his Christophanic references in their particular literary and socio-historical contexts?" This focus should lead to a solidly supported conclusion. Like Gaventa, the author believes that "imitation" may offer a significant answer to the question of purpose; moreover, it will be contended that this imitation is far more substantial and encompassing than Gaventa articulates. The more focused methodology and a slightly different delineation of Christophanic references will lead to exegetical conclusions that differ at key points from those reached by Gaventa.

Methodology

To describe *why* Paul employed Christophanic references in specific literary and socio-historical contexts, this study uses, what is best described as, a "text-centered, author-oriented intertextual" analysis. Of course, asking the question "why?" places the interpreter on speculative ground concerning the possibility of discovering the intended meaning of the author's communication.[92] Therefore, a few methodological considerations must be addressed to avoid the impression that this is an attempt to get into Paul's psyche and discover Paul's feelings about his Christophany.

First, the question of "why" should not be confused with the question of "how."[93] The latter speaks of method and/or manner and the former of reason and/or purpose. Although they should not be confused, they are clearly related. For the modern reader of ancient texts, "how" becomes the means for discovering "why."[94] Therefore, this study analyzes the socio-historical settings of Paul and his audiences alongside the textual elements of such things as vocabulary, syntax, rhetorical device, location within the argument, and the employment of various intertexts in order to better understand the message Paul is trying to communicate.

Second, the methodological approach taken in this study should not be mistaken for a purely literary approach that often seeks meaning only in the modern reader.[95] As Kevin Vanhoozer writes, "it is important to recover

---

92. Thiselton, *New Horizons in Hermeneutics*, 472–73, notes a major shift away from authorial intention and toward a semiotic system in many strands of literary formalism. Nevertheless, Vanhoozer, *Is There a Meaning*, 43–97, 201–80, makes a significant appeal for still considering authorial intention provided one is aware of and avoids the pitfalls of the methodological fallacies of relevancy, transparency, identity, and objectivity, which he outlines (82–85).

93. Additionally, there are the questions of "What constitutes a Christophanic reference for this study?" and "Where and in which Pauline epistles are these Christophanic references to be found?" These questions are addressed in chapter 2.

94. See, for instance, the work of Morse, "What's in a Name?," 243–264. Morse argues that Reception Criticism "designates an approach to biblical studies that asks *how* and *why* the Bible has been, and continues to be, made meaningful for individuals and communities throughout history" (253).

95. For example, Reader-Response Criticism or other postmodern, poststructuralist approaches. See, Thiselton, *New Horizons in Hermeneutics*, 471–555.

the author's thought, but this is best done not by psychological intuition but by historical inference—by an analysis of the author's *public* communicative action."[96] The "text-centered" aspect of the method acknowledges the fact that Paul's available "communicative action" is in the form of a written text. This methodological approach attempts to discover, through the structure and mechanics of the text, what Paul is trying to express. Furthermore, since the text is not simply a series of words detached from a setting, this study carefully considers the historical and social context in which these words were first penned and first read.[97] In sum, the immediate and larger literary setting of the particular texts provides a context for describing why Paul employed his Christophanic references, and the socio-historical context provides a lens through which to interpret the words and images of the text.

In some respects, therefore, this is a historical-critical/grammatical method. However, it is not primarily concerned with some "behind the text" matters such as Source, Form, and Textual Criticisms. Additionally, while the methodology undertaken in this study is primarily concerned with the final form of the text, it does not approach the text from an ahistorical perspective. Neither is it primarily concerned with Canonical Criticism. Rather, it seeks first to examine how Paul employs his Christophanic references in each letter as a particular instantiation within the specific contexts of that communicative event.[98] Additionally, it will be argued that Paul made use of intertexts in many of his Christophanic references, a phenomenon often referred to as intertextuality.[99] Therefore, this thesis will identify and interpret Paul's use of intertexts.

Due to the popularity of intertextuality within biblical studies and the controversies over its methodological validity and functionality, the third concern is to provide an explanation of this phenomenon and why its use in this study is required. The primary argument for the validity of an intertextual analysis is that Paul cites the Jewish Scriptures often and

96. Vanhoozer, *Is There a Meaning*, 230, emphasis his.

97. Jasper, "Literary Readings of the Bible," 27, warns against the loss of focus on the historical context within literary criticism. An overemphasis on the text apart from the context leads to overemphasis on the modern reader.

98. Cf. Brown, *Scripture as Communication*, 225–30, who describes the intersection and difference between Canonical and Intertextual readings of Scripture.

99. This word was coined by Kristeva, *Desire in Language*, 36. Nevertheless, the foundation for the modern concept of intertextuality comes from Bakhtin, *The Dialogic Imagination*. In Bakhtin's words: "Each word tastes of a context and contexts in which it has lived its socially charged life; all words and forms are populated by intentions" (293). For Bakhtin, these various contexts and intentions create other voices (heteroglossia), which force a dialogue with the new context creating both intentional and unintentional meaning for the reader (375).

extensively.[100] Paul's worldview is dominated by a Jewish framework heavily influenced by the Scriptures.[101] The primary challenge of interpreting Paul's use of intertexts is that his hermeneutic process of citing the Jewish Scriptures remained unchanged by his Christophany. However, this radical experience did change *how* he read the Scriptures—through the lens of his conviction that Jesus is the Messiah—and *why* he continued to cite intertexts—to use this reinterpreted narrative to bring further authority and clarity to the gospel he preaches (see Rom 1:3). For Paul, the revelation of the gospel was a continuation of the revelation of Scripture and vice versa. As Markus Bockmuehl writes: "Given the advent of the Messiah, Scripture itself now makes the gospel clear."[102]

The debate regarding the validity and functionality of intertextuality often involves hermeneutical ideologies. Geoffrey Miller has classified intertextuality into two seemingly disparate methodological approaches: "reader-oriented" and "author-oriented."[103] The reader-oriented approach to intertextuality is a postmodern and poststructuralist synchronic approach in which texts continually take on new meaning. As Thomas Hatina writes, "intertexts are viewed as only existing in the actual communicative process—always oscillating, being experienced only in an activity."[104] Conversely, author-oriented intertextuality is a diachronic approach that complements traditional and historically grounded interpretive methods. According to Miller, in this approach the modern reader should look for "markers" left by the author to guide them to the source-text/s and the modern "[r]eaders are not free to explore the inexhaustible plurality of meaning

---

100. Koch, *Die Schrift*, 21–23, lists eighty-nine quotations in the undisputed letters of Paul; Silva, "Old Testament in Paul," 631, lists 102 (nine debated) quotations in the undisputed letters. This does not account for the multitude of possible allusions and echoes. For significant arguments in favor of exploring Paul's allusions and echoes see: Hays, *Echoes of Scripture*; Hays, *Conversion of the Imagination*; Wagner, *Heralds of the Good News*; Ciampa, *Presence and Function*; Ciampa, "Scriptural Language and Ideas," 41–57.

101. What Hays refers to as "Paul's imaginative narrative world." Hays, *Conversion of the Imagination*, x; cf. Hays, *The Faith of Jesus Christ*.

102. Bockmuehl, *Revelation and Mystery*, 154.

103. Miller, "Intertextuality in Old Testament," 283–309.

104. Hatina, "Intertextuality and Historical Criticism," 31. Hatina seems unable to envision a definition or use of intertextuality that is void of its poststructuralist ideology. He, therefore, bids the abandonment of this term by those undertaking an author-oriented intertextuality (42). See also Miller, "Intertextuality in Old Testament," 305; and Yoon, "Ideological Inception of Intertextuality," 71–74. Nevertheless, the term "Intertextuality" to denote a more author-oriented approach has taken root in biblical studies and is not likely to vanish quickly.

of any given text by reading it alongside countless others, but must confine their pursuits to those specific texts the author has in mind."[105]

Richard Hays, a pioneer in applying intertextuality to the interpretation of Scripture, desires to hold these approaches in "creative tension."[106] An important aspect of Hays's interpretative approach is his understanding of the literary trope *metalepsis*. "Metalepsis is a rhetorical and poetic device in which one text alludes to an earlier text in a way that evokes resonances of the earlier text *beyond those explicitly cited*. The result is that the interpretation of a metalepsis requires the reader to recover unstated or suppressed correspondences between the two texts."[107] Metalepsis, at first glance, places a heavy burden on the modern reader that could easily give way to a more reader-oriented interpretation. Nonetheless, Hays insists that "[c]laims about intertextual meaning effects are strongest where it can credibly be demonstrated that they occur within the literary structure of the text and that they can plausibly be ascribed to the intention of the author and the competence of the original readers."[108]

The author-centered aspect of the present methodological approach holds, with Hays, that when evaluating occurrences of intertexts within Paul's Christophanic references, metalepsis requires exploring the literary and socio-historical context of the source-text to see if additional thematic connections are being proposed by Paul, and how such connections aid in understanding why Paul utilized that Christophanic reference. While each of the main exegetical chapters (3–6) evidence some intertextual analysis, this approach is especially relevant to the chapter on Galatians (3) and the chapter on Second Corinthians (6).

Because, in addition to the more easily identified citations/quotations, this thesis seeks to uncover possible OT allusions and echoes[109]

---

105. Miller, "Intertextuality in Old Testament," 287.

106. Hays, *Echoes of Scripture*, 26–28. Hays lists five possible places where a hermeneutical event occurs: (1) in the author's mind; (2) in the original readers of the text; (3) in the text itself; (4) in the modern reader's act of reading; (5) in a community of interpretation (26). Roughly speaking, 1, 2, and 3 corresponds to an author-oriented approach and 4 and 5 to a reader-oriented approach.

107. Hays, *Conversion of the Imagination*, 2, emphasis his. Cf. Moyise, "Intertextuality and Biblical Studies," 418–31. Moyise believes the source-text is not simply altered by its new context or by how a particular author chooses to utilize or reconstitute it. Instead, the source-text "fights back . . . reminding the reader that it once belonged elsewhere and has certain 'rights' . . . [T]he new affects the old while the old affects the new" (424). In this way, not only the words of the source-text but also the contexts (literary, historical, cultural, and social) come forward.

108. Hays, *Echoes of Scripture*, 28.

109. Hays, *Echoes of Scripture*, 29, confesses the difficulty in distinguishing

related to Paul's Christophanic references, Hays's seven criteria are used as a weighted guide.

> (1) *Availability.* Was the proposed source of the echo available to the author and/or original readers? . . . (2) *Volume.* The volume of an echo is determined primarily by the degree of explicit repetition of words or syntactical patters . . . (3) *Recurrence.* How often does Paul elsewhere cite or allude to the same scriptural passage? . . . (4) *Thematic Coherence.* How well does the alleged echo fit into the line of argument that Paul is developing? . . . (5) *Historical Plausibility.* Could Paul have intended the alleged meaning effect? . . . (6) *History of Interpretation.* Have other readers, both critical and precritical, heard the same echoes? . . . (7) *Satisfaction.* With or without clear confirmation from the other criteria listed here, does the proposed reading make sense? Does it illuminate the surrounding discourse? Does it produce for the reader a satisfying account of the effect of the intertextual relation?[110]

Based strictly on Paul's OT citations, apart from any allusions or echoes, criterion 1 may be assumed, at least as it concerns Paul himself. Of the remaining six, more weight is given to 2, 3, 4, and 7.[111] While these criteria are not foolproof and still necessitate a significant amount of subjectivity, they provide a safeguard. In Hays's words: "There are always only shades of certainty when these criteria are applied to particular texts."[112]

As this study unfolds, it is demonstrated that Paul's Christophanic references include significant allusions to Isaiah, especially chapters 40–66. Isaiah provides Paul with a foundation for articulating the identity of Christ,

---

between echo and allusion and utilizes the terminology "flexibly." He does, however, still define allusions as dependent upon authorial intention but says an echo does not necessarily depend on conscious intention. So also Thompson, *Clothed with Christ*, 30. With regard to their use within this book, Hays's general classification will suffice: "*allusion* is used of obvious intertextual references, *echo* of subtler ones" (29, italics his). Still more subtle are *thematic parallels.* Harmon, *She Must and Shall Go Free*, 30, defines thematic parallel as "ideas/concepts shared between texts that transcend precise verbal relationships."

110. Hays, *Echoes of Scriptures*, 29–31, italics his. Cf. Thompson, *Clothed with Christ*, 32–33. Thompson lists 11 criteria for discerning if an allusion or echo to Jesus tradition is found in the epistles. As such, many of these criteria do not apply to the current study. Those remaining are similar to Hays's.

111. The final criterion of satisfaction is often downplayed. However, see Leithart, *Deep Exegesis.* Leithart elevates the criterion of satisfaction arguing that a "hypothesis is compelling because of the over-all coherence of the story, which encompasses many established facts but which goes beyond that mere collection of facts" (134).

112. Hays, *Echoes of Scripture*, 32.

his own apostolic calling, and the role of believers in the eschatological age. Many studies highlight Paul's significant reliance upon Isaiah,[113] and the fact that he quotes it more than any other single book.[114] Hays posits an additional fifty allusions to Isaiah in the undisputed Pauline letters, concluding: "This rough statistical evidence suggests—at the very least—that Paul attributed particular significance to the prophecies of Isaiah."[115] J. Ross Wagner states: "Paul's citations and allusions to Isaiah are not plundered from random raids on Israel's sacred texts. Rather, they are the product of sustained and careful attention to the rhythms and cadences of individual passages as well as to larger themes and motifs that run throughout the prophet's oracles."[116] Furthermore, with respect to Paul's Christophanic references, multiple scholars have emphasized Paul's paralleling of his account to the so-called Suffering Servant passages of Isaiah.[117] For these reasons, significant exploration of how Paul appropriates Isaiah in and around his Christophanic references is undertaken, especially in chapters 3 and 6.

Finally, it should be noted that this study is limited to evaluating the Christophanic references in the so-called undisputed letters.[118] While the pendulum appears to be swinging with regard to Ephesians, Colossians, and Second Thessalonians,[119] there is still much ongoing scholarly debate surrounding the authorship of these and the other so-called disputed letters.

113. E.g., Hays, *Conversion of the Imagination*, 25–49; Wilk, *Die Bedeutung des Jesajabuches für Paulus*; Wagner, *Heralds of the Good News*; Shum, *Paul's Use of Isaiah*; Moyise and Menken, *Isaiah in the New Testament*, 117–58; Gignilliat, *Paul and Isaiah's Servants*.

114. Koch, *Die Schrift*, 21–23, lists twenty-eight; Hays, *Conversion of the Imagination*, 46–47, lists thirty-one; Silva, "Old Testament in Paul," 631, lists twenty-seven, with Psalms the next closest at twenty-three. Furthermore, Harmon, *She Must and Shall Go Free*, 11 n. 41, believes: "Of the thirteen Pauline letters, only Philemon lacks an Isaianic citation, allusion, or echo.

115. Hays, *Conversion of the Imagination*, 25–26.

116. Wagner, *Heralds of the Good News*, 356.

117. Harmon, *She Must and Shall Go Free*, 105–15; Stanley, "Theme of the Servant," 385–425; Dinter, "Paul and the Prophet Isaiah," 48–52; Beker, *Paul the Apostle*, 115–16; Ciampa, *Presence and Function*, 94–95; Newman, *Paul's Glory-Christology*, 206–7.

118. Romans, First Corinthians, Second Corinthians, Galatians, Philippians, First Thessalonians, and Philemon.

119. See Foster, "Who Wrote 2 Thessalonians?," 150–75, and note the survey (171); D. Campbell, *Framing Paul*, esp. 190–338, who makes a strong argument for the authenticity of these three epistles.

Conclusion

This introduction shows the complexities surrounding the evaluation of Paul's Christophany in scholarly study revealing multiple foci and methodologies. In so doing, it exposes the need for a full-length evaluation of the purpose/s behind Paul's employment of his various Christophanic references in their specific literary and socio-historical contexts. Its significant contribution is a rediscovery of how each reference functions integrally within the individual epistolary argument.

2

Prolegomena

THERE IS CONSIDERABLE DEBATE regarding the passages in which Paul makes reference to his Christophanic experience. There is near unanimous agreement[1] on Gal 1:11–17 (vv. 12, 16),[2] 1 Cor 9:1–2 (v. 1), and 1 Cor 15:1–11 (v. 8),[3] with most also accepting Phil 3:4–14 (vv. 7–9, 12). Additionally, 2 Cor 3:1—4:6 (3:16–18; 4:1, 6) has considerable support, whereas 2 Cor 5:16–18, 2 Cor 12:1–4, and Rom 10:2–4 have had limited support. Many scholars also acknowledge the multiple declarations to Paul's "call" (Rom 1:1; 1 Cor 1:1), to "grace" (Rom 1:5; 12:3; 15:15; 1 Cor 3:10; Gal 2:9), to "apostleship" (Rom 11:13; 2 Cor 1:1; Gal 1:1), and to apostolic work (Rom 1:13; 1 Cor 1:17; 2 Cor 10:8; 13:10; cf. Gal 2:2) as Christophanic references. Lastly, there are a handful of acknowledged references from the so-called disputed Pauline letters (Eph 1:1; 3:1–13; Col 1:1, 23c–29; 1 Tim 1:11–14; Titus 1:3), which will not be considered.

Delineation of Christophanic References

Surprisingly, few scholars have established criteria for delineating a Christophanic reference. As a prolegomenon to this study a working definition needs to be proposed against which the passages noted above can be tested.

Christophany can refer to any manifestation/revelation of/from Christ, and since Paul apparently had several such phenomena (2 Cor 12:1; Gal 2:2; cf. Acts 16:9–10; 18:9; 22:17; 23:11), this study limits

---

1. Murphy-O'Connor, *Paul: A Critical Life*, 71, "on which all agree."

2. Parenthetical verses are those on which most agree, whereas contextual ranges vary considerable.

3. Both Bornkamm, *Paul*, 16–25; and Gaventa, *From Darkness to Light*, 21–40, make passing references to the two Corinthian references but focus entirely on Gal 1 and Phil 3.

"Christophany" to speak of Paul's initial encounter with Christ. The following two criteria will be used to confirm whether Paul is making a Christophanic reference: Criterion 1—if there is a reference or allusion to a manifestation/revelation of/from Christ to Paul, and Criterion 2—if the text identified by Criterion 1 can be connected to Paul's initial call/conversion. Both criteria must be met to be considered in this study. Additionally, there is need to categorize confirmed references so as to bring further clarity into the ongoing discussion. This too has rarely been done and when it is, there is no definition of the categories.[4] The broad categories of primary and secondary will be used: primary references are those where Paul is said to refer directly (and thus intentionally) to this event (i.e., Christophany is in the foreground); secondary references are those where Paul is said to refer indirectly (either intentionally or unintentionally) to this event (i.e., Christophany is in the background).

Galatians 1:11–17

In Gal 1, Paul claims his gospel came not from a human source but through an ἀποκαλύψεως Ἰησοῦ Χριστοῦ (v. 12) and that God ἀποκαλύψαι τὸν υἱὸν αὐτοῦ ἐν ἐμοί (v. 16).[5] In the NT, ten of the eighteen uses of ἀποκάλυψις[6] and nine of the twenty-six uses of ἀποκαλύπτω[7] are found in the undisputed Pauline letters. In each of these uses, God is either the direct or the implied agent.[8] The phrase "ἀποκαλύψεως Ἰησοῦ Χριστοῦ" can be viewed as either a subjective ("a revelation from Christ")[9] or objective genitive ("a revelation

4. Dietzfelbinger, *Die Berufung des Paulus*, 44, gives the clearest categorization acknowledging only four direct references (Gal 1:15; 1 Cor 9:1; 15:8; 2 Cor 4:6) and multiple other references where Christophany "*im Hintergrund steht*" (Gal 1:11, 16; 2:2, 7–9; 1 Cor 1:1; 3:10; 2 Cor 3:7–11; Rom 1:1; 11:13; 15:15, 16, 18; Phil 3:4b–11; 1 Thess 2:16). Churchill, *Divine Initiative and Christology*, 99–148, does not directly categorize these references but acknowledges some as more dubious (2 Cor 10:8, 13; Rom 11:13) and uses these as "support" text only.

5. All Greek NT quotations are taken from NA28.

6. Rom 2:5; 8:19; 16:25; 1 Cor 1:7; 14:6, 26; 2 Cor 12:1, 7; Gal 1:12; 2:2; cf. Eph 1:17; 3:3; 2 Thess 1:7.

7. Rom 1:17, 18; 8:18; 1 Cor 2:10; 3:13; 14:30; Gal 1:16; 3:23; Phil 3:15; cf. Eph 3:5; 2 Thess 2:3, 6, 8.

8. Both Smith, "History of ΑΠΟΚΑΛΥΠΤΩ and ΑΠΟΚΑΛΥΨΙΣ," 14, and Bockmuehl, *Revelation and Mystery*, 33, express surprise at the NT, and especially Pauline, use of ἀποκάλυψις and ἀποκαλύπτω to express theological revelation as this is rarely the case in the LXX.

9. Wallace, *Greek Grammar*, 113; Longenecker, *Galatians*, 23–24; Schlier, *Der Brief an die Galater*, 47; cf. Churchill, *Divine Initiative and Christology*, 112–13, who

of Christ").[10] In light of verses 15–16, where God is clearly the agent, the objective genitive reading is preferable.

The prepositional phrase ἐν ἐμοί (v. 16) also raises interpretive questions. It can be translated as a simple dative ("to me"),[11] as locative ("in me"),[12] or as instrumental ("through me").[13] Complicating the decision is debate concerning the kind of appearance Paul experienced, whether internal/spiritual or external/physical. Proponents of the former usually prefer the locative translation[14] while those in support of the latter usually prefer the simple dative.[15] However, one should avoid deriving any conclusions based strictly on ἐν ἐμοί;[16] Paul seems to have been able to speak of his Christophanic experience in multiple ways.[17] As already noted, historical reconstruction based on strained philological methodology is suspect. It seems equally logical that Paul's use of ἐν ἐμοί is making a theological claim rather than a specific Christophanic claim. Whichever way one translates this phrase, the divine agency of this revelation to/in Paul fulfills Criterion 1.

Criterion 2 is clearly met in the rest of the pericope. Paul's "earlier life in Judaism" (vv. 13–14) is set against the report of verse 23—"The one who formerly was persecuting us is now proclaiming the faith he once tried to destroy."[18] Furthermore, the contrast is unmistakably the result of God having set apart, called, and revealed for the purpose of (ἵνα) Paul proclaiming Christ among the Gentiles (v. 16), resulting in God's glorification (v. 24). While Paul speaks often of his call and apostleship and never uses the language of "repentance" or "conversion" about himself,[19] there is evidence to show at least some immediate[20] and significant transformation or alternation took place in light of the Christophany. Paul moved from

---

argues for plenary genitive.

10. Dunn, *Galatians*, 53–54; Martyn, *Galatians*, 144; de Boer, *Galatians*, 77.

11. Martyn, *Galatians*, 158; Gaventa, *From Darkness to Light*, 27.

12. Dunn, *Galatians*, 64; Bruce, *Galatians*, 92–93.

13. Hays, "Christology and Ethics in Galatians," 281.

14. Ashton, *Religion of Paul the Apostle*, 83.

15. Kim, *Origin of Paul's Gospel*, 56–57; cf. Wright, *Resurrection of the Son of God*, 380, who argues it is both "to" and "through."

16. Churchill, *Divine Initiative and Christology*, 119.

17. Wallace, *Snatched into Paradise*, 169–201.

18. Unless otherwise indicated, Scriptural and Apocryphal quotations in English are from the NRSV.

19. See Longenecker, "A Realized Hope," 25–26.

20. This does not discount the strong possibility that Paul's transformation continued and that it may have taken years for him to develop his understanding of how Christ functioned, especially in connection to the law.

viewing Christ as a blasphemous criminal to knowing him as the risen Lord, from persecuting the church to building the church through the proclamation of the gospel.[21]

Galatians 1:11–17 is a Christophanic reference, having met both criteria. Additionally, the context shows this to be a primary reference. Paul intentionally employs his Christophany as part of an extended autobiographical section (Gal 1:11–2:14) that highlights, among other things, the source of his gospel message (cf. Gal 1:1). N. T. Wright has claimed this pericope is "the only time Paul refers explicitly to what *happened to him or in him* on the Damascus Road."[22] As will become evident, this is the clearest and most extensive reference. Whether it is the "only" explicit (primary) reference cannot be substantiated at this point.

First Corinthians 9:1–2 (16–17)

Paul begins 1 Cor 9 with four rhetorical questions, each expecting a positive response.[23] The third question comprises the heart of this proposed Christophanic reference—οὐχὶ Ἰησοῦν τὸν κύριον ἡμῶν ἑόρακα (v. 1). These are significant words, which meet Criterion 1.[24] The verb ἑόρακα is a perfect active indicative form of ὁράω and has been understood to underscore the continued impact of a single event[25]—Paul's having seen the risen Lord.[26]

Criterion 2 is more difficult to establish, as Paul does not directly mention his pre-Christophanic life or his calling; apostleship is simply stated as a present reality. Furthermore, Paul's reference to "seeing" Jesus could point to a subsequent rather than initial event. In light of the positive response expected from Paul's rhetorical questions, one might assume the Corinthians knew of his Christophanic experience and of his transformation. Furthermore, if Paul is speaking about his Christophany then his use of

---

21. For debate over call versus conversion see, Stendahl, *Paul among Jews*, 7–23; Segal, *Paul the Convert*, 7; Chester, *Conversion at Corinth*, 163; Gaventa, "Paul's Conversion," 342–54.

22. Wright, *Faithfulness of God*, Book 2, 1420–421, emphasis his. The reference to Damascus in Gal 1:17 (cf. 2 Cor 11:32) provides possible correlation to the Acts accounts. This may be the justification for Wright's claim.

23. Garland, *First Corinthians*, 403.

24. Cf. Porter, *When Paul Met Jesus*, 100–101 who argues that Paul's use of ἑόρακα indicates stative aspect and is a reference to the past act of having seen the earthly Jesus rather than primarily a reference to his Christophany.

25. Wallace, *Snatched into Paradise*, 171.

26. Wright, *Resurrection of the Son of God*, 382; Thiselton, *First Corinthians*, 668; Fee, *First Corinthians*, 395.

Ἰησοῦν τὸν κύριον ἡμῶν[27] would evidence a significant transformation in his thinking—the earthly Jesus is now his Lord[28] and the one who establishes his apostleship. However, this reading is still too inferential.

Before disqualifying this reference, it is beneficial to evaluate the larger context and especially 1 Cor 9:16–17.[29] Paul states that his gospel proclamation is not of his own will but out of obligation, because he has been entrusted (πεπίστευμαι) with a stewardship (οἰκονομία). The language of obligation and especially οἰκονομία "almost always points to servile status"[30] and "slave" (δοῦλος), a common self-designation for Paul, is usually tied to his call (Rom 1:1; Gal 1:10; Phil 1:1; cf. 1 Cor 9:19; 2 Cor 4:5).[31] Additionally, Paul's use of the perfect passive form πεπίστευμαι points to a specific event in Paul's past where God entrusted him with the ongoing task of proclaiming the gospel. Taking 1 Cor 9:1–2 together with 1 Cor 9:16–17 confirms this is a Christophanic reference.

This passage also falls within the category of primary reference as Paul intentionally invokes his Christophanic reference as part of his current argument, which is part of a larger argument concerning the "rights" and "freedoms" of those in Christ. This primary reference is extremely sparse, especially when compared to Gal 1:11–17.[32] Nevertheless, Paul deems it necessary to point specifically to this experience.

First Corinthians 15:1–11

The whole of 1 Cor 15 focuses on resurrection, with verses 5–8 on resurrection appearances. At the end of a kerygmatic formula (vv. 3–5), Paul gives a list of all those to whom the resurrected Christ appeared. The list can be divided into four lines, each including the verb ὤφθη, the aorist passive form of ὁράω. Paul describes Christ's appearance to him in identical language to the other resurrection appearances. This may strengthen the possibility that

27. Fee, *First Corinthians*, 395 n. 14, argues this is "semitechnical language for speaking of Christ in his resurrection" (cf. Rom 4:24).

28. Thiselton, *First Corinthians*, 668.

29. Kim, *Origin of Paul's Gospel*, 4–5; Matera, *God's Saving Grace*, 19, 27; and Newman, *Paul's Glory-Christology*, 165–66, view this as an additional Christophanic reference.

30. Martin, *Slavery as Salvation*, 74.

31. Beker, *Paul the Apostle*, 115, argues δοῦλος is a prophetic title and not a term of humility. Contra Dunn, *Galatians*, 50.

32. Both Fee, *First Corinthians*, 395 n. 15; Fee, *Galatians*, 43; and Bockmuehl, *Revelation and Mystery*, 136–37, appear to view 1 Cor 9:1 and 15:8 as more certain Christophanic references than Gal 1:11–16.

Paul's experience was an external/physical phenomenon rather than an internal/spiritual one.[33] Regardless, this reference fulfills Criterion 1.

Criterion 2 is also straightforward. Paul's reference to ἔκτρωμα (v. 8) and to having persecuted the church of God (v. 9; cf. Gal 1:13; Phil 3:6) establishes the baseline for the transformation wrought through the divine encounter with Christ. The focus of verse 10 is firmly on God's grace,[34] referenced thrice, which called and enabled Paul to work "harder than any of them,"[35] a reference to his proclamation of the gospel (vv. 1, 2, 11). This is, therefore, a confirmed Christophanic reference, which is also primary; Paul intentionally positions his experience in the midst of his larger argument.

Philippians 3:4–14

Concerning Criterion 1, this reference differs from those above; there is no overt language of a visual or revelatory encounter with Christ. Many make mention of Paul's use of the aorist passive κατελήμφθην in verse 12,[36] and see an allusion to his being apprehended or forcefully seized[37] by Christ. This allusion is weak by itself. A stronger case for meeting Criterion 1 may be made in Paul's language of "knowing" Christ. In verse 8, Paul claims to regard everything as loss διὰ τὸ ὑπερέχον τῆς γνώσεως Χριστοῦ Ἰησοῦ τοῦ κυρίου μου. V. Koperski and others make solid arguments for the Jewish origins of Paul's "knowledge" language,[38] where ידע, and cognates, usually signifies intimacy and the profoundly personal relationship between God and his people[39] (e.g., MT Gen 4:1; Ps 9:11; Jer 31:34; Isa 40:13; Hos 2:21–22; cf. Bar 2:15, 31; Wis 15:3; cf. Gal 4:9). Furthermore, Peter Stuhlmacher suggests that in apocalyptic literature such as Daniel, there is "Die Auswechselbarkeit und Vergleichbarkeit von Erscheinungs-, Enthüllungs- und Erkenntnisterminologie,"[40] as they all derive from the same divine source (Dan 2:21; 8:19; 9:25; 2 Bar.

33. Fee, *First Corinthians*, 732; Wright, *Resurrection of the Son of God*, 327.

34. Fee, *First Corinthians*, 734–35, claims this as the basis for Paul's theology of grace.

35. Wallace, *Snatched into Paradise*, 174–75, argues Paul is emphasizing unworthiness rather than authority.

36. Bockmuehl, *Philippians*, 221; Flemming, *Philippians*, 184; Churchill, *Divine Initiative and Christology*, 147–48.

37. Munck, *Paul*, 22–24; Kim, *Origin of Paul's Gospel*, 4, 108.

38. Koperski, *The Knowledge of Christ*, esp. 20–65; see also Bockmuehl, *Philippians*, 205–6. Contra Dibelius, *An die Thessalonicher I, II.*, 89, who argues a Hellenistic mystical background.

39. Flemming, *Philippians*, 167.

40. Stuhlmacher, *Das paulinische Evangelium*, 76.

56:1–2; 76:1). This close association is also evidenced in the Qumran literature (e.g., 1QpHab 11:1–2; 1QS 2:3; 11:3–4a).[41]

The connection between knowledge and revelation is also clear in the larger context of Philippians. In this letter, Paul employs φρονέω[42] to encourage the Philippians toward a unity of mind/attitude with him, one another (Phil 2:2), and Christ (Phil 2:5; cf. 1 Cor 2:16; Rom 12:2); and Paul concludes the current pericope with these words: Ὅσοι οὖν τέλειοι, τοῦτο φρονῶμεν· καὶ εἴ τι ἑτέρως φρονεῖτε, καὶ τοῦτο ὁ θεὸς ὑμῖν ἀποκαλύψει (Phil 3:15). Just as God revealed the intimate knowledge of Christ to Paul (Phil 3:7–8), thus giving him a unity of mind with Christ, so too God has/will reveal himself to the Philippians (cf. Phil 1:9–10; 1 Cor 1:5–6; 2 Cor 4:6).

Criterion 2 is more easily established. Paul gives a list of his pre-Christophanic merits, both inherited and achieved (vv. 5–6), followed by an "accounting" of their trans-valuation in light of knowing Christ Jesus (vv. 7–9). The dichotomy between past and present does not highlight the difference between Judaism and Christianity; this is too anachronistic. Within the context, the stress lies on the contrast between confidence in the flesh and confidence in Christ. The latter took place as a result of a past event in which Paul "suffered the loss of all things" (note the aorist passive ἐζημιώθην; v. 8).[43] When this is taken together with the aorist passive κατελήμφθην (v. 12) it becomes more likely Paul is reflecting on his Christophanic experience in this pericope. Having met both criteria, Phil 3:4–14 may confidently be included as a Christophanic reference. It is also worth noting the language of call (κλῆσις) in verse 14 is linked to a specific athletic imagery[44] and does not appear to be connected to Paul's Gentile commission.[45]

This is not an explicit reference; Paul's Christophany sits in the background.[46] While Paul's audience likely would have heard an allusion to his Christophany, this recognition is not necessary for his point to be made. Otherwise, Paul would have introduced it in a similar fashion as he did in Gal 1:11–17, 1 Cor 9:1–2, 16–17, and 1 Cor 15:1–11. Neither the audience nor the situation necessitated overtness. Nevertheless, this reference is most likely intentional. There can be little doubt that from Paul's perspective the subject at hand brought his Christophanic experience sharply to his mind.

---

41. Ashton, *Religion of Paul the Apostle*, 124, esp. n. 18.

42. Phil 1:7; 2:2(bis), 5; 3:15(bis), 19, 4:2, 10(bis).

43. O'Brien, *Philippians*, 389.

44. Pfitzner, *Paul and the Agon Motif,* 139–53.

45. But see O'Brien, *Philippians*, 432–33.

46. Ashton, *Religion of Paul the Apostle*, 125.

Second Corinthians 3:1—4:6

There is considerable scholarly support for viewing sections of 2 Cor 3:1—4:6 as a Christophanic reference.[47] Among the most liberal is Kim, who argues that 2 Cor 3:16–18 and 4:4–6 refer to Paul's experience of Christ's glory on the Damascus Road and 2 Cor 3:6 and 4:1, 4–6 refer to his call to be a minister of the new covenant.[48] Both criteria are seemingly met in this expansive pericope. Fulfilling Criterion 1 are the multiple references to what can be understood as a visual/revelatory experience of Christ.[49] Paul speaks of "beholding (κατοπτριζόμενοι)[50] as in a mirror the glory of the Lord" (2 Cor 3:18a, NASB) and of the God "who has shone (ἔλαμψεν) in our hearts to give the light (φωτισμόν) of the knowledge (γνώσεως) of the glory of God in the face (προσώπῳ) of Jesus Christ" (2 Cor 4:6). Fulfilling Criterion 2, Paul speaks of how the surpassing glory has set aside the past glory (2 Cor 3:9–11; cf. Phil 3:7–8), how turning to the Lord removes the old veil (2 Cor 3:16), of "being transformed (μεταμορφούμεθα) into the same image from one degree of glory to another" (2 Cor 3:18b), and of the renouncing of shameful things (2 Cor 4:2).

The difficulty with viewing any part of this pericope as referring to Paul's Christophanic experience is the continuous use of the first person plural/s (*fpp*) in the larger context of 2 Cor 2:14—7:4.[51] Kim argues all of the "we" references in 2 Cor 3:1—4:6, with the exception of the ἡμεῖς πάντες of 3:18,[52] are "stylistic plural[s] referring to Paul himself alone."[53] Regarding 2 Cor 3:18, Kim sees Paul as applying his own Christophany as a "typical" model for believers' conversion, though not including a physical/outward seeing of Christ, and even adds that 2 Cor 4:6 is a "typical"

---

47. E.g., Dietzfelbinger, *Die Berufung des Paulus*, 49–51; Newman, *Paul's Glory-Christology*, 229–35; Ashton, *Religion of Paul the Apostle*, 84–86; Thrall, *Second Corinthians*, 316–19.

48. Kim, *Origin of Paul's Gospel*, 5–13, 193–99, 229–39.

49. Wright, *Resurrection of the Son of God*, 385–86, stresses that this is an "inner" experience rather than visual/physical.

50. There is difficulty in translating this present middle participle with the two strongest interpretations being "beholding" or "reflecting." For the former see, Thrall, *2 Corinthians*, 290–95; for the latter, Belleville, *Reflections of Glory*, 278–82. Cf. Kim, *Origin of Paul's Gospel*, 13 n.2, 232, 237, who holds both interpretations.

51. Harris, *Second Corinthians*, 240–41; Barnett, *Second Corinthians*, 137–45; Thrall, *Second Corinthians*, 188.

52. Belleville, *Reflections of Glory*, 275–76, argues 3:18 only refers to Paul and "all true gospel ministers."

53. Kim, *Origin of Paul's Gospel*, 235; so also Hafemann, *Suffering and Ministry*, 12–16.

apostolic commission.[54] For Kim, however, this appears to be a concession, mostly to account for the πάντες in 2 Cor 3:18. He argues this generalization is tangential to Paul's main concern of "defending himself and his gospel against the charges of his opponents."[55] Kim's proposed "stylistic plural" as a reference to Paul alone does not seem tenable. At the least, it would refer to Paul and the other ministers/apostles,[56] especially in light of the leadership factions Paul sought to lessen in 1 Corinthians (cf. 1:10–17; 3:5–9; 4:9–13; 15:1–11; 16:12). Furthermore, the parallels between 2 Cor 3:16, 18 and 4:4, 6 make it more feasible Paul is speaking in general terms to all believers throughout the pericope.[57]

Wright questions the validity of seeing this pericope as a Christophanic reference precisely because of the inclusive language. His question, aimed at Kim, is apropos: "how could Paul have generalized from his experience—granted his placing of his seeing of Jesus at the end of a one-off sequence in 1 Cor. 15.8—to the experience he and the Corinthians all shared?"[58] Wright may be correct to assume Paul's conversion/call is unique and cannot be *exactly* duplicated. Nevertheless, as will be argued in chapter 4, this is not the point of Paul's Christophanic reference in 1 Cor 15:8–10. Wright also argues that 2 Cor 3:1—4:6 is not concerned with conversion or call but with a constant experience in the life of the believer and, therefore, cannot be a reference to Paul's Christophany.[59] While Wright is accurate concerning the ongoing nature of the experience described in 2 Cor 3:18, this does not negate the possibility that Paul is also speaking of conversion/call in this verse or in the larger pericope, especially in 2 Cor 3:16, 4:4, 6. These verses are too directly related to the initial experience and implications of "turning" to the Lord. It seems more plausible that Paul is explicating the process from conversion/call to continued transformation as a way of helping the Corinthians understand what has taken place and should continue to take place in the life of believers because of the eschatological new creation.

The ongoing scholarly debate concerning the validity of 2 Cor 3:1—4:6 as a Christophanic reference, which derives from the ambiguity

---

54. Kim, *Origin of Paul's Gospel*, 231; cf. Gaventa, "Paul's Conversion," 192; Thrall, *2 Corinthians*, 317.

55. Kim, *Origin of Paul's Gospel*, 5–6 n. 7; cf. 235.

56. Belleville, *Reflections of Glory*, 275–76; Wallace, *Snatched into Paradise*, 179.

57. Meier, *Mystik bei Paulus*, 42, 63; Wright, *Resurrection of the Son of God*, 384–85; Churchill, *Divine Initiative and Christology*, 135.

58. Wright, *Resurrection of the Son of God*, 384–85 n. 37; cf. Furnish, *Second Corinthians*, 250–51.

59. Wright, *Resurrection of the Son of God*, 384–86; cf. Churchill, *Divine Initiative and Christology*, 134–35, who sees this as a reference to 2 Cor 12:1–4.

of the text itself as it pertains to this issue, precludes its categorization as a primary Christophanic reference. Nevertheless, as shown above, there are significant connections between the confirmed Christophanic references and the experience Paul extends to all believers in this pericope. Furthermore, since both criteria appear to have been met, 2 Cor 3:1—4:6 will be deemed a secondary Christophanic reference and this a priori assumption will be confirmed in chapter 6.

Second Corinthians 5:16–18

This pericope has limited[60] support as a Christophanic reference.[61] It does appear to meet Criterion 2 as Paul speaks of a shift in eschatological perspective from "old" to "new." Additionally, there are multiple references in and around this pericope that correlate to apostolic ministry, which could point to Paul's initial call. For example, his reference to being compelled (συνέχει) by God's love could be understood as apostolic obligation (cf. 1 Cor 9:16–17)[62] as well as his references to having been given a "ministry of reconciliation" from God (2 Cor 5:18) and being "ambassadors for Christ" (2 Cor 5:20).

Kim suggests Paul's reference to previously having known Christ "according to the flesh" is an indirect way to speak of his prior persecution of Christ-followers and that Paul's words likely reflect an awareness of his opponents' critique against him on this point. Therefore, argues Kim, Paul's use of ἀπὸ τοῦ νῦν (v. 16; cf. ἀλλὰ νῦν) is a reference to the time of Paul's conversion, which is the moment when Paul stopped viewing Christ according to the flesh and became a new creation (v. 17), having been reconciled to Christ and given a ministry of reconciliation (v. 18).[63] While Kim does acknowledge the eschatological dichotomy being presented in Paul's words, especially verse 17, he once again ignores the *fpp* and thus over-personalizes Paul's new creation language. Rather than thinking "primarily of his own case,"[64] Paul understands the new creation reality to have already been inaugurated through Christ and connected to the eschatological people of God

---

60. Kim, *Paul and the New Perspective*, 223, well overstates his claim that 2 Cor 5:16 is "universally recognized as alluding to" Paul's Christophany.

61. Kim, *Origin of Paul's Gospel*, 13–20; Newman, *Paul's Glory-Christology*, 166; Seifrid, *Second Corinthians*, 248–49; cf. Hafemann, *Second Corinthians*, 244–45.

62. So Kim, *Paul and the New Perspective*, 224–25.

63. Kim, *Origin of Paul's Gospel*, 13–18; cf. Kim, *New Perspective*, 214–38.

64. Kim, *Origin of Paul's Gospel*, 16.

rather than specifically to his own experience; he would of course include himself as part of the eschatological people of God.[65]

Criterion 1 is especially difficult to establish as there is no direct reference to a visible/revelatory experience. There are multiple references to "knowing" (οἴδαμεν, ἐγνώκαμεν, γινώσκομεν) in verse 16, which could compare to those in Phil 3:7–9. However, the emphasis is on "no longer" knowing Christ, or anyone else, according to the flesh. Stanley Porter has recently claimed that verse 16b is actually a reference to Paul's own personal experience of having seen the earthly Jesus prior to his conversion/call.[66] Even if this claim could be substantiated, it would still not fulfill Criterion 1. Mark Seifrid postulates an intriguing proposal that Paul's use of "according to the flesh" is in reference to his opponents' claims to have had similar *post-resurrection* encounters with Christ (cf. 2 Cor 12:1–4); "Paul does not contest the claim of the opponents to have known Christ, but here with his first-person plural, he indicates that he is their equal. His point here, however, is that such knowledge of Christ has been transcended by another."[67] Nevertheless, even if Seifrid's proposal could be verified, the focus would still be on a "knowing" which has been superseded and not specifically on Paul's Christophanic experience of "knowing" Christ.

Therefore, while an argument for Criterion 2 could be made, Criterion 1 has not been met and this pericope must be excluded from consideration as a Christophanic reference. However, the thematic connection of conversion imagery between this pericope and 2 Cor 3:4—4:6, as well as the continuation of the use of the *fpp* language, may give significant insight into understanding the latter. For this reason, 2 Cor 5:16–18 will be further studied as part of the larger context of 2 Cor 3:4—4:6.

Second Corinthians 12:1–4

This passage makes reference to ὀπτασίας καὶ ἀποκαλύψεις (v. 1; cf. v. 7) and to a particular ecstatic experience in which "a person," almost definitely Paul,[68] "was caught up into Paradise and heard things that are not to be told, that no mortal is permitted to repeat" (v. 4). This would appear to satisfy Criteria 1. However, Paul says this event took place "fourteen years ago," and based on the dating of Second Corinthians (ca. C.E. 55–57), most

---

65. While v. 17 is decidedly singular (ὥστε εἴ τις ἐν Χριστῷ), the new creation is a collective reality, which includes all believers as well as the ever-expansive Kingdom.

66. Cf. Porter, *When Paul Met Jesus*, 107–15.

67. Seifrid, *Second Corinthians*, 249.

68. *Pace*, Goulder, "The Visionaries of Laodicea," 15–39, esp. 18.

scholars[69] quickly dismiss the possibility of this being a Christophanic reference,[70] especially since attempts to reconcile the two dates have been unconvincing.[71] There are multiple other points which make this a dubious Christophanic reference. First, Paul speaks of an unutterable event, whereas in Gal 1:11–17 (cf. 1 Cor 15:8–11) the Christophany requires Paul's continued proclamation.[72] Second, nowhere else does Paul overtly connect his Christophany to a heavenly ascent.[73] Third, unlike other confirmed references, here, Paul self-distances himself from the revelation, probably due to the parodic nature of his apologia in this section (chs. 10–13).[74] Fourth, rather than "knowing" (Phil 3:8), Paul claims, "I do not know" (vv. 2–3, bis; cf. 2 Cor 5:16). Finally, the larger context centers on boasting and there is no reference to calling or apostleship.[75] Having not met Criterion 2, this passage is disqualified.

Romans 10:2–4

Romans 10:2–4 is part of large and challenging section of Romans (9:1–11:36) in which Paul's thesis of salvation for both Jews and Gentiles through faith (Rom 1:16) is enunciated[76] and climaxed.[77] On the surface, this passage has very little to do with Paul's Christophany. However, Carey Newman argues in "Romans 10:2–4 Paul reads the history of Israel in light of his own conversion experience."[78] Others have made similar assertions that appear to rely almost entirely on the shared language of ζῆλος in Rom 10:2 and Phil

69. In favor see Enslin, *Reapproaching Paul*, 53–55; Horsley, *First Corinthians*, 124; cf. Ashton, *Religion of Paul the Apostle*, 117–23.

70. Wright, *Resurrection of the Son of God*, 387; Churchill, *Divine Initiative and Christology*, 136; Furnish, *Second Corinthians*, 544; Harris, *Second Corinthians*, 836; Barnett, *Second Corinthians*, 561.

71. Riddle, *Paul*, 63; Buck and Taylor, *Saint Paul*, 220–26; Enslin, *Reapproaching Paul*, 53–55. However, both Segal, *Paul the Convert*, 36–37; and Wallace, *Snatched into Paradise*, 251–52 and esp. n. 57, warn against too quickly dismissing this reference based solely on re/constructed chronology.

72. Baird, "Visions, Revelation, and Ministry," 652.

73. Furnish, *Second Corinthians*, 544; Wright, *Resurrection of the Son of God*, 387. Pace, Newman, *Paul's Glory-Christology*, 202.

74. McCant, *Second Corinthians*, 18–19; McCant, "Paul's Periodic Apologia," 175–92, sees all of Second Corinthians as parodic defense. See also Watson, "Paul's Boasting," 260–75.

75. Gaventa, "Paul's Conversion," 187–88.

76. Dunn, *Romans 9–16*, 519–20.

77. Wright, *Climax of the Covenant*, 234.

78. Newman, *Paul's Glory-Christology*, 165.

3:6 (cf. ζηλωτής in Gal 1:14),[79] which then opens further linguistic connections of "righteousness" and "knowledge" between these pericopae.

But does this passage actually meet the Christophanic criteria set out above? Since Paul makes no reference to his own conversion/call, Criterion 2 is not met. Regarding Criterion 1, a case could be made from Paul's "knowledge" language (ἐπίγνωσιν in Rom 10:2; ἀγνοοῦντες in Rom 10:3); but again, the emphasis is on *not* knowing and thus correlates more with 2 Cor 5:16 and 12:2–3 than with Phil 3:7–9. For Kim, Paul is contrasting the "ignorance" of the Jews in trying to establish their own righteousness through their zeal for the law with God's righteousness, which he received through faith as a result of his Christophany.[80] One of the difficulties with this reading is it presents Paul as one who condemns Israel for doing the very thing (in Kim's reading) he was unable to do apart from the Christophany; this hardly seems just. Nevertheless, it is not this unjustness which disqualifies it from being a Christophanic reference. It does not meet Criterion 2 and likely does not meet Criterion 1, having no manifestation/revelation of/from Christ.

References to Call, Grace, Apostleship, and Apostolic Work

Regarding those passages which make reference to Paul's "call" (Rom 1:1; 1 Cor 1:1), to "grace" (Rom 1:5; 12:3; 15:15; 1 Cor 3:10; Gal 2:9), to "apostleship" (Rom 11:13; 2 Cor 1:1; Gal 1:1), and to apostolic work (Rom 1:13; 1 Cor 1:17; 2 Cor 10:8; 13:10; cf. Gal 2:2), two things are immediately evident. First, each of these references could be seen as pointing to Paul's initial conversion/call and could therefore fulfill Criterion 2. Nevertheless, one would still need to substantiate that each was indeed a reference to Paul's initial conversion/call and not just a general declaration of his present reality. Second, none of these references directly mentions or alludes to a manifestation/revelation of/from Christ. Therefore, they do not meet Criterion 1 and as such cannot be considered Christophanic references.

Conclusion

From the evaluation of the proposed Christophanic references, it has been concluded that 2 Cor 5:16–18, 2 Cor 12:1–4, Rom 10:2–4, and the various

---

79. Kim, *Origin of Paul's Gospel*, 3–4, 298; Kim, *Paul and the New Perspective*, 112; Bruce, *Romans*, 200; Stuhlmacher, *Romans*, 154; Greathouse and Lyons, *Romans 9–16*, 73.

80. Kim, *Paul and the New Perspective*, 79–81.

references to call, grace, apostleship, and apostolic work do not meet one or both of the stated criteria and have therefore been disqualified. On the other hand, Gal 1:11–17, 1 Cor 9:1–2, 16–17, 1 Cor 15:1–11, and Phil 3:4–14 each meet both criteria and are therefore confirmed Christophanic references. The first three have been categorized as primary references and the final as secondary. Finally, 2 Cor 3:1—4:6 was deemed a secondary Christophanic reference although the presence of the *fpp* brings continued ambiguity to this status. Nevertheless, an a priori judgment of 2 Cor 3:1—6:4 will be confirmed in the evaluation of this epistle.

Outline of the Study

Chapters 3–5 will evaluate the now-confirmed Christophanic references in their larger literary and socio-historical contexts to understand exactly why Paul employs them. This evaluation will take place chronologically. Therefore, chapter 3 will look at Gal 1:11–17, chapter 4 at 1 Cor 9:1–2, 16–17 and 1 Cor 15:1–11, and chapter 5 at Phil 3:4–14. Next, chapter 6 will be devoted to the complexity of 2 Cor 3:1—4:6 and will provide evidence which confirms its Christophanic status. Finally, chapter 7 will bring the finding of chapters 3–6 together and compare them to see if a more general consensus for why Paul employs his Christophanic references can be reached.

3

Paul's Christophanic Reference in Galatians

GALATIANS 1:11–17 IS PAUL's most overt reference to his Christophanic experience and is contained in his most extensive autobiographical narrative (Gal 1:11—2:21). However, many scholars have lost sight of the context and purpose of the autobiographical statements focusing on the apologetic nature of Gal 1–2 and divorcing them from what they consider the theological arguments found in Gal 3–4.[1] As Gaventa writes, "it is not surprising that Galatians 1 and 2 are used extensively, and almost exclusively, for writing the history of primitive Christianity."[2] In light of these emphases, Paul is often depicted as a maverick apostle seeking to demonstrate his independence from and dominance over the Jerusalem church and its leaders,[3] and this is also viewed as the primary purpose behind Paul's Christophanic reference.[4] As noted in chapter 1, Gaventa argues for a reading of Galatians which takes seriously the integral place of Gal 1–2 within the whole epistle and for viewing Paul's Christophanic reference as functioning paradigmatically.[5] This chapter builds upon

---

1. Lightfoot, *Galatians*; Burton, *Galatians*; Duncan, *Galatians*; Schmithals, *Paul & the Gnostics*; Betz, *Galatians*; Bruce, *Galatians*; Longenecker, *Galatians*; Dunn, *Galatians*; Malina and Pilch, *Social-Science Commentary*; Schreiner, *Galatians*.

2. Gaventa, "Galatians 1 and 2," 311. See also Gaventa, "Singularity of the Gospel," 147–59.

3. So Barrett, *Freedom and Obligation*; Dunn, *Jesus, Paul and the Law*, 108–82; Dunn, *Galatians*, 12–131. Contra: Verseput, "Paul's Gentile Mission," 36–58; Lategan, "Is Paul Defending," 411–30.

4. Sandnes, *Paul—One of the Prophets*, 67; Newman, *Paul's Glory-Christology*, 204–5.

5. Gaventa, "Galatians 1 and 2"; Gaventa, "Paul's Conversion," 237–46. A paradigmatic function behind Gal 1–2 is also posited by: Lyons, *Pauline Autobiography*,

and extends beyond Gaventa's work. Beforehand, some preliminary concerns must be addressed, which help to lay the groundwork for evaluation of the Christophanic reference. This includes a brief introduction to the overall theme of Galatians and an extended analysis of Isaiah as an important intertextual background for understanding Paul's autobiographical section in Galatians.

Preliminary Considerations

The Occasion and Theme of Galatians

The impetus for Paul's writing of Galatians is found in Gal 1:6–7. "Agitators"[6] had entered into the Galatians' community and were perverting the gospel of Christ. As a result, the Galatians were in the process of "turning to a different gospel." Paul writes in reaction to this incident and his letter evidences his passion for the gospel and for the church in Galatia. This passion is often mistaken for a kind of reckless haste.[7] While the situation may have necessitated swiftness, the epistle as a whole evidences a careful and planned response[8] with a deliberative approach.[9]

It has been noted that the thanksgiving sections of Paul's letters are more than mere epistolary requirement; they set the tone and theme for the whole epistle.[10] In the case of Galatians, the lack of a thanksgiving[11] itself provides the tone; when it is coupled with Paul's astonishment (Gal 1:6)

123–76; Cummins, *Paul and the Crucified*, 93–137.

6. The identity of these agitators is unimportant for this study. For a brief survey of the arguments see, Jewett, "The Agitators," 198–212; Hurd, "Reflections Concerning Paul's," 129–48. Cf. Martyn, *Galatians*, 122; and Nanos, *Irony in Galatians*, 193–283, who both paint a less negative picture of the opponents. Also note, Lyons, *Pauline Autobiography*, 79, who warns about the dangers of "mirror reading" that, while not fully convincing, should be considered.

7. Richards, *Paul and First-Century Letter*, 123–33, is incorrect that Paul was too rushed to write a thanksgiving.

8. Bryant, *The Risen Crucified Christ*, 115, argues that Paul's reference to καὶ οἱ σὺν ἐμοὶ πάντες ἀδελφοί in Gal 1:2a is proof that Paul discussed the situation and his response with others.

9. Hansen, *Abraham in Galatians*, 57–72; Witherington, *Grace in Galatians*, 25–41; Smit, "The Letter of Paul," 1–26; Kennedy, *New Testament Interpretation*, 144–52.

10. O'Brien, *Introductory Thanksgivings*, 13–15; Schubert, *Form and Function*.

11. Lietzmann, *An die Galater*, 5, concerning Gal 1:5 writes: "sie ist hier eine Art Ersatz für den sonst typischen Dank an Gott." Schubert, *Form and Function*, 162, makes a similar remark. Hansen, "A Paradigm of the Apocalypse," 143–54, argues θαυμάζω (Gal 1:6) has the same function as εὐχαριστέω in the Greek letter.

and double curse (Gal 1:8–9), the audience would have quickly deduced the gravitas of the situation.[12] Concerning theme, it is argued by many that Gal 1:6–9 encompasses the theme of "gospel"[13] and the tone and content shows that Paul is defending his gospel.[14] Others have pointed to Gal 1:1, 11–12 arguing that Paul's emphasis on his Christophanic experience correlates to the theme of apostolic apologia.[15]

However, there is another possible location for establishing the epistle's theme, namely Gal 1:1–5.[16] Modern epistolary and rhetorical studies have often relegated this pericope to the place of "introduction" or "prescript." Nevertheless, Paul's extended opening may provide far more than introduction. It will be argued that rather than defending his apostleship and distancing himself from the Jerusalem church, Paul seeks to persuade the Galatians that a new eschatological age had dawned, and what they experienced while Paul was present was still true in his absence. Paul's Christophanic reference, as well as the whole of the autobiographical narrative of Gal 1–2, is brought into the discussion as proof of this eschatological reality and as an example of how one transitions between these two ages.

---

12. So Stowers, *Letter Writing in Greco-Roman*, 22. Although, Van Voorst, "Why is There No Thanksgiving," 160, claims "a thanksgiving period was not in fact customary in letters of the time, so that the Galatians in all likelihood would not have noted Paul's not giving thanks for them, much less viewed it as meaningful."

13. O'Brien, *Thanksgiving*, 265, writes: "No thanksgiving period omits a reference to the gospel" and that "Thanksgiving and the gospel are inextricably linked." Thus, he insinuates that Gal 1:6–9 functions as Paul's thanksgiving section.

14. Lightfoot, *Galatians*; Burton, *Galatians*; Duncan, *Galatians*; Schmithals, *Paul & the Gnostics*; Betz, *Galatians*; Bruce, *Galatians*; Longenecker, *Galatians*; Dunn, *Galatians*; Malina and Pilch, *Social-Science Commentary*; Schreiner, *Galatians*.

15. So Barrett, *Freedom and Obligation*; Dunn, *Jesus, Paul and the Law*, 108–82; Dunn, *Galatians*, 12–131. Contra: Verseput, "Paul's Gentile Mission," 36–58; Lategan, "Is Paul Defending," 411–30.

16. Many scholars note correlations between themes found in Gal 1:1–5 and those found throughout the letter: e.g., Betz, *Galatians*, 37–43; Kennedy, *New Testament Interpretation*, 147–148; Martyn, *Galatians*, 92–106. However, few scholars argue that Gal 1:1–5 provides the theme. Two exceptions are: Van Voorst, "Why is there No Thanksgiving," and Cook, "The Prescript as Programme," 511–19. Cf. Nanos, *Irony in Galatians*, 71.

Intertextual Reliance upon Isaiah 40–66[17]

The importance of Isaiah for Galatians may be brought into question because it contains only one direct citation (Gal 4:27, cf. Isa 54:1).[18] However, if one includes possible allusions, echoes, and thematic parallels then the role of Isaiah within Galatians must be reconsidered.[19]

Important to the current study on Paul's Christophanic reference is a well-noted allusion in Gal 1:15 to Isa 49:1[20] or Jer 1:5[21] or both.[22] There are at least two reasons to see Isa 49:1 as the primary referent.[23] First, the verbal connection is greatest between 1:15 and Isa 49:1, the former quoting verbatim four words from the latter and both utilizing the verb καλέω (cf. Isa 49:6).[24]

Galatians 1:15	Isaiah 49:1
ὁ ἀφορίσας με ἐκ κοιλίας μητρός μου καὶ καλέσας διὰ τῆς χάριτος αὐτοῦ	Ἀκούσατέ μου, νῆσοι, καὶ προσέχετε, ἔθνη, διὰ χρόνου πολλοῦ στήσεται, λέγει κύριος. ἐκ κοιλίας μητρός μου ἐκάλεσεν τὸ ὄνομά μου

17. Debate concerning authorship and unity/division of Isaiah is not pertinent to this thesis. For recent trends see: Williamson, "Recent Issues in Isaiah," 21–39. For Paul and his contemporaries this was not a topic of discussion and they most likely possessed what we now know as canonical Isaiah. Proof of this may be gleaned from Qumran manuscript evidence. See Swanson, "The Text of Isaiah at Qumran," 191–212. I find most persuasive those arguing for literary unity with multiple authors or redactors. E.g., Seitz, "Isaiah, Book of," 3:472–88, 501–7; Rendtorff, "The Composition of Isaiah," 146–69; Routledge, "Is There a Narrative Substructure," 183–204. Less convincing are arguments favoring a single-author unified Isaiah. So Oswalt, *Isaiah: Chapters 1–39*, 17–28; Beale, *The Erosion of Inerrancy*, 123–59; cf. Watts, *Isaiah 1–33*, xxiv–xlvi.

18. J. Ross Wagner, "Isaiah in Romans and Galatians," 129, writes: "Isaiah plays a relatively minor role in Galatians."

19. So Harmon, *She Must and Shall Go Free*.

20. Sandnes, *Paul—One of the Prophets*, 61–65; Aernie, *Is Paul also among the Prophets?*, 136–37; Harmon, *She Must and Shall Go Free*, 78–79.

21. Segal, *Paul the Convert*, 13–14; Jervis, *Galatians*, 43; Witherington, *Grace in Galatians*, 105.

22. Munck, *Paul*, 24–26; Gaventa, "Paul's Conversion," 231; Fung, *Galatians*, 63–64; Martyn, *Galatians*, 156–57. Cf. Kim, *Paul and the New Perspective*, 201–6, who suggests a combined allusion to Isa 41:8–9, 42:1 and Jer 1:5.

23. This does not negate the possibility that Jer 1:5 or other call narratives also shaped Paul's understanding.

24. All LXX quotes are taken from Rahlfs-Hanhart *Septuaginta*.

Second, there are multiple other connections between the larger contexts of these two pericopae. Paul's self-description as δοῦλος (Gal 1:10; cf. Rom 1:1; Phil 1:1; 2 Cor 4:5) appears to correlate with the servant of Isa 49:3, 5, who was called to glorify Yahweh (καὶ ἐν σοὶ δοξασθήσομαι; Isa 49:3) by being a light to the nations (εἰς φῶς ἐθνῶν; Isa 49:6; cf. 49:8b) and who grieved over labor given in vain (κενῶς ἐκοπίασα; Isa 49:4). Similarly, Paul's call is to proclaim Christ among the nations (ἵνα εὐαγγελίζωμαι αὐτὸν ἐν τοῖς ἔθνεσιν; Gal 1:16), which has led the churches in Judea to glorify God (ἐδόξαζον ἐν ἐμοὶ τὸν θεόν; Gal 1:24). Additionally, Paul mentions going to Jerusalem to make sure he has not run in vain (εἰς κενόν; Gal 2:2).

These striking parallels lead many scholars to conclude that Paul is seeking to represent his own call in the form of an OT prophetic call narrative,[25] perhaps in order to establish and legitimize his authority.[26] However, attempts to categorize Paul's Christophanic reference into the various *formgeschichtlichen* elements outlined by Norm Habel[27] are neither convincing nor consistent.[28] This does not negate the possibility that Paul understood himself as fulfilling some type of prophetic role; it is only a question of the necessity of making Paul's words conform to a particular narrative form. Others have argued Paul understood himself as fulfilling the specific role of the Isaianic servant.[29] In light of the multiple allusions to Isa 49, the latter proposal appears more convincing. However, before drawing conclusions, it is beneficial to see if there are additional Isaianic allusions or echoes that may shed light on the importance of Isaiah for this epistle and which may, therefore, help to interpret Paul's use of Isa 49 as part of his Christophanic reference.

25. Baird, "Visions, Revelation, and Ministry," 656–57; Sandnes, *Paul—One of the Prophets*, 49–70; Aernie, *Is Paul also among the Prophets?*, 136–39; Ciampa, *Presence and Function*, 119–20.

26. Sandnes, *Paul—One of the Prophets*, 67; Newman, *Paul's Glory-Christology*, 204–5; cf. Hafemann, *Paul, Moses*, 92–110.

27. Habel, "Form and Significance," 297–323. Although see, Guyette, "Genre of the Call Narrative," 54–58, who argues that there is not a single form to which all call narratives conform.

28. Baird, "Visions, Revelation, and Ministry," 656–57; Newman, *Paul's Glory-Christology*, 204.

29. Harmon, *She Must and Shall Go Free*, 105–15; Stanley, "Theme of the Servant," 385–425; Dinter, "Paul and the Prophet of Isaiah," 48–52; Beker, *Paul the Apostle*, 115–16; Ciampa, *Presence and Function*, 94–95; Newman, *Paul's Glory-Christology*, 206–7. Cf. Kim, *Origin of Paul's Gospel*, 93–99, who also sees an echo to Isa 6 and more specifically to the divine council scene therein. Similarly, Sandnes, *Paul—One of the Prophets*, 64–68.

Another important Isaianic allusion comes in the prescript, which comprises the theme of this epistle. Multiple scholars argue that Gal 1:4 (cf. Gal 2:20) contains an allusion to Isa 53,[30] with the exact verse being contested.

Galatians 1:4	Isaiah 53:6	Isaiah 53:10	Isaiah 53:12
τοῦ δόντος ἑαυτὸν ὑπὲρ τῶν ἁμαρτιῶν ἡμῶν	καὶ κύριος παρέδωκεν αὐτὸν ταῖς ἁμαρτίαις ἡμῶν	ἐὰν δῶτε περὶ ἁμαρτίας, ἡ ψυχὴ ὑμῶν ὄψεται σπέρμα μακρόβιον, καὶ βούλεται κύριος ἀφελεῖν	καὶ αὐτὸς ἁμαρτίας πολλῶν ἀνήνεγκεν καὶ διὰ τὰς ἁμαρτίας αὐτῶν παρεδόθη

Here, it is unnecessary to rehash the debates offered for the various referent[31] if it can be shown that the Jewish idea of vicarious suffering stems from Isa 53. Hermann Spieckermann has traced the prehistory of vicarious suffering in the OT, arguing that it resembles the prophetic intercession and prophetic suffering evidenced in Deuteronomic Moses, Amos, Jeremiah, and Ezekiel.[32] However, Spieckermann believes Isa 53 evidences a new and unique sense in at least four ways: (1) "It becomes suffering for the guilt of others that is intended by God and the Servant together";[33] (2) it is concentrated on the role of a single figure who is able to remove guilt for all time; (3) "God makes the Servant's righteousness a part of the vicarious event";[34] and (4) it is for the "many," which includes other nations. Spieckermann is correct in highlighting these significant differences, many of which appear to continue until the NT period.[35] Therefore, caution should be taken be-

30. Ciampa, *Presence and Function*, 51–61; Harmon, *She Must and Shall Go Free*, 56–66; Bruce, *Galatians*, 75; Longenecker, *Galatians*, 7; Hays, "Galatians," 203; Rohde, *Galater*, 35; Fee, *Galatians*, 19, also proposes Isa 53:4.

31. Among the most significant arguments see: Ciampa, *Presence and Function*, 51–61, who favors Isa 53:6; Harmon, *She Must and Shall Go Free*, 56–66, who favors Isa 53:10; Rohde, *Galater*, 35, who favors Isa 53:12.

32. Spieckermann, "Vicarious Suffering," 1–15. Also see Scharbert, "Stellvertretendes Sühneleiden," 190–213, for an argument against viewing Babylonian traditions as a background for the phenomenon of *Stellvertretung* found in Isa 53.

33. Spieckermann, "Vicarious Suffering," 13–14.

34. Spieckermann, "Vicarious Suffering," 14.

35. For a history of the use of Isa 53 in the intertestamental period see: Hengel with Bailey, "Effective History of Isaiah 53," 75–146. They argue the exaltation motif of Isa 52–53 is strongest in these later writings and "the motif of vicarious atoning death . . . recedes more or less into the background in other pre-Christian texts" (146). See also Hooker, *Jesus and the Servant*, 53–61.

fore assuming any kind of solidified concept behind the identity and work of the Servant; these were still very much *in statu nascendi*.[36]

The absence of a prehistory does not exclude the possibility of a subsequent (possibly independent) source for Paul's understanding of vicarious suffering. Many have suggested Maccabean Martyr Theology (*MMT*).[37] Of particular importance is 2 Macc 7:37–38, 4 Macc 6:28–29, and 4 Macc 17:21–22. There are, however, significant difficulties in viewing these as a source for Paul's understanding of Christ's vicarious suffering. First, 4 Maccabees, which evidences the clearest and more developed *MMT*, is dated much too late to be considered a source for Paul.[38]

Second, *MMT* fails to meet important elements found in Isa 53 and in Paul's writings.[39] For example, the martyrs' sacrifice is not necessarily intended by God for the purpose of atonement; rather, the martyrs themselves make an appeal to Yahweh that their actions might provide atonement for others. Additionally, and of great importance to Paul, this sacrificial act is only for the Jewish nation and not for the "many" (cf. Dan 11:34–35).

Third, many have correctly asserted *MMT* "is itself based on exegetical reflection upon scriptural material in general relating to sacrifice and redemption and Isaiah 53 in particular."[40] The fact Paul's words in 1:4 show a greater linguistic[41] and thematic connection to Isa 53 than to 2 Macc 7:37–38 may suggest Paul is doing his own exegetical reflection on the former text rather than on the latter. This assertion may be strengthened by Paul's multiple other allusions to Isa 53 in places where he refers to Christ's vicarious suffering (Rom 4:24–25; 5:15–19; 1 Cor 15:3–4; Gal 2:20; Phil 2:7–9; cf. Eph 5:2, 25; 1 Tim 2:6; Titus 2:14).

Fourth, the recognition that Isa 53 was a significant text for the early church's understanding of the person and work of Christ (Mark 10:45; Matt 20:28; Luke 22:37; John 1:29, 36; Heb 9:28; 1 Pet 2:21–25; 3:18),[42] coupled

---

36. Spieckermann, "Vicarious Suffering," 14; Wright, *Climax of the Covenant*, 60.

37. See de Jonge, "Jesus' Death for Others," 142–51; Heard, "Maccabean Martyr Theology"; Williams, *Maccabean Martyr Traditions in Paul.*; Cummins, *Paul and the Crucified*, 19–90.

38. D. Campbell, *Rhetoric of Righteousness in Romans*, 219–28; van Henten, "Vierten Makkabäerbuches," 136–49. Contra Bickerman, "The Date of IV Maccabees," 275–81; deSilva, *4 Maccabees*, 14–18.

39. Khobnya, *The Father Who Redeems*, 146–48.

40. Ciampa, *Presence and Function*, 58–59; so also Williams, *Maccabean Martyr Traditions in Paul*, 72–84; Heard, "Maccabean Martyr Theology," 185–393.

41. However, 2 Macc 7:37 does include the verb προδίδωμι.

42. Stuhlmacher, "Isaiah 53 in the Gospels," 147–62; Hofius, "The Forth Servant Song," 163–88; Stanley, "Theme of the Servant," 386–412; Gignilliat, "Isaiah's Servant," 125–36.

with the recognition that some of the Pauline references evidence pre-Pauline kerygmatic tradition (esp. 1 Cor 15:2–3; cf. Phil 2:6–11; and possibly Gal 1:4[43]), lends itself to the conclusion that if Paul is borrowing from a source other than Isa 53, it is likely from early church Christology, which itself is based on Isa 53.[44]

There is, therefore, strong evidence for viewing Isa 53 as a significant foundation text for Paul's interpretation and understanding of Christ's atonement and for viewing 1:4 (and 2:20[45]) as alluding to parts or all of Isa 53. Matthew Harmon's point is significant: "The fact that a plausible case can be made for an allusion to three different portions of the same passage of scripture indicates the probability that the allusion itself is to the totality of the passage rather than to just a specific line from it."[46]

Harmon argues for three additional references to Isa 53 in Gal 3. First, he views Paul's use of ἐξ ἀκοῆς πίστεως in Gal 3:2, 5 as an allusion to Isa 53:1 (τίς ἐπίστευσεν τῇ ἀκοῇ ἡμῶν).[47] This connection is made by others,[48] and should be seen as a strong possibility in light of Rom 10:16–17. Second, Harmon makes a case for seeing an allusion to Isa 53 in Gal 3:13, although not denying the citation from Deut 21:23, which he believe is best interpreted in light of the Isaiah passage.[49] Harmon's argument is mostly reliant upon the parallels he perceives between Gal 1:4 and 3:13. Roy Ciampa makes a similar appeal adding a comparison between the language of "curse" in Deut 21:23 and the description of the Servant in Isa 53:2–3.[50] While this appears to be a faint echo, rather than a solid allusion, it should not automatically be dismissed.

Finally, Harmon sees a thematic parallel between Paul's reference to Christ as the singular seed (σπέρμα) in Gal 3:16 (cf. Gal 4:1–7) and Isaiah's references to Abraham's seed (σπέρμα Ἀβρααμ) in Isa 41:8, which is later

---

43. So argues Bovon, "Une formule prépaulinienne," 91–107.

44. Of course, Paul could have both Jesus tradition and *MMT* in the back of his mind as he himself evaluates Isa 53. Cf. Ciampa, *Presence and Function*, 52–59; Dunn, *Galatians*, 35.

45. Those favoring an Isa 53 allusion in Gal 2:20 include: Harmon, *She Must and Shall Go Free*, 101–2; Ciampa, *Presence and Function*, 212; Bruce, *Galatians*, 145–46; cf. Hays, "Galatians," 244 n. 126.

46. Harmon, *She Must and Shall Go Free*, 65.

47. Harmon, *She Must and Shall Go Free*, 129–32.

48. E.g., Hays, *The Faith of Jesus Christ*, 128–31; Bruce, *Galatians*, 149

49. Harmon, *She Must and Shall Go Free*, 142–46.

50. Ciampa, *Presence and Function*, 59. Here, Ciampa is reliant upon Hanson, *The People Called*, 245–46.

understood as the Servant's seed (σπέρμα; Isa 53:10; 54:3).[51] Harmon notes the more obvious connection between Paul's words and Gen 17:7–12, 19 (cf. Gen 12:7; 13:15; 15:18), but argues Paul reads the Genesis passage through the lens of Isaiah and in so doing transforms the narrative of Gen 12–25 in a way which benefits his "faith" perspective rather than his opponents' "law" perspective.[52] Harmon's argument has some weaknesses.[53] Nevertheless, the Servant of Isa 40–66 may be the most profitable imagery for working through Paul's difficult reading of Christ as the singular seed over and against the seed as collective faithful Israel (cf. Gal 3:29; Rom 4:18; 9:7).

It has become evident thus far that Paul does make multiple references to Isaiah in general and to the Servant texts in particular.[54] Additionally, since Paul applies aspects of the Servant's identity and work to both Christ and himself, further work must be undertaken before conclusions can be drawn concerning why Paul utilizes this imagery in his Christophanic reference. In light of the emphasis on the Isaianic Servant, a brief analysis of this subject will precede the exegesis of Galatians.

The Servant and the Servants

The Hebrew word עֶבֶד is used thirty-one times in Isa 40–66 (MT): twenty times in the singular, all in chapters 41–53, and eleven times in the plural, all in chapters 54–66. The LXX makes use of four different words to encompass these same references (παῖς [fourteen times[55]]; δοῦλος [nine times[56]]; δουλεύω [seven times[57]]; θεραπεύω [once[58]]). However, the LXX adds Isa 45:14 and omits 66:14; it also pluralizes Isa 42:19[bis] and 49:7 and singularizes 65:8. The MT's abrupt and decisive shift from the singular to the plural, the LXX's blurring of these lines, and the multiple singular references

51. Harmon, *She Must and Shall Go Free*, 150–58; similarly, Pyne, "The 'Seed,' the Spirit," 214–16.

52. Harmon, *She Must and Shall Go Free*, 154–55.

53. For example, Harmon's reading of Isaac as the singular seed in Gen 17:19 is not convincing and may undercut his main agenda of arguing for the necessity of Isaiah in Paul's reading.

54. By "Servant texts," I am not referencing the so-called "Servant Songs" (Isa 42:1–4; 49:1–6; 50:4–9; 52:13—53:12) of Duhm, *Das Buch Jesaia*. I am speaking about the multiple references, both stated and inferred, to the Servant/servants throughout Isa 40–66 in their literary context.

55. Isa 41:8, 9; 42:1, 19; 43:10; 44:1, 2, 21(bis), 26; 45:4; 49:6; 50:10; 52:13.

56. Isa 42:19; 45:14; 48:20; 49:3, 5, 7; 56:6; 63:17; 65:9.

57. Isa 53:11; 65:8, 13(thrice), 14, 15.

58. Isa 54:17.

in both, which appear to function as a collective, have led to great confusion concerning the identity or identities of the servant/s.

Chapters 40–48 continually designate the singular servant collectively as Israel or Jacob.[59] Even in chapter 42, which includes the first so-called "Servant Song," the identity of the servant is collective Israel whose main role is to bring justice to the nations (Isa 42:1, 3, 4) because Yahweh has given them as "a covenant to the people, a light to the nations" (Isa 42:6). H. G. M. Williamson has established multiple connections between Isa 42:1–4 and the role of Israel as described in Isa 1–39.[60] Furthermore, Peter Wilcox and David Paton-Williams demonstrate that while there is a difference in the character between the servant in chapter 42 and Israel's character in chapters 40–48, the identity is the same. "[T]he prophet looks forward to a time when passive Israel will take up his [sic] mantle once more, as Yahweh's active servant among the nations."[61] In the words of Goldingay, "It is . . . because Israel cannot fulfil the servant role which is her responsibility, that the identity of the servant which was explicit in chapter xli is open in chapter xlii. The picture of the servant has become a role seeking for someone to fulfil it."[62]

This "someone" is introduced in chapter 49. Although still named Israel (Isa 49:3), this Servant[63] is clearly represented as an individual who speaks in the first person singular about his being called by Yahweh (Isa 49:1–5) "to raise up the tribes of Jacob and to restore the survivors of Israel" and to be "a light to the nations, that [Yahweh's] salvation may reach to the end of the earth" (Isa 49:6). The Servant being both called Israel[64] and called to restore Israel creates confusion. The LXX complicates this further by pluralizing servant (τῶν δούλων) in Isa 49:7. Wilcox's and Paton-Williams's proposal makes the most sense of this passage and its correlation to Isa 42. They take the יִשְׂרָאֵל of verse 3 not as a vocative ("You are my servant, [O] Israel") but as a predicative, thus rendering it "You are my [S]ervant, [you are] Israel."[65] The Servant becomes representative of the whole. The Servant does not replace Israel; the Servant "remains

---

59. Wilcox and Paton-Williams, "Servant Songs in Deutero-Isaiah," 82–84.

60. Williamson, *Variations on a Theme*, 130–46.

61. Wilcox and Paton-Williams, "Servant Songs in Deutero-Isaiah," 88.

62. Goldingay, "The Arrangement of Isaiah," 292.

63. Here, Servant with a capital "S" represents the individual servant.

64. Westermann, *Isaiah 40–66*, 209. Westermann's suggestion that v. 3 is a later interpolation is not convincing.

65. Wilcox and Paton-Williams, "Servant Songs in Deutero-Isaiah," 93; so also Seitz, "Isaiah 40–66," 429; Childs, *Isaiah*, 384–85; Gignilliat, *Paul and Isaiah's Servants*, 73–74.

inseparable from Israel—but as a faithful embodiment of the nation Israel who has not performed its chosen role."[66]

The exact (historical) identity is not the primary goal of the texts.[67] The obscurity surrounding the Servant actually serves to emphasis his role[68] and his connection to Yahweh. The anonymity of this singular Servant throughout chapters 49–54 emphasize Yahweh's working through the Servant to bring his covenant promises to fruition. There are places where the lines are blurred to such an extent that one might see Yahweh as the Servant (e.g., Isa 49:7; 51:4–6; 52:13).[69] Almost metaphorically, the Servant represents the suffering Yahweh has endured at the hands of Israel's disobedience. In Richard Bauckham's words: "The Servant, in both his humiliation and his exaltation, is therefore not merely a human figure distinguished from God, but, in both his humiliation and his exaltation, belongs to the identity of the unique God."[70] This does not negate the participation of the Servant, nor of Israel as a whole.[71] Yahweh, through the Servant, is seeking to awaken Israel to embrace her calling and embody her covenant commitment (Isa 51:9; 52:1–2). One can even see a corporate call to consecration (Isa 52:11) and covenant renewal for Israel (Isa 55:1–12), which is extended to all obeying nations (Isa 56:1–8; 66:18–21).

This constitutes a final shift in the identity of the servant; namely, an expanded return to the collective servant, here represented with the plural (e.g., Isa 54:17; 55:6). The plural "servants" is foreshadowed in Isa 53:10 as the singular Servant's suffering results in "offspring" or "seed" (זֶרַע; cf. Isa 44:3) who prolong his days.[72] This protraction does not refer to the Servant's escape from death but to the offspring who turn from their transgressions and receive the same Spirit that guided the singular Servant (Isa 59:20–21; cf. 11:2; 42:1), the same mission[73] (Isa 61:1–2, 9; 62:2, 10–12), and possibly the same suffering (Isa 57:1–2).[74] Isaiah 65–66 concludes with a glorious

66. Childs, *Isaiah*, 385.

67. Westermann, *Isaiah 40–66*, 93; Gignilliat, "Isaiah's Servant," 134; Seitz, "How is the Prophet Isaiah Present," 239. Cf. Clines, *I, He, We, and They*, 33, 46.

68. Gignilliat, *Paul and Isaiah's Servants*, 88 and n. 147; Wilcox and Paton-Williams, "Servant Songs in Deutero-Isaiah," 98.

69. Wilcox and Paton-Williams, "Servant Songs in Deutero-Isaiah," 95.

70. Bauckham, *Jesus and the God of Israel*, 36–37; cf. Gignilliat, *Paul and Isaiah's Servants*, 88–89.

71. Childs, *Isaiah*, 402–4.

72. Beuken, "Main Theme of Trito-Isaiah," 67–87, argues the question driving Isaiah 56–66 is: "who are his offspring, in whom does he go on living?" (73).

73. Childs, *Isaiah*, 446; McKenzie, *Second Isaiah*, lvii.

74. Seitz, "Isaiah 40–66," 490–91; Gignilliat, *Paul and Isaiah's Servants*, 116–17.

picture of God's faithfulness and restoration of his creation, in which the servants hold a special place (Isa 65:8–9, 12–15; 66:14).[75]

Summary

The ambiguity of identity as well as the connection between the singular Servant and his seed (the servants), appears to have provided Paul with a significant foundation for his understanding of Christ's identity, his own identity, and the identity of all believers. In what follows, it will be demonstrated that an understanding of this Isaianic Servant/s and his/their role aids the modern reader in interpreting Paul's Christophanic reference as well as other significant sections of Galatians.

One further point needs to be articulated. This reading does not necessitate a recognition or understanding of the various Isaianic allusions and echoes by the Galatians. This neither discounts the possibility for such Isaianic underpinnings, nor does it mean the Galatians would have missed Paul's point. Paul's argument contains multiple layers and one such layer is Paul's understanding of the Jewish Scriptures, which naturally moves behind the text and surfaces both intentionally and unintentionally from time to time. Nevertheless, there does appear to be some assumed knowledge of various OT passages and especially the Abrahamic narrative (Gal 3:6–9, 16–19; 4:21–31).[76] Paul quotes the OT at least ten times[77] from at least five different books. Although Paul's familiarity with this group cannot easily be deduced, it would appear the Galatians had at least a basic familiarity with the OT,[78]

---

75. Beuken, "Main Theme of Trito-Isaiah," 76–85.

76. Marshall, *New Testament Theology*, 216, comments on how Paul's use of Scripture "dominates much of the discussion, almost providing the structure of the argument as well as the basis for it."

77. Silva, "Old Testament in Paul," 631, lists: Gen 15:6 (Gal 3:6); Gen 12:3 + 18:18 (Gal 3:8); Deut 27:26 (Gal 3:10); Hab 2:4 (Gal 3:11); Lev 18:5 (Gal 3:12); Deut 21:23 (Gal 3:13); Gen 13:15 (Gal 3:16); Isa 54:1 (Gal 4:27); Gen 21:10 (Gal 4:30); Lev 19:18 (Gal 5:14); and Ps 143:2 (Gal 2:16) as debated. Cf. Koch, *Die Schrift*, 22–23.

78. *Pace*, Stanley, *Arguing with Scripture*, 114–35, who argues Paul's audience did not know the OT Scriptures well otherwise they would have "noted grave problems with the arguments that he erects" (135). Contra Ciampa, *Presence and Function*, 267, who goes so far as to say: "It is clear from the content of the letter that the Galatian churches were definitely involved in vigorous study of the Scriptures."

which may have come from Paul's teaching,[79] from the Agitators' teaching,[80] from synagogue teaching,[81] or from a combination thereof.

Exegesis of Paul's Autobiographical Data

Galatians 1:1–5

Paul's opening words (Gal 1:1–5) encompasses the theme of Paul's Jewish eschatological gospel and the Galatians' place within it. In these five short verses Paul reveals that (1) Christ the Lord (2) has been raised from the dead (3) by God the Father; that (4) the churches of Galatia are recipients of (5) God's grace and peace, which has been extended through (6) Christ having given himself for sins (7) in order to rescue humanity from the present evil age; and that this was (8) the will of God.

1. Although Χριστός (Gal 1:1, 3) is often viewed simply as a cognomen,[82] it arguably has some messianic connotations, at least for Paul.[83] While diverse in meaning,[84] the concept shares the overarching themes of

79. Ciampa, *Presence and Function*, 268–70.

80. Martyn, *Galatians*, 281–373, 431–66; Barclay, *Obeying the Truth*, 52–56; cf. Ciampa, *Presence and Function*, 261–64.

81. Nanos, *Irony in Galatians*, 6–9; cf. Davies, review of *Galatians* by H. D. Betz, 311–12.

82. Dunn, *Christ and the Spirit*, 212–28; Jonge, "The Earliest Christian Use of *Christos*," 321–43.

83. Wright, *Climax of the Covenant*, 46; Wright, *Faithfulness of God*, Book 2, 817–25, is a strong proponent of this view believing that for Paul, Χριστός is incorporative and has not lost the titular sense of 'Messiah.' See also: de Boer, *Galatians*, 24; Ciampa, *Presence and Function*, 38–39. Contra Chester, *Messiah and Exaltation*, 383, who argues Paul's primary use of Χριστός is not titular and that for Paul's Gentile audience the use of Χριστός as a title would not be a commendable designation (cf. 102–3 n. 228). Nevertheless, Chester does believe Paul viewed Jesus as the fulfilment of a particular Jewish messianic category, namely, "where the Messiah is a human or angelic figure belonging . . . in the heavenly world, a figure who at the same time has had a specific, limited role on earth" (394–95; cf. 307). Cf. Novenson, *Christ Among the Messiahs*, 88–97, who argues that in Paul, Χριστός is not a name or a title but an honorific. Novenson's work has had a significant impact on Wright's later work: see Wright, *Faithfulness of God*, Book 2, 824–25.

84. There is ongoing debate over the scope and impact of messianism in the various streams of Judaism. Two collected works highlight the complexity of the issue and argue there was no uniform or definitive messianic expectation within Judaism. See: Neusner, Green, and Frerichs, *Judaisms and Their Messiahs*; Charlesworth, *The Messiah*. Still, Chester, *Messiah and Exaltation*, argues that in the 1st Century BCE and 1st and 2nd Century CE "there was clearly a generally widespread acquaintance with royal messianic expectation" (282; see also 356–62) and that while there may appear

God's future intervention through some Davidic connected figure, whether human or angelic (e.g., 2 Sam 7:8–16; Isa 9:2–7; 11:1–9; Jer 23:5–8; Ezek 34:23–24).[85] On its own, this titular reference may carry little significance for Paul's audience. Nevertheless, what Paul connects to this title, and thus to the historical person of Jesus, is significant. This "anointed one" is referenced as κυρίου Ἰησοῦ Χριστοῦ (v. 3). The background for Paul's understanding of the language and concept of κύριος is thoroughly Jewish.[86] While this dictum may have conjured imperial overtones and thus anti-imperial connotations in the minds of the Galatians,[87] Paul uses it to construct a particular picture of the Christ.[88]

2. Reference to Christ's resurrection in a Pauline prescript is rare (cf. Rom 1:4) and, here, gives further definition to Christ. If Paul is reading Isa 40–66, then reference to Christ's resurrection in Gal 1:1 may be an allusion to LXX Isa 52:13 where the Servant is said to be ὑψωθήσεται καὶ δοξασθήσεται. The word ὑψωθήσεται (from ὑψόω, a translation of the Hebrew רום) is often translated as "raised" or "exalted" and is closely linked with Christ's resurrection (cf. Phil 2:9; Acts 2:32–33; 5:30–31).[89] Most interesting is the LXX's translation of the Hebrew נָשָׂא (lifted up) with δοξάζω (glorified; cf. Gal 1:5, 24), which is unprecedented[90] and may have been selected because of its relationship to the Servant figure.

---

to be a "messianic vacuum" from 500–200 BCE, it is more proper to think of a "latent messianism" (283–84 and n. 293). Chester is able to reach this conclusion, in part, by moving beyond philological studies, which rely exclusively on passages containing the term "messiah" (204).

85. See Wright, *The New Testament*, 307–20.

86. Fitzmyer, *To Advance the Gospel*, 220–23; Wright, *Jesus and the Victory of God*, 477–539.

87. Wright, "Paul's Gospel and Caesar's Empire," 160–83.

88. For argumentation in favor of a Pauline divine-Christology see: Bauckham, *Jesus and the God of Israel*, 182–232; Fee, *Pauline Christology*; Tilling, *Paul's Divine Christology*. For argumentation in opposition to a Pauline divine-Christology see: Dunn, *Theology of Paul*, 234–93; McGrath, *The Only True God*, 38–54; Casey, *From Jewish Prophet to Gentile God*, 121–40.

89. Lüdemann, "ὑψόω," *EDNT* 3:410. Within the Johannine literature, ὑψόω expresses the full event of crucifixion and exaltation (John 3:14; 8:28; 12:32, 34). Collins, *Apocalypticism*, 121–22, argues that רום is used in 1QH 14:34 as either a literal or metaphoric reference to resurrection.

90. The four other translations of נָשָׂא (nif'al, passive) are as follows: 1 Chr 14:2 with the verb αὐξάνω; Isa 2:12 with the noun ὑψηλός; Isa 6:1 with the verb ἐπαίρω; and Isa 33:10 with the verb ὑψόω. The closest correlation is the LXX translation of Isa 33:10, which contains both ὑψόω and δοξάζω, but where they are used to translate the opposite Hebrew word (i.e., δοξάζω from רום and ὑψόω from נָשָׂא).

Regardless of whether or not Paul intentionally alludes to Isa 52:13, his mention of Christ's resurrection serves as a significant eschatological marker.[91] God has done a new thing in raising Christ from the dead and this "new thing" is just the beginning of what God is doing in and through Christ. Paul sets the stage for a new reality that sits both within and without of the Galatians' present reality.

3. Paul's multiple references to God as father (Gal 1:1, 3, 4; cf. 4:2, 6) is a relatively common concept within Judaism, which is usually either connected to corporate Israel (e.g., Ps 68:5; Isa 63:16; 64:8; Jer 31:9; Mal 1:6; cf. Exod 4:22; Deut 14:1; Hos 11:1) or to an individual within the line of the Davidic kingship (e.g., 2 Sam 7:14; 1 Chr 17:12; Ps 89:26).[92] This concept also takes on possible messianic overtones by the Second Temple Period (cf. 4QFlor 1 I, 11), which has its origin in the OT and especially 2 Sam 7:14. James Scott argues 2 Sam 7:14 contains an adoption formula that is taken up in subsequent Jewish tradition and applied "eschatologically either to the Messiah (4QFlor 1:11), to Israel (*Jub.* 1:24), or to both (*T. Jud.* 24.3)."[93] It is not difficult to see how Paul could utilize fatherhood and sonship/child-ship language in relation to Christ (Gal 1:16; 2:20; 4:4, 6) and in relation to collective Israel (cf. Gal 4:5). Nevertheless, Paul's purpose for employing this concept in Galatians is to remind them of their eschatological inclusion through Christ (Gal 1:1–4; 4:4–7).

Within Jewish literature, the universality of God's fatherhood is reflected in general terms (e.g., Wis 14:3; *Ant.* 1:20, 230; 2:152) and Gentile inclusion is attested on an individual basis reliant upon repentance and conversion to Judaism (*Jos. Asen.* 12:8, 12–14).[94] Nevertheless, the large-scale universal adoption of Gentiles in a manner similar to that of Israel's adoption appears to be missing. There is, however, the concept of the eschatological inclusion of the Gentiles, which crops up in Isa 2:2–4 and is later connected to the role of the Servant/servants (e.g., Isa 45:20–23; 49:6; 55:5; 56:1–8; 60:3; 66:18–21). Thematically, an argument can be made that the Isaianic Servant is the Davidic heir

---

91. Cf. Beker, *Paul the Apostle*, 152.

92. Khobnya, *The Father Who Redeems*, 19–44. Examples of this concept in STJL include: Tob 13:3–4; 3 Macc 6:3; *Jub.* 19:29.

93. Scott, *Adoption as Sons of God*, 104. Scott argues *T. Jud* 24:1–3 is not a Christian interpolation (109–12). However, this view is highly debated. For instance, see: de Jonge, "Christian Influence in the Testaments," esp. 210–16. But see also: deSilva, "The *Testaments of the Twelve Patriarchs*," 21–68.

94. See Khobnya, *The Father Who Redeems*, 42–44.

(cf. Isa 7:13–14; 9:6–7; 16:5; 55:3).[95] But whereas the Davidic heir of 2 Sam 7:14 is punished for his iniquity (ἀδικία) the Isaianic Servant is righteous (δίκαιος) and makes others righteous (δικαιῶσαι) through his bearing of their sin (Isa 53:11). In this way, the Isaianic Servant is antithetical to the Davidic heir; "this future Ruler will carry out his responsibilities with a fidelity that was lacking in Judah's contemporary kings."[96] Unlike David's offspring (σπέρμα), the Isaianic Servant produces offspring (σπέρμα) that will continue Yahweh's righteous mission. Paul's justification for the inclusion of the Gentiles as children of God the father may be birthed in this eschatological picture of the new Servant-Davidic King who is adopted by God and brings others into the family by their connection to him.

4. Paul's use of ἐκκλησία[97] (Gal 1:2,[98] 13, 22) is likely grounded in the Jewish concept of the יְהוָה קְהַל (Deut 23:2–4, 9; 1 Chron 28:8; Mic 2:5) or קְהַל הָאֱלֹהִים (Judg 20:2; Neh 13:1), which the LXX renders ἐκκλησία κυρίου (cf. Gal 1:13). Within their contexts, reference to the ἐκκλησία κυρίου refers to the assembly or congregation of Israel. It is not surprising the Hebrew phrase קְהַל יִשְׂרָאֵל and the Greek phrase ἐκκλησία Ἰσραηλ are also well attested (Deut 31:30; Josh 8:35; 1 Kings 8:14; 1 Chron 12:2; 2 Chron 6:3). Paul's use of ἐκκλησία in relation to the Gentiles does not necessarily denote a replacement of Israel.[99] Nor does it mean that Paul is only employing the word in the generic Hellenistic sense of "assembly" or "gathering" (cf. Acts 19:32, 39, 40–41).[100] Paul's words serve to remind the Galatians of their new identity as the people of God, both Jew and Gentile (cf. Gal 1:13, 22).[101] Rather than focusing on nationality, this concept reminds the Galatians of the dawning of a new eschatological reality[102] in which Gentiles become the ἐκκλησία of God as they simultaneously become children of God the Father.

---

95. See Chisholm, "The Christological Fulfillment," 387–404. Chisholm notes Isa 42:7, 49:7, 52:13–15, and 53:11–12 as passages that emphasize the Servant's royalty.

96. Schultz, "The King in the Book of Isaiah," 158–59.

97. Used forty-four time in the undisputed Pauline epistles.

98. In Gal 1:2 ἐκκλησία is used in the plural but it carries the same basic meaning as the other uses. For LXX uses of the plural see: Ps 25:12; 67:27.

99. Dunn, Theology of Paul, 539, is correct to note that Paul is "representing the more inclusive strand of Israel's heritage over against those who emphasized its exclusiveness."

100. Contra Beker, Paul the Apostle, 313–17; Park, Paul's Ekklesia.

101. Cf. de Boer, Galatians, 26–27.

102. Cf. 1QM 4:10; 1QSa 2:4; and see, Roloff, "ἐκκλησία," 1:411.

5. The grace and peace "formula," assumed to be an adopted and adapted part of the Hellenistic epistolary form,[103] may signal the disclosure of God's new reality to the recipients.[104] Ulrich Mauser notes that this formula (or variations of it) is frequent in Jewish literature apart from letters and speaks of God's imparted blessings on his people. He further notes how grace is often connected with persons who have been given a revelation from God.[105] In this benedictory statement, Paul extends a revelation of God's grace and peace to the Galatians, where "grace" refers to "an activity and a sphere, by and in which believers are privileged to live" and "peace" is "that condition of eschatological well-being ('salvation') that only God can bring about."[106]

6. Reference to Christ's sacrificial death for sin not only highlights the work of this Christ, a concept Paul is continuing to construct, it also emphasizes the Galatians' corporate sin in conjunction with Israel's.[107] Paul is effectively writing Gentiles into Israel's story, not as the "other nations," before whose eyes Israel is called to evidence the glory of God, but as the people of God, who have disobeyed and who have required a Servant figure to redeem them and to remind them of their covenant commitment. Thus, Paul places the Galatians within the sphere of the eschatological redemption of the Servant (cf. Isa 53) and challenges them to embrace the Servant's mission in this new eschatological reality.

7. This phrase τοῦ αἰῶνος τοῦ ἐνεστῶτος πονηροῦ (Gal 1:4) is Paul's most blatant declaration of his eschatological framework (cf. Rom 12:2; 1 Cor 1:20; 2:6, 8; 3:18; 2 Cor 4:4).[108] Paul has already alluded to and now clearly announces the apocalyptic in-breaking of a new age in which the Christ event has enabled the participation of the Gentiles into the eschatological Kingdom. The word ἐξαιρέω is rare in the NT and only used here by Paul (Gal 1:4). It frequently occurs in the LXX as a reference to deliverance or rescue from one's enemy (e.g., Exod 3:8; 18:4; Deut 23:15; Isa 50:2; 60:16; Dan 3:17) and this same use is well attested in Acts (Acts 7:10, 34; 12:11; 23:27; 26:17). In Matthew, it carries

---

103. Doty, *Letters in Primitive Christianity*, 21–47, esp. 29–31.

104. Barclay, *Paul & Gift*, 352–53, speaks of Christ and the Christ-event as God's beneficence and highlights the radicalness of this Christ-gift being given to such unrighteous beneficiaries as the Gentiles.

105. Mauser, *The Gospel of Peace*, 108.

106. De Boer, *Galatians*, 28.

107. See Ciampa, *Presence and Function*, 60 and n100.

108. See esp. Martyn, *Galatians*, 97–105; de Boer, *Galatians*, 31–36.

rather violent and graphic connotations (Matt 5:29; 18:9), which may be closer in meaning to how Paul utilizes it. The Galatians have been plucked from[109] the present evil age and this is said to be the purpose (ὅπως) of Christ's sacrificial giving (cf. Isa 53:10–11).

The reality of two ages is a fundamental part of Paul's eschatological understanding but these "ages" cannot be viewed as strictly temporal categories. "[T]hey are also spatial categories, referring to two spheres or orbs of power, both of which claim sovereignty over the world."[110]

8. That these events take place as part of "the will of God" is significant; it buttresses Paul's conviction of Gentile inclusion as part of God's overarching plan (cf. Isa 2:2; 45:20–25; 49:6, 8; 56:3–8; 60:1–6; 66:18–23). Furthermore, this phrase τὸ θέλημα τοῦ θεοῦ parallels Paul's opening words in Gal 1:1 concerning his own calling (cf. 1 Cor 1:1; 2 Cor 1:1) and together highlight an important supporting theme for this epistle; namely, the dichotomy between divine and human actions and desires, henceforth referred to as divine–human dichotomy.[111] This concept is integrally tied to Paul's eschatological framework as Paul aligns his divine gospel with the new age and the agitators' human gospel with the present evil age.

Paul's opening words provide the context for the whole letter. As Ciampa writes: "Paul is clarifying right from the start the 'necessary presuppositions' or 'background knowledge' necessary to properly understand and follow his discourse and the 'conceptual framework' within which it will develop."[112] Paul begins by assuring the Galatians of the new eschatological reality which has come about through the Servant Christ. The Galatians themselves are proof of this new reality. Their own adoption into the family of God, the ἐκκλησία, bears witness to the glory of God's revelation of himself through Christ (Gal 1:5; cf. 1:24).[113] Paul addresses the Galatians'

109. Cf. Martyn, *Galatians*, 90–91, who translates ἐξαιρέω as "snatch us out of the grasp of."

110. De Boer, *Galatians*, 33. See also Schütz, *Paul and the Anatomy*, 116–17; Gammie, "Spatial and Ethical Dualism," 356–85. Gammie suggests at least ten different types of dualism in apocalyptic literature. Of special importance to this study are temporal, spatial, and theological dualisms.

111. Lategan, "Is Paul Defending," 418–30, argues the "God-man tension" is the main theme of the whole epistle. While his analysis is good, he misses the larger eschatological function of the divine–human motif. See also Lyons, *Pauline Autobiography*, 152–56.

112. Cf. Ciampa, *Presence and Function*, 68.

113. So Aalen, "Glory, Honour," 2:45.

perilous situation by giving them further proof of this new eschatological reality and of their inclusion in it. Paul knows that if the Galatians embrace their eschatological identity in Christ, then they will also accept Paul's gospel and live in accordance with it. Paul addresses a concrete situation with a theological argument[114]—even his autobiographical section is theologically purposed to reveal this eschatological reality.

Galatians 1:6–10

The gospel which the Agitators are "perverting"[115] is the eschatological gospel Paul laid out while present (Gal 1:8) and has once again articulated in the prescript. In Gal 1:6–10, the content of the gospel takes backstage to Paul's main concern of establishing the source of the true gospel vis-à-vis the source of other gospels. Paul elevates his proclaimed gospel to the status of direct revelation from God; God is τοῦ καλέσαντος[116] ὑμᾶς ἐν χάριτι [Χριστοῦ].[117] In this way, Paul intentionally shifts the focus off himself (cf. Gal 1:1).[118] The Galatians have been called by God through grace and specifically through the revelation of God's son before their very eyes (Gal 3:1b). That Paul is the voice-piece is only significant as he places himself under the same authority to which he calls the Galatians to submit. The validity of Paul's previously preached gospel is seen in its original effectiveness to call the Galatians into a new reality.

Galatians 1:6 references several shifts in location. The Galatians have already been plucked *out of* (ἐξαιρέω; Gal 1:4) the present evil age and brought *in* the sphere of Christ's grace (ἐν χάριτι Χριστοῦ); now they find themselves quickly returning (οὕτως ταχέως μετατίθεσθε) *into* a different gospel (εἰς ἕτερον εὐαγγέλιον).[119] Although Paul does not explicitly

114. W. Campbell, *Paul and the Creation*, 161, is correct when he writes: "Theologizing in Paul is designed to change people, to transform communal life and to create a Christ-like pattern of life within his communities."

115. Martyn, *Galatians*, 106, 112–13, translates Gal 1:7b as "they wish to change the gospel of Christ into its opposite," which captures the dichotomy between Paul's gospel and the Agitators.

116. Moo, *Galatians*, 77, notes that God is always the subject of the verb καλέω when used by Paul in a theological sense.

117. While Χριστοῦ is absent in a few important mss (P46vid, G, Hvid), it is found in many other important mss (P51vid, ℵ, A, B, Ψ).

118. Cf. Witherington, *Grace in Galatians*, 83, who says, "it is the message not the messenger which matters."

119. The dative preposition ἐν carries the idea of 'in the realm of' and is usually understood as being statically located. The prepositions ἐκ and εἰς denote movement. See Porter, *Idioms of the Greek*, 152–59.

reference the age to come, the "ἐν Χριστῷ" formula[120] (cf. Gal 1:22; 2:4, 17; 3:26, 28) is Paul's way of talking about participation and location within the coming age. "Present evil age" and "a different gospel" also appear to function as parallels. The Galatians are in danger of returning to their previous state and to their previous location outside of the eschatological reality brought forth through Christ. Paul may also be insinuating that those who participate in a different gospel join those who espouse this gospel in their eventual anathema.

Here, Paul must remind the Galatians of their original calling to participate in the eschatological kingdom and challenge them to explore the source and effectiveness of other gospels. The severity of perverting the gospel is seen in Paul's double anathema (Gal 1:8–9),[121] to which he intentionally submits his own subsequent proclamation. Reference to ἢ ἄγγελος ἐξ οὐρανοῦ possibly proclaiming a different gospel has been understood as either functioning hyperbolically[122] or as referring to Paul's opponents who may have claimed such authority concerning their own proclamations.[123] Kjell Morland argues that Paul includes angels as a way of evidencing the source of this curse as coming directly from God who is the only one capable of rendering such a judgment upon heavenly beings.[124] If Morland is correct, then the divine–human dichotomy Paul is establishing is significantly narrowed; Paul places every other living creature under the authority of God the father and the Lord Jesus Christ. If the opponents are claiming some type of angelic authority (cf. Gal 3:19), then even this must be brought under the authority of the God who has already revealed the true gospel to the Galatians as evidenced through their reception (Gal 1:9).

When read in correlation with Gal 4:14, Paul's recollection of the Galatians' welcoming him ὡς ἄγγελον θεοῦ . . . ὡς Χριστὸν Ἰησοῦν, may solidify this reading. Reference to an angel in Gal 1:8 may be another reference to Paul himself.[125] The *fpp* in Gal 1:8–9 would then be taken

---

120. For an excellent evaluation of Paul's use of this language see, C. Campbell, *Paul and Union with Christ*.

121. See Sandnes, *Paul—One of the Prophets*, 70–73, for the possible connection between Gal 1:6–9 and Deut 13.

122. So Moo, *Galatians*, 81; Hays, "Galatians," 206.

123. Betz, *Galatians*, 53; Martyn, *Galatians*, 113; de Boer, *Galatians*, 48. Contra Ehorn, "Galatians 1:8," 439–44.

124. Morland, *The Rhetoric of Curse*, 148–50.

125. Ciampa, *Presence and Function*, 90, notes that if Paul is alluding to Deut 13, reference to an angel "could reflect an apocalyptic echo of the reference to prophets as heavenly messengers."

as genuine plurals[126] referring to Paul and his companions, possibly even other apostles, and the reference to himself (ἄγγελος) would show the Galatians that Paul holds himself to this same standard; he is not excluded from the possibility of this divine anathema. The Galatians would also be reminded that while they may have viewed Paul ὡς ἄγγελον θεοῦ, through Paul's proclamation of the gospel (Gal 4:13),[127] they came to a revelation of Christ himself (ὡς Χριστὸν Ἰησοῦν).

Paul's two rhetorical questions in verse 10 are essentially synonymous[128] and serve a significant paradigmatic purpose. The sternness of Paul's words and the insinuation that the Galatians are in danger of entering into the anathema may have seemed overly harsh to Paul's audience. However, Paul seeks to model a truth—those who have entered the eschatological age no longer live by the worldly standards of the present evil age. Instead, they have begun the process of being reshaped by Christ and have been called to become servants of this Christ rather than servants of human beings (cf. 1 Cor 7:23; 2 Cor 4:5).[129] The concluding sentence of the pericope solidifies the incompatibility of these two realities—εἰ ἔτι ἀνθρώποις ἤρεσκον, Χριστοῦ δοῦλος οὐκ ἂν ἤμην (Gal 1:10c).

Paul's reference to being a "servant of Christ" is not primarily a reference to his apostleship[130] or his prophetic position;[131] it carries a more general invitation for all believers,[132] here the Galatians specifically, to embrace fully the Lordship of Christ as part of their new eschatological identity (cf. Rom 12:11; 14:18; 1 Cor 7:22; Phil 1:1; 1 Thess 1:9). The use of δοῦλος, when read in correlation with Gal 1:15–16, is an allusion to the Isaianic Servant (esp. Isa 49:1–6). However, if the reference to Christ's atoning action in Gal 1:3–4 is seen as an allusion to Isa 53 and the role of the Isaianic Servant, it may be better to understand Paul's use of Χριστοῦ δοῦλος as a reference

126. So Dunn, *Galatians*, 44–45; de Boer, *Galatians*, 49; Nanos, *Irony in Galatians*, 43–44 n. 45. Contra Moo, *Galatians*, 80; Martyn, *Galatians*, 113; Lyons, *Pauline Autobiography*, 10–16.

127. See Dunn, *Galatians*, 44–45, 188–92.

128. Lyons, *Galatians*, 68; de Boer, *Galatians*, 62–63; Betz, *Galatians*, 54–56.

129. Longenecker, *Galatians*, 19, is correct to emphasize that Paul is not specifically speaking against pleasing others (cf. 1 Cor 10:33; Gal 5:13) "but against gaining the favor of others for one's own advantage and as the motivation and goal of Christian ministry."

130. *Pace*, Longenecker, *Galatians*, 19; Fung, *Galatians*, 50; McKnight, *Galatians*, 63. Nor is it a way of claiming status. Cf. Martin, *Slavery as Salvation*, 51.

131. *Pace*, Beker, *Paul the Apostle*, 115–18; Moo, *Galatians*, 84; Ciampa, *Presence and Function*, 94–95 and n. 87.

132. Cf. Dunn, *Galatians*, 50; Clarke, *A Pauline Theology*, 96–97; Harris, *Slave of Christ*, 87–105.

to Paul's role as one of the servants of the Servant. This hypothesis will be further evaluated in the following section.

Galatians 1:11–24

This autobiographical section, which contains Paul's Christophanic reference, comes only after he has placed himself under God's divine authority, thus locating himself on the correct side of the eschatological divide. This recognition helps avoid reading the pericope as primarily an apostolic apologia. If a defense, it is a defense of the gospel.

Paul begins the body of this letter by referring to the Galatians as ἀδελφοί (Gal 1:11; cf. 3:15; 4:12, 28, 31; 5:11, 13; 6:1, 18), which appears to be a shift in tone. It draws the audience back to the prescript and reminds them that, despite a stumble in judgment, they are still the ἐκκλησία, those set free from the present evil age. This section focuses on the divine source of the gospel[133] and equally upon the revelatory aspect of God (cf. Gal 1:1). Dunn may be correct to note the phrase "to make known" is often used in apocalyptic thought concerning "the revelation of heavenly mysteries."[134] More noteworthy is Paul's phrase τὸ εὐαγγέλιον τὸ εὐαγγελισθὲν ὑπ' ἐμοῦ (Gal 1:11b).

Paul makes significant use of both the noun εὐαγγέλιον[135] and the verb εὐαγγελίζω[136] in his letters; Galatians is no exception (εὐαγγέλιον: 1:6, 7, 11; 2:2, 5, 7, 14; εὐαγγελίζω: 1:8(bis), 9, 11, 16, 23; 4:13). Although the Galatians may originally have understood this language through the interpretive lens of the Emperor Cult,[137] Paul draws on the language of the prophets (LXX Joel 3:5; Nah 2:1), specifically Isaiah (LXX 40:9[bis]; 52:7[bis]; 60:6; 61:1; cf. MT 41:27),[138] a suggestion strengthened by Paul's quotation of Isa 52:7 in Rom 10:15. There are three notable features of the Isaianic εὐαγγελ-. First, it is always used in verb form. Second, in all but one instance (Isa 60:6), the verb is directly or indirectly connected to the action of the Servant/servants (cf. 11QMelch II.16–24). Finally, the verb is always used in reference to a

---

133. So de Boer, *Galatians*, 72; Gaventa, "Paul's Conversion," 199.

134. Dunn, *Galatians*, 52. Dunn relies mostly on Theodotian's Greek translation of Daniel citing 2:23, 28–30, 45; 5:7–8, 15–17; 7:16, but also cites 1QpHab 7:4–5; 1QH 4:27–28; 7:27.

135. Forty-eight times in undisputed letters.

136. Nineteen times in undisputed letters.

137. Strecker, *Das Evangelium Jesu Christi*, 503–48; cf. Martyn, *Galatians*, 127–32.

138. Stuhlmacher, "The Pauline Gospel," 160–66; Stuhlmacher, *Das paulinische Evangelium*, 109–206. Jesus draws from this same language. Cf. Matt 5:3–4; 11:5; Luke 4:18; 6:20–21; 7:22; Acts 10:36.

revelation of Yahweh's eschatological deliverance (cf. *Pss. Sol.* 11:1).[139] This last point speaks to why the Septuagintal interpreters of Isaiah understood this message to be "good news" and utilized the verb εὐαγγελίζομαι.[140]

Similarly, Paul's use of the verb form carries a revelatory connotation. This is evident when Paul utilizes the noun and verb forms together, as in Gal 1:11—τὸ εὐαγγέλιον τὸ εὐαγγελισθὲν (cf. 1 Cor 15:1; 2 Cor 11:7). Paul understands the proclamation of the gospel to be a dynamic and revelatory event in which salvation is made known and made possible (cf. Rom 1:16–17).[141] While the prepositional phase ὑπ' ἐμοῦ, in correlation with the passive participle εὐαγγελισθέν, denotes Paul as the direct agent, it may be possible to see a divine agent sitting behind Paul's actions (cf. Rom 3:21; 2 Cor 1:4; 3:3; 8:19); this appears to be the emphasis of Gal 1:11–12.

Together, these verses form an important chiastic structure,[142] which elucidate Paul's understanding of God's revelation of Christ.

> [11]Γνωρίζω γὰρ ὑμῖν, ἀδελφοί,
>
> τὸ εὐαγγέλιον τὸ εὐαγγελισθὲν ὑπ' ἐμοῦ
>
> ὅτι οὐκ ἔστιν κατὰ ἄνθρωπον
>
> [12]οὐδὲ γὰρ ἐγὼ παρὰ ἀνθρώπου παρέλαβον αὐτὸ οὔτε ἐδιδάχθην,
>
> ἀλλὰ δι' ἀποκαλύψεως Ἰησοῦ Χριστοῦ.

Paul makes known to the Galatians the ἀποκαλύψεως Ἰησοῦ Χριστοῦ, which takes place through τὸ εὐαγγέλιον τὸ εὐαγγελισθὲν. It is clear Paul parallels εὐαγγέλιον and Ἰησοῦ Χριστοῦ (Gal 1:7; cf. Rom 1:9; 15:19; 16:25; 1 Cor 9:12; 2 Cor 2:12; 4:4; 9:13; 10:14; Phil 1:27; 1 Thess 3:2); Christ is the *auto-euangelion*.[143] What is less clear is the strong possibility Paul is equating εὐαγγελίζω and ἀποκάλυψις.[144] If so, then Paul makes a significant parallel between his own Christophanic experience and the Galatians' experience mediated through Paul's preaching of the gospel; in both cases, Christ is be-

---

139. Cf. Koole, *Isaiah III*, 72, who argues the Hebrew בְּשֵׂר of Isaiah points to the fall of Babylon and with it "the dawning revelation of Yahweh's kingship."

140. Baltzer, *Deutero-Isaiah*, 61 n. 75.

141. Bockmuehl, *Revelation and Mystery*, 138.

142. Gaventa, "Paul's Conversion," 203, notes a chiastic structure but hers if focused on source versus method. She therefore argues for a subjective genitive reading of ἀποκαλύψεως Ἰησοῦ Χριστοῦ seeing a contrast between the sources of "humanity" and "Christ."

143. Chamblin, "Revelation and Tradition," 6–8; cf. Bruce, *Tradition Old and New*, 31.

144. Cf. Sturm, "Paul's Use of *Apokalyptō/Apokalypsis*," 248.

ing revealed by God.[145] This is why Paul can so adamantly deny the human origins behind his gospel.

The language of ἀποκάλυψις[146] and ἀποκαλύπτω[147] is significant in Paul. However, great debate arises over how best to interpret these words in their historic and literary contexts. This is compounded by the now commonplace use of "apocalyptic" as an adjective describing a particular literary genre as well as a particular Jewish theological framework.[148] However, this subset of apocalyptic literature and the worldview which either births it or is birthed from it does not actually employ this language to describe itself prior to the book of Revelation (1:1).[149] Additionally, while the ἀποκάλυ- lexeme shows up ninety times in the LXX OT, with an additional fourteen times in the apocrypha, the majority of these uses are connected to human "uncovering." In the relatively few cases where God is the subject of this uncovering, it is rarely an apocalyptic-type revelation[150] (although see Num 22:31; 1 Sam 3:21; 9:15).[151] There are, however, a handful of places which speak of God's revealing of himself and/or his salvation to the masses and three out of the four instances take place in Isaiah (52:10; 53:1; 56:1; cf. Ps 97:2).

Since an intertextual reliance upon Isaiah has already been established, it is wise to explore further connections in Paul's ἀποκάλυ- language. Isaiah 52:7, 10 directly connects the *proclamation* (εὐαγγελίζω) of God's eschatological salvation with the *revelation* (ἀποκάλυψις) of this salvation,[152]

145. I interpret ἀποκαλύψεως Ἰησοῦ Χριστοῦ as an objective genitive, especially in light of Gal 1:16. So also Bruce, *Galatians*, 89; Schreiner, *Galatians*, 97; Martyn, *Galatians*, 144; Hays, "Galatians," 211. Contra Longenecker, *Galatians*, 23–24; Fee, *Pauline Christology*, 229; cf. Moo, *Galatians*, 95; Silva, *Galatians*, 45.

146. Rom 2:5; 8:19; 16:25; 1 Cor 1:7; 14:6, 26; 2 Cor 12:1, 7; Gal 1:12; 2:2; cf. Eph 1:17; 3:3; 2 Thess 1:7. Found five times in the rest of the NT (Luke 2:32; 1 Pet 1:7, 13; 4:12; Rev 1:1).

147. Rom 1:17, 18; 8:18; 1 Cor 2:10; 3:13; 14:30; Gal 1:16; 3:23; Phil 3:15; cf. Eph 3:5; 2 Thess 2:3, 6, 8. Found thirteen times in the rest of the NT (Matt 10:26; 11:25, 27; 16:17; Luke 2:35; 10:21, 22; 12:2; 17:30; John 12:38; 1 Pet 1:5, 12; 5:1).

148. For explanation of apocalyptic literature and apocalypticism see: Rowland, *The Open Heaven*; Stone, "Apocalyptic Literature," 383–441; Collins, *The Apocalyptic Imagination*; Koch, *The Rediscovery of Apocalyptic*. "Apocalyptic" is a significantly nuanced concept in Pauline studies. See Struff, "Defining the Word 'Apocalyptic,'" 17–48.

149. Smith, "ΑΠΟΚΑΛΥΠΤΩ and ΑΠΟΚΑΛΥΨΙΣ," 14.

150. Num 24:4, 16; 1 Sam 2:27; 3:7; 9:15; 2 Sam 7:27; 22:16; Ps 28:9; Isa 3:17; Jer 13:26; Ezek 16:37; Hos 2:12; 7:1; Amos 3:7; Micah 1:6; Nah 3:5; Sir 42:19.

151. Cf. Smith, "ΑΠΟΚΑΛΥΠΤΩ and ΑΠΟΚΑΛΥΨΙΣ," 9–10; Bockmuehl, *Revelation and Mystery*, 32–33, 101–2.

152. Cf. Childs, *Isaiah*, 406, "The reign of God has not just been announced, but the prophetic drama testifies to its actual reception by Zion for all the earth to see."

strengthening the plausibility for the same connection in Gal 1:11–12 and providing the locus for Paul's understanding.

Isaiah 52:7	Isaiah 52:10
like season upon the mountains, like the feet of one bringing glad tidings (εὐαγγελιζομένου) of a report of peace, like one bringing glad tidings (εὐαγγελιζόμενος) of good things, because I will make your salvation (σωτηρίαν) heard, saying to Sion, "Your God shall reign" (NETS)	And the Lord shall reveal (ἀποκαλύψει) his holy arm (βραχίων) before all the nations (πάντων τῶν ἐθνῶν), and all the ends of the earth shall see the salvation (σωτηρίαν) that comes from God. (NETS)

Additionally, within Isaiah, there is a significant connection between Isa 52:7–10 and 40:1–11. In the latter, the author speaks of the divine comfort (Isa 40:1; cf. 52:9) Israel will soon experience resulting in the glory of the Lord being revealed (ὁράω[153]) and all flesh seeing God's salvation (ὄψεται πᾶσα σὰρξ τὸ σωτήριον τοῦ θεοῦ; Isa 40:5). Israel is the one who is to proclaim the good news (εὐαγγελιζόμενος; Isa 40:9[bis]) of God's coming strength, his arm (βραχίων; Isa 40:10). It is this "arm of the Lord" that Isa 53:1 directly connects with the singular Servant who has been revealed to those who have believed what they have heard (κύριε, τίς ἐπίστευσεν τῇ ἀκοῇ ἡμῶν; καὶ ὁ βραχίων κυρίου τίνι ἀπεκαλύφθη;). The final Isaianic use of ἀποκάλυ- in Isa 56:1 is also significant; it relates the coming revelation of God's salvation and mercy (γὰρ τὸ σωτήριόν μου παραγίνεσθαι καὶ τὸ ἔλεός μου ἀποκαλυφθῆναι) to the eunuchs and to the foreigners who join themselves to the Lord and become his servants (Isa 56:6).

Several links can be made between Paul's train of thought in Gal 1 and Isaiah. Here, Paul finds a place of clarity for interpreting his own Christophanic experience. Christ is the long awaited Servant who has ushered in God's eschatological salvation and reign through his atoning death (Gal 1:4) and who has made possible the inclusion of the Gentiles (Gal 1:16). Paul now finds himself one of the servants of the Servant (Gal 1:10) and, therefore, one of the heralds of this eschatological salvation (Gal 1:1, 11), which is simultaneously the revelation of Christ to those who believe what they hear (Gal 1:6; cf. 1 Cor 1:18–25). Now, in the whole of this letter, Paul seeks to convince the Galatians they too have become servants of the Servant and to warn them against straying from this new eschatological identity.

---

153. The Hebrew word נִגְלָה, here translated as ὁράω is translated elsewhere in the LXX as ἀποκαλύπτειν (most notably Isa 53:1; 56:1).

In many ways, Gal 1:11–12 actually stands as the conclusion of Gal 1:6–10 while simultaneously providing a springboard for Gal 1:13–24.[154] Paul concludes Gal 1:6–10 by inviting the Galatians to remember and to embrace their own eschatological calling, which was highlighted in Gal 1:6. Paul's intentional use of παραλαμβάνω in Gal 1:12b is meant to point back to παραλαμβάνω in Gal 1:9. In the latter, Paul speaks of the Galatians having "received" the authentic gospel through Paul's proclamation. In the former, Paul speaks of himself having received Christ through a revelation from God. Paul now makes clear that these two experiences are identical, not in their particulars but in their content, source, and dynamism; both are revelations of Christ from God.

Some scholars argue Paul avoids using παραλαμβάνω to speak of his Christophanic experience believing he makes a distinction between the received tradition of the Galatians and his own divine revelatory experience (cf. 1 Cor 15:1–3).[155] The Greek does not warrant such as distinction and the ellipsis of Gal 1:12b naturally points back to the verb παραλαμβάνω (and possibly also ἐδιδάχθην) in Gal 1:12a.[156] The irony of Gal 1:8–9 now comes to the forefront.[157] It is impossible that a contrary gospel could be "gospeled" (εὐαγγελίζω) to the Galatians[158] because God is the source behind all revelations of Christ whether they be received by Paul or by the Galatians, and whether they be proclaimed by Paul or others (Gal 2:7–9; cf. Phil 1:15–18; 1 Cor 15:11).

An analysis of Gal 3:1–5 will help solidify the connection Paul makes between his own Christophanic experience and the Galatians' experience. While Gal 3:1–5 serves to introduce a new but interconnected part of Paul's argument, it also intentionally points back to and parallels Gal 1:6–12. First, in Gal 3:1–5, Paul returns to the Galatians' current predicament; they have been "bewitched"[159] and are in danger of acquiescing to a human rather than divine gospel (Gal 1:6–9).[160] The language shifts to Spirit and flesh but

154. Cf. Lyons, *Pauline Autobiography*, 131–32.

155. Winger, "Tradition, Revelation and Gospel," 65–86; Fung, *Galatians*, 52–53; Furnish, *Second Corinthians*, 142–44, 148–51; Moo, *Galatians*, 93–95; Dunn, *Galatians*, 53.

156. deSilva, *Galatians*, 14; so also Williams, *Galatians*, 43; Oakes, *Galatians*, 51; Betz, *Galatians*, 62; de Boer, *Galatians*, 82.

157. Cf. Nanos, *Irony in Galatians*, 296–98.

158. Cf. Gaventa, "Singularity Revisited," 188–89.

159. See Longenecker, *Triumph of Abraham's God*, 150–55, for exposition on βασκαίνω and the "evil eye."

160. Martyn, *Galatians*, 281, "Paul employs for a second time the epistolary rebuke (cf. 1:6)."

the dichotomy is the same. Second, Paul's reference to the Galatians' initial experience of Christ significantly parallels Paul's Christophany.

Galatians 3:1c	Galatians 1:12b
κατ᾽ ὀφθαλμοὺς Ἰησοῦς Χριστὸς προεγράφη ἐσταυρωμένος	δι᾽ ἀποκαλύψεως Ἰησοῦ Χριστοῦ

Linguistically there is a link between ὁράω and ἀποκάλυψις, which is clear from Paul's other Christophanic references (1 Cor 9:1; 15:8). The parallel becomes more obvious when read with Isa 40:5 and 52:10, which both emphasize "seeing" God's salvation.

Isaiah 40:5	Isaiah 52:10
καὶ ὄψεται πᾶσα σὰρξ τὸ σωτήριον τοῦ θεοῦ	καὶ ὄψονται πάντα τὰ ἄκρα τῆς γῆς τὴν σωτηρίαν τὴν παρὰ τοῦ θεοῦ.

This salvation is specifically tied to the work of the Servant in Isa 52:13—53:12; a connection Paul has already alluded to in Gal 1:4 and 2:20. The latter is significant as it posits a personal element to Christ's crucifixion. Although little is known of what transpired during Paul's Christophanic experience, it may be safe to assume it was here that Paul came to understand Christ as "the Son of God who loved [Paul] and gave himself for [Paul]" (Gal 2:20). In sharing this personal revelation, Paul hopes to move the Galatians toward embracing co-cruciformity with Christ (Χριστῷ συνεσταύρωμαι; Gal 2:19; cf. 5:24; 6:14). In light of Paul's ensuing argument (Gal 3:10–14), it makes sense that Paul would closely tie Christ's crucifixion to the Galatians' salvation.

The justification for returning to Isaiah for interpreting Gal 3:1–5 is found in Paul's echoing of Isa 53:1 in Gal 3:2, 5. The possibility for such a connection was mentioned above and now appears surer. Harmon notes that Isa 53:1 is the only place in the whole LXX where the combination of ἀκοή and πίστις/πιστεύω appears.[161] In its context, the "hearing" relates to proclamation of the gospel (Isa 52:7), which has already been shown to equate with God's revelation of his salvation (Isa 52:10; 53:1; 56:1). This is also the case in Gal 3:2, 5. The focus appears firmly on divine action over human action. "Paul's emphasis lies . . . upon the proclaimed *message* (ἀκοή), which calls forth faith, as the means by which the Spirit is given."[162]

---

161. Harmon, *She Must and Shall Go Free*, 130.

162. Hays, *The Faith of Jesus Christ*, 132, emphasis his. See also Lull, *The Spirit in*

The final parallel between Gal 1:6–12 and 3:1–5 is found in Paul's use of λαμβάνω in reference to the Galatians reception of the Spirit (Gal 3:2, 14; cf. 1:9, 12), which introduces another divine–human dichotomy. Like his own Christophanic reference, the dichotomy is focused on the source of the reception rather than the object of reception. Thus, the contrast is not between πνεῦμα and ἔργων νόμου, but between the human source of ἔργων νόμου and the divine source of ἀκοῆς πίστεως. The latter has already been seen to equate with gospel proclamation and in Isa 53:1 is directly paralleled with God's revelation. Therefore, it appears surer in Gal 3:1–5 that Paul is aligning the Galatians' conversion experience with his own Christophanic experience.

	Human source	Divine source	Object of reception (παραλαμβάνω/λαμβάνω)
Gal 1:12 (cf. 1:11)	παρὰ ἀνθρώπου	δι᾽ ἀποκαλύψεως (εὐαγγελίζω)	Ἰησοῦ Χριστοῦ (εὐαγγέλιον)
Gal 3:2 (cf. 3:5)	ἐξ ἔργων νόμου	ἐξ ἀκοῆς πίστεως	τὸ πνεῦμα

This chart raises a question concerning the relationship between Christ and the Spirit. Paul does not deny the Galatians' reception of Christ in his language of their reception of the Spirit; it is Christ who was displayed before their eyes (Gal 3:1) and it is the gospel of Christ which was received by both Paul and the Galatians (Gal 1:9, 12). Nor does Paul deny his own reception of the Spirit (cf. Gal 3:14; 4:6; 5:5). As Dunn writes, "in Paul's experience Christ and the Spirit [are] one, and . . . Christ [is] experienced through the Spirit."[163] Thus, Paul can refer to the Spirit as τὸ πνεῦμα τοῦ υἱοῦ (Gal 4:6; cf. Rom 8:9; 2 Cor 3:17, 18; Phil 1:19). However, when it comes to the particulars of Paul's Christophanic experience as they relate to believers' conversion experience, there are differences. Foremost is the reality that Paul considers his Christophany to be in a rare category of believers (cf. 1 Cor 15:6–8) who experienced a more direct revelation of Christ. Nevertheless, Paul does not overemphasize these differences. Instead, Paul creates a new but related category to articulate the revelation of Christ from God through the Spirit which all believers experience—a Pneuma-Christophany.

Galatians 1:13 marks a slight shift in purpose from the preceding two verses, which were meant to more closely align the experiences of Paul and the Galatians. Gaventa highlights the disruption of Gal 1:13–14 in the midst

---

Galatia, 54–59. Contra Harmon, *She Must and Shall Go Free*, 130–33.

163. Dunn, *Baptism in the Holy Spirit*, 148.

of what otherwise would be a continuation of Paul's Christophanic reference between 1:11–12 and 1:15–17.[164] Gaventa believes Paul calls upon his own experience as a paradigm to show how the Christophany radically changed his direction away from something otherwise seen by Paul as a "good and obedient life."[165] "What the Galatians can imitate is Paul's single-minded response to the gospel that was revealed to him . . . To become as Paul is[,] means to allow Christ to live in oneself (cf. 2:20) to the exclusion of the Law or of any other tradition or category (cf. 3:27–28)."[166]

Gaventa's observations are important and help move the conversation away from an apostolic apologia reading of Paul's Christophanic reference.[167] Two things are worth highlighting and extending. First, Paul does not present Judaism in a negative light; his own past actions are stated pragmatically, even with a hint of pride (cf. Phil 3:4–6).[168] Paul's previous mode of existence is not introduced in order to denounce as much as to provide a foundation for Paul's reversal in light of the new eschatological reality which has dawned in Christ. Gaventa overextends when she makes "exclusion of the Law" a focal point in this reversal. Galatians 1:13–14 present a particular picture of law observance from which Paul shifts, namely, an over reliance upon works of the law (cf. Gal 2:15–17). The law itself is not bad (cf. Gal 3:19–29; Rom 7:7–12). Paul's reference to "zeal" (cf. Num 25:10–13; 1 Macc 2:26) in relation to τῶν πατρικῶν μου παραδόσεων (Gal 1:14) should not be read as a direct antithesis to the gospel.[169] Instead, Paul expresses how his past life was steeped in human achievement (cf. Rom 10:2–3). Paul walks a thin line between seeking to articulate his own Christophanic experience in terms of a divine–human dichotomy while not completely dismissing his Jewish heritage (cf. Rom 9:4–5) or Jewish law observance. Remember, Paul is speaking to a Gentile audience and one of his primary foci is to evidence the dawning of the new eschatological reality and the inclusion of the Gentiles into the eschatological people of God apart from works of the law.

The second important aspect of Gaventa's reading is her focus on Paul's desire for the Galatians to imitate his "response to the gospel." By this, Gaventa means the singular focus on Christ apart from any other worldly

---

164. Gaventa, "Paul's Conversion," 238–40, 244–45.

165. Gaventa, "Paul's Conversion," 139.

166. Gaventa, "Galatians 1 and 2," 322.

167. Gaventa, "Galatians 1 and 2," believes apostolic apologia is not the primary purpose behind Paul's Christophanic reference but allows for it as a secondary purpose. Cf. Hays, "Galatians," 213, who also includes both but reverses the order.

168. Cf. Bockmuehl, *Revelation and Mystery*, 130–31.

169. See Ortlund, *Zeal without Knowledge*, 137–50. Contra Dunn, *New Perspective on Paul*, 242, 289, 478.

distraction;[170] it is "Christ-faith alone."[171] However, Gaventa appears to bring the discussion of Gal 2:15—5:1 into what Paul is doing in Gal 1:13–24. While agreeing that Paul seeks imitation of his response to the gospel, the focus is not on the content of the gospel but upon the source behind it and the action such a source elicits. Thus, Paul continues the divine–human dichotomy began in Gal 1:1, 11–12. This is seen in at least three ways.

First, Paul's narration of his "reversal" in Gal 1:13–16a resolves in the rather odd declaration of 1:16b–17—"I did not confer with any human being . . . but I." Whereas the "old" Paul would have sought human approval before beginning such a mission (cf. Acts 9:1–2; 22:5; 26:10, 12), the divine Christophany needed no further consultation but moved Paul to immediate action. While the purpose of Paul's trip to Arabia cannot be fully known, Paul links it to the mission he has just received, proclamation of the gospel among the Gentiles.[172]

Second, the disruptive interjection of Gal 1:20—"In what I am writing to you, before God, I do not lie!"—appears to function as an alibi for Paul's divine commission and moreover for his divine gospel message.[173] It is assumed such an alibi is only necessary if Paul is seeking to defend his apostleship.[174] This need not be the case. If indeed Paul is continuing a divine–human dichotomy, then it is possible that in his historical retelling of the events surrounding his call, Paul deems it necessary to reaffirm what was said in Gal 1:16b. Moreover, the focus may not be on the oath itself but rather on the phrase ἰδοὺ ἐνώπιον τοῦ θεοῦ, note its emphatic location in the Greek. This phrase would then function to emphasize God's presence (cf. LXX Exod 3:6; 2 Sam 6:7; Ps 60:8) within Paul's autobiographical narrative and even to stress the revelation of this God in Paul's actions (cf. Gal 2:2). Paul may also be juxtaposing the "face" of God, which had been made known to Paul through the Christophanic event, with his own unknown face—ἀγνοούμενος τῷ προσώπῳ (Gal 1:21).[175] At the least, the last point functions to place the focus on God rather than Paul.

Third, this section ends in the same way it begins, with the contrast between a "former" way of living—persecuting the church (Gal 1:23; cf.

170. See Gaventa, "Singularity Revisited."

171. Gaventa, "Singularity Revisited," 190.

172. Bruce, Galatians, 96; Fung, Galatians, 68–69. For a fuller discussion of Gal 1:17 in correlation to Acts 9:19b–22 see Hengel and Schwemer, Paul Between Damascus and Antioch, 106–26.

173. Sampley, "Before God," 477–82.

174. Sampley, "Before God"; Dunn, Galatians, 77–78.

175. There is the possibility of an echo to Moses's call in Exod 3:6 (LXX): ἀπέστρεψεν δὲ Μωυσῆς τὸ πρόσωπον αὐτοῦ, εὐλαβεῖτο γὰρ κατεμβλέψαι ἐνώπιον τοῦ θεοῦ.

1:13)—and a "now" way of living—proclaiming the faith (Gal 1:23; cf. 1:16)—with the stress falling on the resultant glorification of God (Gal 1:24). The dual time markers ποτε and νῦν stress the "time/locus" shift which has taken place in Paul's own life.[176] Additionally, Paul's dual reference to having "persecuted" (διώκω; Gal 1:13, 23) the church begins an often neglected feature in the epistle (cf. Gal 4:29; 5:11; 6:12).[177] It illustrates the difference in attitude and action between those residing in the "present age" and those residing in the "coming age."

Gal 1:13, 23	Paul persecuted (ἐδίωκον/διώκων) the church prior to his Christophanic experience.
Gal 4:29	The child born of the flesh persecuted (ἐδίωκε) the child born of the Spirit.
Gal 5:11	Paul is now being persecuted (διώκομαι) for not preaching circumcision by those who preach circumcision.
Gal 6:12	Paul's opponents preach circumcision in order to avoid being persecuted (διώκωνται) for the cross of Christ.

The dichotomy is clear. The *persecutor* is one who is ignorant of the eschatological reality (Gal 1:13, 23; 4:29) while the *persecuted* are those residing in this new reality (Gal 4:29; 5:11). The irony of the agitators is that in seeking to be included in the eschatological promises of God they have inadvertently denied its reality; they have become persecutors in order to avoid being persecuted (Gal 6:12). They failed to see the eschatological reality and freedom afforded by the cross of Christ (cf. Gal 3:13–14).[178]

Through Paul's Christophanic narrative, he places his previous life in pharisaical Judaism on the wrong side of the divine–human divide and actually aligns his old self with the agitators.[179] However, Paul's point is not that his previous way of life was wrong in and of itself. Rather, it is the presence of a new eschatological reality made possible through Christ that has changed everything. Paul will make this important distinction clear when

176. See Lyons, *Pauline Autobiography*, 147, see also 146–152; Lyons, *Galatians*, 67–68.

177. Baasland, "Persecution: A Neglected Feature," 135–50; see also Gorman, *Inhabiting the Cruciform God*, 130.

178. Baasland, "Persecution: A Neglected Feature," 140–41, shows the link between "persecution" and "curse" in Galatians and its connection to OT curse motifs, esp. Deuteronomy.

179. Cf. Ciampa, *Presence and Function*, 110–11; Ebeling, *Die Wahrheit des Evangeliums*, 104.

he speaks of how the law was given as a guardian until the "fullness of time had come" in God's sending of his Son (Gal 3:23—4:7). Paul's calling and his mission to the Gentiles is irrefutable proof that this time has indeed come. Additionally, the Galatians' conversion and calling, which Paul intentionally parallels to his Christophanic experience in Gal 1:6–12 (cf. Gal 3:1–5), is also irrefutable proof of this new eschatological reality.

The divine–human dichotomy is employed by Paul to stress human-ity's inability to grasp God's salvific act in Christ without the relocation of the individual/group into the sphere of a new reality. Since Paul has already included the Galatians in this new reality as part of the eschatological people of God (Gal 1:2–6), they should have already recognized the incompatibility of the agitators' message with the gospel that has been divinely revealed to them through the proclamation of the gospel. Paul's astonishment at the cur-rent predicament is meant to shame the Galatians for not recognizing what should have been clear to them (Gal 1:6; cf. 3:1, 3; 5:7–8) and to move them toward right action in the future. Rather than trying to defend his apostle-ship, Paul attempts to demonstrate how his calling originates and continues to be guided by a divine source in order to provide the Galatians with a para-digm to imitate. Galatians 1:6–24 can be charted as follows:

	divine revelation	leads to	eschatological people of God	leads to	continued hu-man guidance	equals	possible anathema
Galatians	divine revelation	leads to	eschatological people of God	leads to	*continued hu-man guidance*	equals	*possible anathema*
Paul	divine revelation	leads to	eschatological people of God	leads to	*continued divine guidance*	equals	*glory to God*

One question remains; why does Paul allude to Isa 49:1–6 as part of his Christophanic reference? As noted, most scholars understand this as part of Paul's apostolic apologia emphasizing his prophetic-like calling in general or his Isaianic Servant role specifically and functioning to prove his authority. How does this reading change if apostolic apologia is not the purpose behind Paul's Christophanic reference? As evidenced above, Paul has constructed a picture of Christ as the messianic savior who atones for sin by his sacrificial death and resurrection (Gal 1:1–5); Christ is the singular Isaianic Servant. Furthermore, Paul is one of the servants of the Servant Christ (Gal 1:10). These factors should guide ones' interpretation of Paul's allusion to Isa 49:1–6 in Gal 1:15–16.

Some clarity may be found in the prepositional phrase ἐν ἐμοί (Gal 1:16). As noted in chapter 2, this phrase has sparked much debate, which are mostly attempts at historical reconstruction of Paul's Christophanic ex-perience. However, there may be a more theological reason Paul employs this phrase. Newman argues ἀποκαλύψαι . . . ἐν ἐμοί is an echo of ἐν σοὶ δοξασθήσομαι (Isa 49:3).[180] Newman links ἀποκαλύπτω and δοξάζω by showing how the latter often "denotes the manifestation of God's visible presence" in the prophetic writings (cf. LXX Isa 24:21–23; Ezek 28:22; 39:13; Hag 1:8).[181] For Newman, ἐν ἐμοί is proof that Paul's Christophany was an ecstatic throne room experience where he came to know Christ as the divine glory (glory-Christology), and the link to Isa 49:3 shows that Paul interprets his "apostolic ministry as a conduit for divine Glory."[182]

Newman's proposed echo is intriguing and is strengthened when read in correlation with Paul's rather odd statement in Gal 1:24—καὶ ἐδόξαζον ἐν ἐμοὶ τὸν θεόν. This ἐν ἐμοί is usually translated causally,[183] which is logical unless one views 1:24 as also echoing Isa 49:3.[184] Taken together and read through the lens of Isa 49, Gal 1:16 and 1:24 could be read as further proof that Paul understood himself as the Isaianic Servant and God's glorification in Paul was proof of his divine calling. However, this reading forgets the references to Christ as the Servant already mentioned above. Paul reminds us of this fact in Gal 1:16; it is τὸν υἱὸν αὐτοῦ who was revealed "in Paul." The parallel between Gal 1:16 and 1:12 is assurance the "son" is a reference to Christ.

Harmon acknowledges the difficult tension between Christ as Servant and Paul as Servant and believes Gal 2:20 provides the key for unlocking this conundrum.[185] This verse brings together Christ's sacrificial death, his sonship, and his location in Paul. For Harmon, Paul understood Christ's dwelling in him through the Christophanic experience as a participation in Christ's crucifixion (Gal 2:19) leading to his own worldly death. Harmon writes:

> Because of this truth, Paul can refer to his own apostolic mission
> as the fulfilment of the Servant's commission in Isa 49 to be a
> light to the nations, since it is ultimately Christ who fulfils the
> mission through him. As a result, God's intention of revealing
> his Son "in" Paul (Gal 1:16) reaches its intended goal of God be-
> ing glorified "in" Paul (Gal 1:24), because Christ lives "in" Paul

180. Newman, *Paul's Glory-Christology*, 204–7; so also Harmon, *She Must and Shall Go Free*, 82–83; Ciampa, *Presence and Function*, 124–25; Moo, *Galatians*, 115; Lindars, *New Testament Apologetics*, 223.

181. Newman, *Paul's Glory-Christology*, 206.

182. Newman, *Paul's Glory-Christology*, 207.

183. So NASB, NRSV, NIV, ESV.

184. So Harmon, *She Must and Shall Go Free*, 88–89.

185. Harmon, *She Must and Shall Go Free*, 100–102, claims Gal 2:20 also echoes Isa 49:3 but it may be better to understand it as an echo of Gal 1:16, 24.

(Gal 2:20) to fulfil the Servant's commission to be a light to the nations.[186]

Harmon's reading is astute, taking seriously the role of Christ as well as the unique aspects of Paul's apostolic commission. Harmon also notes the possibility that Paul understood this mission extending to at least other apostles and possibly to all believers. However, Harmon finds little proof of this idea in Galatians.[187]

Nevertheless, the work already carried out in this section makes the likelihood of the Servant's mission being extended to all believers more plausible. It has been shown Paul closely links his own Christophany in Gal 1:11–12 to the Galatians' experience of Christ through the Holy Spirit in Gal 3:1–5. It also has been shown that Paul provides his own divine–human reversal as a paradigm for the Galatians to imitate, making it possible for them to have the same outcome as Paul (Gal 1:13–24). To this can be added three additional supports. First, in Gal 1:15 Paul once again parallels his own Christophany with the Galatians (Gal 1:6); both have been called (cf. Gal 5:8, 13) by God as an act of grace (cf. Gal 2:9; 5:4).[188]

Galatians 1:15	Galatians 1:6
καλέσας διὰ τῆς χάριτος αὐτοῦ	τοῦ καλέσαντος ὑμᾶς ἐν χάριτι

Second, Paul's ἐν ἐμοί language in Gal 1:16 (cf. Gal 1:24; 2:20) finds a probable parallel in Gal 4:19 where Paul expresses his deep desire for Christ to be formed ἐν ὑμῖν, referring to the Galatians. Additionally, in Gal 4:19 Paul uses motherhood language calling the Galatians τέκνα μου and referring to his labor pains (ὠδίνω), which may be an echo of Gal 1:15; Paul now provides the motherly womb but it is Christ who is being formed in the Galatians.[189]

Finally, Paul calls the Galatians to imitation in Gal 4:12—Γίνεσθε ὡς ἐγώ, ὅτι κἀγὼ ὡς ὑμεῖς (cf. 1 Cor 4:16; 11:1; Phil 3:17; 4:9; 1 Thess 1:6). The context of this imperative raises the question of what exactly Paul desires the Galatians to imitate and the causal phrase "for I also have become as you are" raises the question of how Paul has become like the Galatians. Galatians 3:6—4:11 articulates a new eschatological reality where Christ's atoning death has brought the blessings of Abraham to the Gentiles and

186. Harmon, *She Must and Shall Go Free*, 119.

187. Harmon, *She Must and Shall Go Free*, 119–20 n. 257.

188. Cf. Barclay, *Paul & Gift*, 332.

189. Cf. Gaventa, *Our Mother Saint Paul*, 29.

with it the Holy Spirit (Gal 3:14). It is a reality where the Gentiles are not obligated to carry out the law in order to be included in the family of God, but through the faithfulness of Christ they are adopted as children and heirs (Gal 4:6–7). This theologically rich section unpacks Paul's autobiographical statements in Gal 2:18–21, which functions paradigmatically. In Gal 4:12, Paul reminds the Galatians he has already become like them. In dying to the law (Gal 2:19), Paul has effectively become a Gentile sinner (Gal 2:16). As Dunn writes: "Paul, though himself a Jew, had become as one who was (like the Galatians) 'without the law', 'outside the law', in order to bring the gospel to them as 'lawless' Gentiles."[190] This does not negate the law or even Paul's observance of the law in certain circumstances (cf. 1 Cor 9:20–23); it is simply part of Paul's missionary strategy. What Paul indeed comes to reject is "his zeal for the Law and the traditions."[191] In this, Paul speaks of having been co-crucified with Christ, dying to self, and allowing God to reveal/glorify himself in Paul (Gal 2:20). This is what Paul invites the Galatians to imitate. Although they begin from different places, they all must die to self and allow Christ to live in them. This takes place as God's revelation of Christ through the Spirit, which in their case took place through Paul's proclamation of the gospel, transforms all believers into servants of the Servant who share in the general mission of being a light to the nations by allowing God's glory to be evidenced in them and through them.

Throughout this pericope (Gal 1:11–24), Paul has consistently invited the Galatians to share in aspects of his Christophanic experience. There are certain particulars unique to Paul in which the Galatians cannot share—his Jewish nationality, his past Pharisaical and zealous actions, and his exact encounter of Christ. However, Paul introduces his Christophany in such a way as to downplay these particulars making it possible for the Galatians to see in Paul's experience something of their own. At points, Paul's Christophanic reference invites the Galatians to imitation and in so doing draws them into deeper understanding of their eschatological identity through Christ and of the actions this new identity requires. At other times, his Christophanic reference is more than paradigmatic; he invites them to participate in a shared eschatological reality. Paul's autobiographical narrative reveals the certainty of God's dynamic revelation, transformation, and calling in all believers.

---

190. Dunn, *Galatians*, 232; cf. Moo, *Galatians*, 281–82.
191. Gaventa, "Galatians 1 and 2," 321.

Galatians 2:1–10

Although the main task of the chapter has been accomplished through the preceding exegesis of Gal 1:11–24, the continued evaluation of Paul's entire autobiographical narrative will help to reinforce the above findings. In Gal 2:1–10 Paul continues his autobiographical narrative in order to solidify the reality of Gentile inclusion in the eschatological age. This is accomplished through a continued "revelation motif" and through an intricate redescribing of Isa 49:6. The question of whether Gal 2:1–10 refers to the Jerusalem Counsel of Acts 15[192] or the relief efforts of Acts 11–12[193] is unimportant for Paul's theological point.

Paul's use of δοκέω in reference to the Jerusalem leaders (Gal 2:2, 6a, 6c, 9) is the source of much angst. The dominate interpretation sees Paul walking a tightrope between independence from and endorsement by the Jerusalem church.[194] However, this may be understood as a continuation of the divine–human dichotomy. The focal point of this argument comes in Gal 2:6b with the phrase πρόσωπον θεὸς ἀνθρώπου οὐ λαμβάνει, an idiomatic expression referencing the impartiality of God.[195] All human acknowledgements of position or stature mean nothing, only God's approval counts. This is why Paul has no need to consult flesh and blood after his revelation (Gal 1:16) and why the Jerusalem leaders added nothing to the gospel Paul proclaims (Gal 2:6c).[196]

This divine–human dichotomy is strengthened by the continuation of the "revelation motif" introduced in Gal 2:2a. Martinus De Boer notes the ambiguity of the phrase κατὰ ἀποκάλυψιν, where the preposition with the accusative can assume several meanings: "in accordance with," "as a result of," or "for the purpose of."[197] The last of these options has had little recognition, but may bring clarity to the passage. De Boer, taking ἀνέβην as

---

192. See Betz, *Galatians*; de Boer, *Galatians*; Dunn, *Galatians*; Phillips, *Paul, His Letters, and Acts.*

193. See Bruce, "Galatians Problems: 1. Autobiographical Data," 292–309; Marshall, *Acts*; Longenecker, *Galatians*; and Witherington, *Grace in Galatians*; Witherington, *The Paul Quest.*

194. Dunn, *Jesus, Paul and the Law*, 118–22; Dunn, *Galatians*, 85–115; Betz, *Galatians*, 92; de Boer, *Galatians*, 115–19.

195. See de Boer, *Galatians*, 118; and Dunn, *Romans 1–8*, 88–89.

196. Dunn's evaluation of προσανεθέμην in 1:16 as having a technical meaning of "consulting with someone who is recognized as a qualified interpreter about the significance of some sign—a dream, or omen, or portent . . ." (*Jesus, Paul and the Law*, 110), lends weight to this interpretation.

197. De Boer, *Galatians*, 108; cf. Köhler, "κατά," 2:253–354.

a complexive aorist,[198] paraphrases 2:2a: "My whole journey to Jerusalem, including what happened during my stay there, was a matter of God's revelatory activity and intention."[199] Thus De Boer writes: "In Paul's account, then, his second visit to the church in Jerusalem functioned as an apocalyptic revelation for the pillar apostles, as the means whereby God invaded their world to disclose to them—concretely in the persons of Paul, Barnabas, and Titus—the truth of the gospel."[200] This interpretation provides a clear dichotomy between God's "revelatory activity" and the "acknowledged leaders" and may explain Paul's use of δοκέω to solidify the contrast. Rather than seeking the approval of the Jerusalem church, this narrative speaks of Paul bringing a further revelation from God to them.

This "revelation" is actually a continuation and furtherance of Paul's Christophanic narrative accomplished by the continuance of Paul's initial allusion to Isa 49 in Gal 1:15. Several connections appear. First, echoing Isa 49:4, Paul references the possibility of having run in vain (κενόν; Gal 2:2). Although Paul may genuinely fear that his Gentile mission would not be recognized by the Jerusalem church,[201] it may also be a way of keeping Isaiah front and center. Second, Paul's reference to the "grace given to me" (Gal 2:9) points back to Gal 1:15 and thus to Isa 49:1. These two echoes make the final echo more feasible. Three times in quick succession, Paul mentions the dual missions of Peter and Paul (Gal 2:7, 8, 9); Peter to the circumcised and Paul to the Gentiles/uncircumcised (ἔθνος; cf. Gal 1:16). Is it possible this is a reference to the dual mission of the Servant who was called to restore Israel and be a light to the nations (ἔθνος; Isa 49:6)?[202] Paul could be redescribing the Servant's mission into two semi-distinct missions.

This reading has several ramifications. First, it buttresses the above argument that Paul sees himself as one of the servants of the singular Servant Christ. If Paul is only fulfilling half of the Servant's mission then he cannot possibly be the singular Servant.[203] Second, it solidifies the extension of the Servant's mission to at least other apostles; they too are servants. Third, it demonstrates the unity between the two parties (cf. Gal 2:10) and intensifies the disharmony between them and the "false believers" (cf. Gal 2:4). Finally, the acceptance of a mission to the Gentiles and moreover the

---

198. See Wallace, *Greek Grammar*, 557.

199. De Boer, *Galatians*, 109.

200. De Boer, *Galatians*, 109. Cf. Martyn, *Galatians*, 200–203.

201. So Fung, *Galatians*, 90; Bruce, *Galatians*, 111.

202. Harmon, *She Must and Shall Go Free*, 90–91, notes the possible echo of Paul's mission to the Gentile but does not mention the mission to Israel.

203. An argument could be made from Rom 9–11 that Paul saw his Gentile mission as part of his Jewish mission. However, this is nowhere to be found in Galatians.

recognition of God's current work is significant proof to the Galatians that the eschatological age had indeed dawned. But why would the Jerusalem leaders accept such a mission?

The Jewish tradition of an eschatological inclusion of the Gentiles is seen in Isa 2:2–4, where a Gentile pilgrimage to Zion serves as a marker to the eschatological reality. The theme is prevalent in the second half of Isaiah (e.g., 55:5; 56:1–8; 60:3; 66:18–21; cf. 40:5; 49:22–26; 52:10). While there are certainly other strands of Jewish thought concerning the eschatological fate of the nations, the Gentile pilgrimage motif is also attested in other places of Scripture (e.g., Mic 4:1–3; Zech 2:11; 8:20–23) and in STJL (e.g., Tob 13:11; 14:5–7; *Sib. Or.* 3:710–721[204]).

Sanders,[205] Wright,[206] and Fredriksen[207] are but a few[208] of the many scholars who believe this tradition lies behind Paul's Gentile mission. Fredriksen's reading is most intriguing since she argues the relevant literature lacks any reference to Gentile halakhic conversion; they do not become Jews. "Their redemption, rather, depended upon their spiritual and hence moral, 'conversion': Gentiles were expected when the Kingdom came, to *turn from* idolatry . . . and *turn to* the worship of the True God . . . They would remain Gentiles and *as Gentiles* would they be saved."[209]

If Fredriksen is correct, then Paul's law-free gospel for the Gentiles would *not* be a new concept to the Jerusalem leaders. The gospel Paul lays before them is not the kerygma about Christ which they already knew and which Paul at least partially received from Peter.[210] Rather, it was the "revelation" that the dawning of the eschatological Kingdom also meant law-

---

204. While parts of the *Sibylline Oracles* bear Christian marks, the majority of chapter three, including the noted section, appears to be of Jewish origins. For a short history of the debate surrounding the date and provenance of Book III see: Buitenwerf, *Book III of the Sibylline*, esp. 124–136.

205. Sanders, *Paul, the Law*, 171.

206. Wright, *Climax of the Covenant*, 150–51.

207. Fredriksen, "Judaism, the Circumcision of Gentiles," 532–564; Fredriksen, *From Jesus to Christ*, 84, 146–76.

208. Cf. Donaldson, "The Curse of the Law," 94–112, who previously advocated but later changed his mind. For this change see, Donaldson, *Paul and the Gentiles*, 187–97, esp. 194. Contra Novenson, "The Jewish Messiahs," 357–73, who argues against Donaldson's later claim and shows a link between Isa 11 and Rom 15. See also Whittle, *Covenant Renewal*, esp. 31–75.

209. Fredriksen, *From Jesus to Christ*, 150, emphasis hers.

210. Dunn's analysis of Paul's use of ἱστορέω in 1:18 of "gaining information" (*Jesus, Paul and the Law*, 110–13) is convincing; Paul didn't need to "consult" anyone concerning his revelation. However, it seems improbable that Paul would visit Peter for fifteen days and not seek to learn from his vast knowledge and experience of Christ (cf. 1 Cor 15).

free Gentile inclusion; Paul helped to reveal the implications of the new age. It must have been Paul's witness to Gentiles having received the Holy Spirit apart from works of the flesh (Gal 3:2–5), and the witness of this indwelling through various signs in their midst, which helped the Jerusalem leaders connect the dots. This is why the Jerusalem leaders did not compel Titus to be circumcised (Gal 2:3), why they rejected the circumcision group (Gal 2:4–5), and why they recognized Paul's mission to the Gentiles (Gal 2:7, 8, 9). It seem improbable, if not impossible, that the Jerusalem leaders believed they were only endorsing "God-fearing" status to the Gentiles or that Paul would have been "ambiguous" about Gentiles gaining "full status as members of the covenant and full heirs of its promises."[211] If Scot McKnight,[212] Michael Bird[213] and Fredriksen[214] are correct in their assessment that Judaism was not a missionary religion which actively proselytized,[215] then Paul's mission would have been unique.[216] The endorsement of Paul's mission by the Jerusalem leaders would thus stand out to the Galatians not because it certified Paul's apostleship or because it appropriated Paul's gospel, but because it concretely demonstrated that the eschatological reality of Isa 49 had come to fruition.

One further point needs addressing. Paul's reference to the dual missions of Peter and himself (to Jews and Gentiles respectively) is not an inference there were two different covenants or two different paths for salvation.[217] Paul understood the Jews as entering the covenant through God's grace and not through the law. The law was simply an identity and boundary marker, which allowed Israel to participate in the covenant relationship. Nevertheless, Paul's Christophanic experience radically shifted his reality. Jesus was the long awaited messiah and his life was the *telos*, the

---

211. *Pace*, Dunn, *Galatians*, 15.

212. McKnight, *A Light among the Gentiles*.

213. Bird, *Crossing Over Sea and Land*.

214. Fredriksen, "Judaism, the Circumcision of Gentiles," 532–64; Fredriksen, *From Jesus to Christ*, 84, 146–76.

215. This does not mean Jews did not proselytize or that Gentiles did not convert; there is plenty of evidence of both. Rather, it means the majority of these conversions took place passively as Gentiles became intrigued with Judaism, started attending synagogue, became God-fearers, and then made the decision to become full members.

Dickson, *Mission-Commitment in Ancient Judaism*, 11–50: provides an interesting alternative evaluation from that of McKnight, et al., although much of the difference is based on contrasting definitions of "mission/missionary."

216. Contra Donaldson, *Paul and the Gentiles*, 273–307, who believes Paul was a Jewish proselytizer before and after his conversion/call.

217. *Pace*, Gaston, *Paul and the Torah*; Gager, *Reinventing Paul*.

consummation, of the law[218] (Rom 10:4; cf. Gal 3:24; 6:2; Matt 5:17). As such, Christ became the new identity and boundary marker for both Jews and Gentiles. The Christophany required Paul to re-examine his previous reading of the Jewish Scriptures through the lens of Christ. Paul discovered Christ had taken on the role of the Isaianic Servant and with it the curse of the law, providing once-for-all atonement for sin and allowing his offspring to live in and live out his righteousness and thus his righteous mission to be a light to the nations and to bring glory to God.

Galatians 2:11–17

The Antioch incident (Gal 2:11–17) is often viewed as a contradictory episode to the one reported in Gal 2:1–10. Whereas the latter confirms Paul's mission, presents a unity among the various leaders, and discloses a dependence on Paul's part, the former rejects the mission, creates division among the leadership, and solidifies Paul's independent mission. Perhaps the greatest modern proponent of this view is Dunn, who views Paul's "defeat" at Antioch[219] as the watershed moment in early church history.[220] He writes: "It shaped the future of Paul's missionary work, it sparked off a crucial insight which became one of the central emphases in Paul's subsequent teaching, and consequently it determined the whole character and future of that young movement which we now call Christianity."[221]

This is an arduous load for the present pericope to bear. Dunn's interpretation has at least two flaws: (1) it assumes *ex silentio* Paul's defeat; and (2) it ignores the context of Paul's argument.[222] Concerning the former, Ciampa convincingly argues Paul's language deliberately implies his victory at Antioch. At hand is the idiomatic phrase κατὰ πρόσωπον αὐτῷ ἀντέστην (2:11). "Κατὰ πρόσωπον modifies ἀνθίστημι eight times in the LXX: Deut 7:24; 9:2; 11:25; 31:21; Judg 2:14; 2 Chr 13:7–8;[223] Jdt 6:4. Each example of

---

218. Bockmuehl, *Revelation and Mystery*, 150–53.

219. Dunn, *Galatians*, believes what is lacking in Gal 2:11–14 provides evidence of Paul's defeat. "Had Peter and the other (Christian) Jews backed Paul on that occasion, he could hardly have failed to draw attention to and underline that fact" (12); Dunn, *Jesus, Paul and the Law*, 160.

220. Cf. Bockmuehl, *The Remembered Peter*, 61–70.

221. Dunn, *Jesus, Paul and the Law*, 162–63.

222. See also the critic by W. Campbell, *Paul and the Creation*, 51.

223. Although not clear in Ciampa's quote, this reference accounts for two of the eight.

the idiom communicates the idea of making a successful resistance to an opposing power or force."[224]

Concerning context, Dunn's interpretation contends the Jerusalem leaders changed their mind and now sided with the "false believers" (Gal 2:4–5). This would suggest the "circumcision faction" and the "people from James" (Gal 2.12) are one and the same.[225] This would equate them with the "agitators" (Gal 1:7; cf. 6:11–13) and mean they too were ἀνάθεμα (Gal 1:8–9). According to Dunn's rationale, part of Paul's apologia is to seek the endorsement of those he is about to condemn. It is more plausible Paul's retelling of the event serves to link Peter and the Jerusalem leaders to the Galatians rather than to the opponents. If Paul is seen to be "victorious" in the situation, then Peter becomes a positive example[226] of one who has properly responded to Paul's correction, and the Galatians should follow his lead. In this way, Peter's and Paul's example are also analogous.

Both the Galatians and Peter were in the process of turning from "the truth of the Gospel" (i.e., their position ἐν Χριστῷ) to "a different gospel" (i.e., "the present evil age") based on the influence of those advocating circumcision. Mark Nanos argues that Peter's actions were denying the eschatological equality of the Gentile brought about through Christ, which demanded that "they must live together as one, as social equals, Jews and Gentiles living righteoused [sic] together by God in Christ."[227]

Several points should be highlighted. First, the "condemning" (Gal 2:11) is not by Paul but by God.[228] Here Paul continues the divine–human contrast. Second, the issue of mixed table-fellowship[229] is noteworthy if one assumes Paul knew of Peter's vision and previous confrontation with the circumcision group over this same issue (Acts 10:9—11:18). This would signal a continuation of the revelation motif.[230] Peter would then be understood as being guilty of turning from the revelation God had already given him (cf. Gal 3:1–5). Third, the action of "compelling" (ἀναγκάζω; Gal 2:14b) in Galatians is always in reference to circumcision (cf. Gal 2:3; 6:12) and is equated with the false believers (Gal 2:4–5). Paul's interrogative in Gal 2:14b

224. Ciampa, Presence and Function, 157–58.

225. So de Boer, Galatians, 133–34. Contra Witherington, Grace in Galatians, 154–56.

226. This may account for the positive references to Peter in First Corinthians. Cf. Bockmuehl, The Remembered Peter, 69.

227. Nanos, "What Was at Stake," 317.

228. The participle κατεγνωσμένος is passive and assumes a divine agent. Contra NRSV, which appears to view this as a middle participle rendering it "self-condemned."

229. Contra Nanos, "What Was at Stake."

230. This is not an absurd assumption especially in light of Gal 1:18.

suggests the "compelling" had not actually taken place, but rather Peter's actions were leading him in this direction. Paul's question is meant to shame Peter before it is too late (cf. Gal 3:1–5). The last assertion is strengthened when Gal 2:15–17[231] is read as part of the current pericope. Since Gentiles are no doubt included in the ἔμπροσθεν πάντων (Gal 2:14), and since Paul's words are directed toward "a Jew by birth" (φύσει Ἰουδαῖοι; Gal 2:15), it seems unlikely Paul is addressing the general audience.[232] The "we" includes Peter. Paul's shift from third person singular to second person plural signals a change in attitude on the part of Peter.[233]

There is an obvious contrast between "works of the law"[234] and "faithfulness of Christ"[235] and it revolves around the verb δικαιόω. From the context, it seems logical to conclude δικαιόω equals salvation and inclusion in the covenant people. "Works of the law" (ἔργων νόμου) is not a negative commentary on the law but an idiomatic expression for "doing the law." Therefore, the contrast is not between law and faith, but between those who seek to be included in the covenant through doing the law and those who seek to be included by the faithfulness of Christ. The key is seen in the divine–human contrast. It is the choice of inclusion via God through Christ or inclusion via human effort through works of the law.

Galatians 2:17 is an important verse, which ties this discourse to Peter's actions and also serves to inform the Galatians of their own actions. Here the passive δικαιωθῆναι in correlation with ζητοῦντες should be understood as expressing human agency and thus conveying the idea that the act of "justifying" is being sought through human effort (i.e., ἐξ ἔργων νόμου) even if it is erroneously thought to be done ἐν Χριστῷ. It seems unlikely those who sought to be "justified" by God (i.e., διὰ πίστεως Ἰησοῦ Χριστοῦ) would find themselves ἁμαρτωλοί. Peter has made this negative shift and Paul is reminding him his actions are making him a servant of sin. The Galatians should thus come to recognize their own

231. So also Jervis, *Galatians*; Schmithals, *Paul and James*. Cf. Cole, *Galatians*; and Lategan, "Is Paul Defending," who both divide 2:11–16 and 2:17–21.

232. This is an additional argument against seeing these verses as being directed at the Galatians.

233. Jervis, *Galatians*, 70, "[T]he *absolutely not!* at the end of the verse [v. 17] would be Peter's exclamation as he comes to grips with the theological consequence of separating himself from Gentiles [*sic*] believers" (emphasis his). Jervis goes so far as to attribute all of 2:15–16a to Peter, stating Paul's view was somewhat different (72).

234. For a summary of the phrase "works of the law," see Ciampa, *Presence and Function*, 186–191. See also Dunn, "4QMMT and Galatians," 147–53.

235. On the subjective genitive see, Hays, *The Faith of Jesus Christ*; Hays, "PISTIS and Pauline Christology," 35–60. Contra Dunn, "Once More, PISTIS XRISTOU," 61–81. For further debate see, Bird and Sprinkle, *The Faith of Jesus Christ*.

shift is potentially making them servants of sin rather than servants of Christ. They are seeking inclusion in the covenant people but their actions are having the opposite effect, moving them toward the "present evil age" rather than helping them to remain ἐν Χριστῷ.

Galatians 2:18–21

Paul's use of the first person singular marks a move from the Antioch narrative to a direct address to the Galatians while still referencing Peter's *lapsus*. The "I" should be understood as "universal"[236] while still being very personal as it relates to Paul's own experience.[237] In these verses the temporal and spatial realty of the two ages and the divine–human contrast coalesce as Paul brings this first part of his polemic to a close and simultaneously jumpstarts the next.

De Boer shows several parallels between Gal 2:19–21 and Gal 1:13–16 and argues the former "constitute[s] Paul's (further) interpretation of his conversion and call."[238] Paul recognizes that if he was to build up his previous life then he would become a transgressor, not of the law, but of Christ (Gal 2:18). The eschatological reality inaugurated through Christ has brought about a separation between Paul and works of the law[239] (Gal 2:19a) and simultaneously a union between Christ and Paul (Gal 2:20a). This mysterious relocation took place as a result of Paul having been "crucified together with" Christ (Gal 2:19b).

The link between Gal 2:20 and Gal 1:4 brings the Galatians back to the eschatological focus of the gospel. Galatians 2:20 also brings the divine–human contrast to a head.[240] The only possible way of escaping the present evil age is by allowing the divine to reside within humanity (ἐν ἐμοὶ Χριστός; cf. Gal 1:16); it is by dying to self and residing in the "faithfulness of the Son of God"[241] that one experiences the eschatological reality of the resurrection in the present body (νῦν ζῶ ἐν σαρκί).

Paul's statement about not invalidating the grace of God (Gal 2:21) confirms the acceptance of the eschatological grace received by him (Gal 1:15) and the Galatians (Gal 1:6) at their calling. The contrast between

---

236. So Lategan, "Is Paul Defending," 427; Betz, *Galatians*, 122.

237. So Dunn, *Galatians*, 142.

238. De Boer, *Galatians*, 159.

239. "Law" is shorthand for "works of the law." So de Boer, *Galatians*, 159.

240. Cf. Lategan, "Is Paul Defending," 428–29.

241. Hays, *The Faith of Jesus Christ*, 167–69, 250; de Boer, *Galatians*, 162. Contra Dunn, *Galatians*, 146.

grace and law in relation to justification parallels the contrast made above between Christ's faithfulness and works of the law (Gal 2:16). The line between validation and invalidation of God's grace (i.e., Christ's death) is clearly drawn and there can be no mistaking the seriousness of crossing this marker (cf. 5:4).

Conclusion

The purpose of Paul's autobiographical narrative and of the epistle as a whole is to persuade (remind) the Galatians that the eschatological age has been inaugurated through the death and resurrection of Christ and that this reality means the Galatians are already the ἐκκλησία of God. This one theological truth and the reality it brings is so world-changing that the Galatians' grasp of it should convince them to reject the law-observant gospel preached by the agitators and fully embrace the truth of the gospel preached by Paul, Peter, and the Jerusalem leaders—the gospel of Christ that allows for a law-free inclusion of the Gentiles in the eschatological age.

In the first two chapters, Paul's method for carrying out this purpose is six-fold: (1) to articulate a particular picture of Christ as the Isaianic Servant who atones for sin and ushers in a new eschatological reality; (2) to articulate a particular picture of the Galatians as those who through Christ have become recipients of God's grace and peace and have assumed a new identity as God's children, the eschatological church; (3) to articulate a significant divine–human dichotomy whereby all things and persons on the "divine" side are part of the eschatological age and all things or persons on the "human" side are part of the present evil age; (4) to provide his own Christophanic experience as proof of the eschatological age, proof of the revelatory aspects of the gospel of Christ, proof of the Galatians' calling as the eschatological people of God, proof of Paul's calling to be one of the servants of the Servant Christ, and proof of the Galatians' same calling; (5) to provide his account of his encounter with Peter and the Jerusalem leaders as proof of the eschatological age, proof of Gentile inclusion into the eschatological people of God apart from works of the law, and proof of the unity of this message among the church leaders; and (6) to provide his account of the Antioch incident in order to offer Peter as a positive example of one who, like the Galatians, comes close to accepting a "different gospel" but ultimately returns to the truth of the gospel of Christ.

Of these six points, number four, which contains five elements, is the most pertinent to the current study as it postulates particular purposes for Paul's Christophanic reference. First, Paul recounts his Christophany to emphasize that it is a revelation of the crucified and now resurrected Christ, which can only mean that this Christ is the long-awaited messiah. From Paul's Jewish perspective, this is proof that the eschatological age has broken into the present. Additionally, the present aspect of this eschatological reality is not only made possible *through* Christ but moreover *in* Christ. Second, Paul recounts his Christophany in order to emphasize its divine source. This emphasis is not self-serving. Paul does not use it to defend his apostleship. Instead, Paul levels the playing field by arguing that the proclaimed gospel is also a divine revelation equal to the revelation Paul himself has experienced. This means all believers, including the Galatians, experience their initial calling by way of divine revelation. Third, Paul recounts his Christophany in a way that intentionally parallels the Galatians' experience to his own. Through the Holy Spirit, the Galatians received a manifestation of Christ, which was simultaneously a calling to become the eschatological people of God. Fourth, Paul recounts his Christophany with strong allusion to the Isaianic Servant. As such, Paul is able to confirm the identity of Christ as the singular Servant and simultaneously identify himself as one of the eschatological servants of the Servant who is called to carry out the mission of being a light to the nations and bringing glory to God. Finally, Paul recounts his Christophany in such a way as to invite the Galatians to embrace the same calling he has embraced to become eschatological servants of the Servant Christ.

All five elements hold a common thread. They show the corporate nature of Paul's Christophanic reference. This corporate aspect goes well beyond Paul's viewing of his calling as designated for the purpose of bringing others into the eschatological Kingdom; although, this is definitely part of his understanding. Paul actually uses his Christophanic reference didactically and paradigmatically. He uses it to teach the Galatians about their identity in Christ and to provide a paradigm for the Galatians to follow. He is willing to highlight the human frailty of his past action and identity in order to provide an example for the Galatians' same reversal. He models transformation away from human/fleshly understanding and actions to divine/Spirit-led understanding and actions. Furthermore, he is willing to parallel his own calling as one of the servants of the Servant Christ in order to help the Galatians understand this same calling in their own lives. This does not negate his unique apostolic calling. Nevertheless, this does not appear to be the focus of his Christophanic reference.

Finally, the most radical and most corporate part of Paul's Christophanic reference is how he intentionally downplays the particulars of his own event in order to emphasize the shared elements of the experiences. At multiple points, Paul's Christophanic reference moves beyond paradigm and articulates a oneness in conversion/calling, experience, and mission. The Galatians are not just invited to emulate a particular action or theology of Paul's. They are invited to recognize the analogous parts of their eschatological conversion/calling. As they are relocated in Christ, they share together with Paul and all believers a dynamic revelation of Christ, co-crucifixion with Christ, the indwelling of God through the Holy Spirit, and a oneness with each other.

4

Paul's Christophanic References in First Corinthians

THIS CHAPTER EVALUATES PAUL'S two Christophanic references in First Corinthians (9:1–2, 16–17; 15:1–11). First Corinthians evidences possible signs of a Corinthian challenge to Paul's authority and is often viewed as an apostolic apologia whereby Paul seeks to persuade the Corinthians to accept his authority over that of other Christian leaders. Both Christophanic references bear the weight of the reading. This study argues that the majority of the Corinthians are not challenging Paul's authority and Paul is not primarily defending his apostleship. It shows how moving beyond this hypothesis allows for a more consistent and theologically focused reading of this epistle in general and of Paul's Christophanic references specifically. First Corinthians does contain multiple OT quotations,[1] allusions, and echoes, which may suggest the Corinthians have a basic understanding of at least some OT texts.[2] Nonetheless, unlike Galatians, Paul's Christophanic references in First Corinthians do not rely heavily on a particular OT text for their interpretation. For this reason, intertextual issues will be addressed as needed. Before an exegetical evaluation of the two Christophanic references can take place, some preliminary issues need to be addressed. These will provide a context and foundation for interpreting these references.

---

1. Koch, *Die Schrift*, 22–23, identifies eighteen quotations; Stanley, *Arguing with Scripture*, 78, seventeen quotations; Silva, "Old Testament in Paul," 631, eighteen quotations; Heil, *First Corinthians*, 14–15, twenty-one quotations.

2. Cf. Ciampa and Rosner, *First Corinthians*, 28–32; Heil, *First Corinthians*, 7–10. Contra Stanley, *Arguing with Scripture*, 75–78.

Preliminary Considerations

The Occasion and Theme of First Corinthians

The immediate occasion for Paul's writing of First Corinthians[3] is almost certainly the need to address issues brought by Chloe's people (1 Cor 1:11; cf. 5:1; 11:18, 15:12) and by the Corinthians' own letter (1 Cor 7:1; cf. 8:1; 12:1; 16:1).[4] It should be remembered that this letter "is the continuation of an ongoing conversation between Paul and the church"[5] (1 Cor 5:9; 7:1; cf. 2 Cor 2:3–4). Paul is relationally investing in this community (1 Cor 4:14–15) and appears to know them relatively well (cf. Acts 18:1–18). Unlike the Galatians, who were in danger of succumbing to "a different gospel" from an outside source, the Corinthians are dealing with internal, interpersonal, and ethical issues, which are threatening to tear the body apart and hurting their testimony in the larger community. Paul addresses ethical and relational missteps as symptoms of deeper theological misunderstandings, while simultaneously tackling surface issues.

Taken together, the prescript (1 Cor 1:1–3) and thanksgiving (1 Cor 1:4–9) sections contain the theme and strategy of the epistle.[6] Paul begins with a reference to his apostolic calling, which took place διὰ θελήματος θεοῦ (cf. 2 Cor 1:1).[7] Several points suggest this prepositional phrase is not inserted as part of an apostolic apologia. For example, Paul has already shown himself capable of using identical language in reference to Christ's atoning sacrifice (Gal 1:3–4). Additionally, Paul employs this language to speak of God's will for believers' transformation (1 Thess 4:3; 5:18), the need for believers to discern God's will together (Rom 12:2), and as a way of center-

3. This study assumes the integrity of First Corinthians. With Fee, *First Corinthians*, 15–16, I agree that any seeming issues can be worked out exegetically. For arguments of unity, which take seriously the complexities of the issue see, Collins, *First Corinthians*, 10–14; Mitchell, *Rhetoric of Reconciliation*; cf. de Boer, "Composition of 1 Corinthians," 229–45.

4. It is possible that additional concerns where brought to Paul by Stephanas, Fortunatus, and Achaicus (1 Cor 16:17). Paul may also glean further information from Apollos (1 Cor 16:12).

5. Garland, *First Corinthians*, 20.

6. Contra Mitchell, *Rhetoric of Reconciliation*, 198–200; Witherington, *Conflict & Community in Corinth*, 94; Thiselton, *First Corinthians*, 111–13, who all view 1 Cor 1:10 as containing the main thesis of unity. However, this focuses on a surface issue rather than on the deeper theological issues Paul is addressing throughout. For a view similar to the one argued in this study, see Ciampa and Rosner, *First Corinthians*, 61.

7. This is also a common phrase in the so-called disputed Pauline epistles, where the author/s does not appear to be mounting a self-defense (cf. Eph 1:1; Col 1:1; 2 Tim 1:1; cf. 1 Tim 1:1; and Titus 1:3).

ing his (Rom 15:32) and believers' actions (2 Cor 8:5) in the realm of God's authority. There can be little doubt that Paul understood the Corinthians calling (1 Cor 1:2, 9, 24) as also taking place by the will of God.[8] Therefore, the primary antithesis is not between Paul's position and the Corinthians' or between Paul's apostolic calling and others' apostolic calling, but between divine agency and human agency. As in Galatians, Paul quickly establishes the divine–human dichotomy in order to aid the Corinthians in understanding the eschatological reality in which they are called to live.

Paul's words in 1 Cor 1:2b allude either to Mal 1:11[9] or Joel 3:5 LXX (Joel 2:32 MT). There are multiple reasons to see the latter as the primary referent.

1 Corinthians 1:2b	Joel 3:5
σὺν πᾶσιν τοῖς ἐπικαλουμένοις τὸ ὄνομα τοῦ κυρίου ἡμῶν Ἰησοῦ Χριστοῦ ἐν παντὶ τόπῳ αὐτῶν καὶ ἡμῶν	καὶ ἔσται πᾶς, ὃς ἂν ἐπικαλέσηται τὸ ὄνομα κυρίου, σωθήσεται

Besides the near identical language, Anthony Thiselton notes Paul's quotation of this same text in Rom 10:13 and argues the reference to day of the Lord in 1 Cor 1:7–8 makes the allusion more sure since Joel is specifically describing this eschatological event (Joel 3:4 LXX; cf. 1 Cor 1:15; 2:1–2; 4:14, 18).[10] Paul's mention of the Spirit's endowment of χαρίσματα (1 Cor 1:7; cf. Joel 3:1–5 LXX) in connection with this day also correlates with Joel (3:1–5 LXX; cf. 1 Cor 1:15; 2:1, 11; 4:14). Additionally, Paul's reference to the Corinthians as ἐκκλησία τοῦ θεοῦ who have been ἡγιασμένοις ἐν Χριστῷ Ἰησοῦ, κλητοῖς ἁγίοις (1 Cor 1:2a) possibly correlates to Joel's call to gather and ἁγιάσατε ἐκκλησίαν in preparation for Yahweh's return (Joel 2:16 LXX). Finally, the larger context of Joel speaks of the people turning (or returning) to the Lord because the Lord is ἐλεήμων καὶ οἰκτίρμων (Joel 2:13 LXX). The adjective ἐλεήμων carries similar connotations to how Paul uses χάρις as referring to the act of God rescuing his people because of his covenant faithfulness (1 Cor 1:3–4).[11]

---

8. Cf. Ciampa and Rosner, *First Corinthians*, 56–57.

9. Ciampa and Rosner, *First Corinthians*, 57–58.

10. Thiselton, *First Corinthians*, 78.

11. The adjective ἐλεήμων is a translation of חַנּוּן in the MT. The Hebrew word חַנּוּן is the adjectival form of חנן and appears thirteen times in the MT, always as an attribute of God and more specifically to his hearing and responding to the cries of his people in accordance with his חֶסֶד (cf. Exod 34:6; Jonah 4:2; Pss 86:15; 103:8; 145:8; Neh 9:17).

It becomes evident that Joel's eschatology has invaded not only 1 Cor 1:2b but the whole of Paul's introduction and thanksgiving (1 Cor 1:1–9). Paul uses this as a way of framing the direction of the epistle as a whole. The issue at hand is theological and principally eschatological. Paul begins by reminding the Corinthians that the eschatological age has *already* dawned and that the Corinthians are *already* part of the eschatological people of God, having experienced God's grace given in Christ Jesus, God's Spirit as evidenced by the gifts of the Spirit, and God's calling into the fellowship of his Son. Nevertheless, Paul juxtaposes this *already-ness* with the reality of the *not-yet-ness*. The Corinthians are reminded that they await τὴν ἀποκάλυψιν τοῦ κυρίου ἡμῶν Ἰησοῦ Χριστοῦ (1 Cor 1:7; cf. Gal 1:12). This is traditionally understood as a reference to Christ's second coming[12] and in light of 1 Cor 1:8 this reading may be sound. However, ἀποκάλυψις is not Paul's normal language for speaking of the second coming (although cf. 1 Cor 3:13; Rom 8:19).[13]

Paul may be highlighting the Corinthians' deficiency with regard to their understanding of Christ and the eschatological age as evidenced by their lack of unity and care for one another (1 Cor 1:10). Thus, even as they are *already* sanctified in Christ Jesus and called to be holy (1 Cor 1:2), they are *not yet* fully embracing this reality.[14] This accounts for what would otherwise be repetition in 1 Cor 1:8, with Paul's reference to the "day of the Lord." Instead, 1 Cor 1:8 anticipates the *not yet* consummation of the eschatological age and balances Paul's last statement by its assurance that it is God's[15] continued work in the Corinthians that is strengthening them and is able to make them blameless till the end. Paul maintains the *already/not yet* tension of both the eschatological age and of the Corinthians own transformation in this age and maintains the divine–human dichotomy.

Paul also addresses the corporate nature of the eschatological age and of the Corinthians' eschatological identity. Through reference to Joel 3:5 LXX, Paul stresses the reality that the Corinthians' inclusion into the eschatological people of God is not unique to them. They join the whole ἐκκλησία of God in Corinth; they join Paul and Sosthenes; and they join "all those who in every place call on the name of our Lord Jesus Christ, both their Lord and ours" (1 Cor 1:2b). They must be reminded that the eschatological reality in which they participate is neither defined by them

---

12. Hays, *First Corinthians*, 18; Ciampa and Rosner, *First Corinthians*, 65–66; Fee, *First Corinthians*, 41–43; Thiselton, *First Corinthians*, 100; Barrett, *First Corinthians*, 38–39.

13. This is noted by both Fee, *First Corinthians*, 42; and Horsley, *First Corinthians*, 40.

14. Cf. Thiselton, *First Corinthians*, 76–77.

15. So Fee, *First Corinthians*, 43–44.

nor theirs to define. Instead, in Christ, they share in something much bigger than themselves, something only God can bring about.

Paul's purpose is disclosed in this reading of the prescript and thanksgiving sections. Paul addresses a deficiency in the Corinthians' eschatological understanding, which is resulting in concrete ethical issues and causing disunity in the church. As Hays aptly articulates, "Paul [is] trying to teach the Corinthian church to think eschatologically."[16] Key to a proper eschatological worldview is a grasping of various dichotomies between divine and human, already and not yet, and corporate and individual. Paul's strategy for carrying out this purpose is also seen in 1 Cor 1:1–9. First, Paul employs OT quotations and allusions as a way of constructing a foundation for the Corinthians to understand their new eschatological identity.[17] Second, Paul sets forth his own life as a model of this new identity and as impetus for present transformation. It will be argued that both of Paul's Christophanic references contribute to this end.

Corinthian Challenge and Apostolic Apologia?

Many scholars see in First Corinthians evidence of a "Corinthian Challenge" and, therefore, read the epistle as an "Apostolic Apologia" (CCAA).[18] While the interpretation of Paul's Christophanic references posited in this chapter do not rise or fall on a non-CCAA reading, it is important to acknowledge the impact of a CCAA reading on 1 Cor 1:10—4:21, which often becomes the hermeneutical lens for interpreting the whole of the epistle (esp. 1 Cor 9:1–23; 15:1–11). The most influential CCAA reading of 1 Cor 1:10—4:21 is found in Nils Dahl's "Paul and the Church at Corinth According to 1 Corinthians 1:10—4:21."[19] Dahl's conclusions,[20] while pos-

16. Hays, *Conversion of the Imagination*, 6.

17. Hays, *Conversion of the Imagination*, 6.

18. Dahl, "Paul and Corinth," (1967), 313–35; Fee, *First Corinthians*; Hays, *First Corinthians*; Chow, *Patronage and Power*; Furnish, *Theology of First Corinthians*; Fitzmyer, *First Corinthians*.

19. Dahl, "Paul and Corinth," (1967), 313–35.

20. Dahl, "Paul and Corinth," (1967), 329, lists four conclusions; (1) that 1 Cor 1:10–4:21 is most definitely an apostolic apologia; (2) quarrels are mainly the result of opposition against Paul; (3) the quarrels are likely occasioned by the letter and delegation sent to Paul; and (4) the function of this section in the epistle is to re-establish his authority before he can address the issues raised. Many of Dahl's conclusions are based on a belief that the slogans found in 1 Cor 1:12 represent four concrete factions with only the "Paul group" in support of Paul (similarly, Fee, *First Corinthians*, 8 and n. 22). Several have convincingly argued that Paul's reference to the Christ-group is his own corrective to the divisions and does not represent a separate group (e.g.,

sible, fail to do justice to the full content of this large unit, not least the wisdom sections (1 Cor 1:18–31; 2:6–16; 3:18–23). He treats the entire unit as preliminary, serving only to position Paul for what follows. Dahl himself notices weaknesses in his argument and in a later republication of this essay writes: "colleagues and students have convinced me that the characterization of 1 Cor. 1:10—4:21 as an apologetic section is one-sided and may be misleading."[21] Sadly, this quote takes place in a final footnote and the content of the essay remains unchanged. Still, many continue to rely heavily on Dahl's earlier argument.[22]

For some, the strongest evidence of CCAA is found in 1 Cor 4:1–5. Of this pericope, Hays writes: "This is our first unambiguous indication that the Corinthians are in fact second-guessing Paul's apostolic labors and questioning his authority."[23] Yet, Paul's reference to being judged (ἀνακρίνω) does not automatically suggest the Corinthians are questioning his authority. Ben Witherington believes this judgment is only in reference to Paul's speech and rhetorical ability and has nothing to do with questioning his apostolic authority.[24] Furthermore, Paul's use of the subjunctive mood with ἵνα may suggest a hypothetical situation.[25]

David Kuck argues the key to understanding all of 1 Cor 1:10—4:21 is found in 3:5—4:5 and the theme of apocalyptic judgment.[26] He views Paul's appeal to divine judgment as a way to "combat the detrimental social effects of the individual pursuit of spiritual wisdom."[27] "Paul uses judgement language not as a threat but as a positive motivation for his parenesis."[28] The primary function of 1 Cor 4:3, argues Kuck, is for Paul to apply 1 Cor 2:15 personally to stress the dichotomy between human reason and God's judge-

---

Mitchell, *Rhetoric of Reconciliation*, 86; Garland, *First Corinthians*, 49). Additionally, while, Dahl and Fee are correct that this letter is mostly directed to the whole congregation and not to a specific group, the few exceptions to this (1 Cor 4:18–19; 9:2–3) suggest Paul's opposition is limited (cf. Ciampa and Rosner, *First Corinthians*, 54, 172). It should also be noted that if Paul were defending himself, his reprimanding of all parties, including the Paul-group, would seem counterproductive. However, if Paul is primarily concerned with correcting the Corinthians' erroneous ethical missteps and theological misunderstandings, then human judgments against Paul would be of little concern to him (cf. 1 Cor 4:3–4).

21. Dahl, "Paul and Corinth," (1977), 61, n. 50.

22. Most recently see, Fitzmyer, *First Corinthians*, 136–40.

23. Hays, *First Corinthians*, 65–66; cf. Fitzmyer, *First Corinthians*, 213.

24. Witherington, *Conflict & Community in Corinth*, 137.

25. Thiselton, *First Corinthians*, 338; cf. Wallace. *Greek Grammar*, 462, 475.

26. Kuck, *Judgment and Community Conflict*, 150–222.

27. Kuck, *Judgment and Community Conflict*, 156.

28. Kuck, *Judgment and Community Conflict*, 222.

ment.[29] Paul's hypothetical judgment drives home the point that Paul makes throughout this section; God's power alone judges and justifies not human wisdom. Paul's own model of divine reversal needs to be embraced (1 Cor 4:16) if the Corinthians are truly to be part of the eschatological people of God who evidence the mind of Christ (1 Cor 2:16).

While chapters 1–4 deal with the issue of Corinthian division, it is not a struggle between Paul and Apollos. Throughout this section Paul downplays any apostolic disagreements by his consistent use of the *fpp* pronoun to speak of the apostles' common proclamation (1 Cor 1:21–23; 2:6–7), position (1 Cor 3:9; 4:1), and suffering (1 Cor 4:9–13). Paul's affirmation of Apollos (1 Cor 3:5–9; 16:12) reveals there is "not the slightest hint that the teachers [are] themselves party to this quarrelling."[30] Nor does the text evidence that the conflict is primarily between Paul and the Corinthians,[31] at least not from Paul's perspective. Instead, the divisions in the church represent an internal power struggle, most likely based on social stratification rather than theological doctrine,[32] which come out of a deficient eschatological understanding.

The theme of "power" (δύναμις) appears throughout this section (1 Cor 1:18, 24; 2:4, 5; cf. 4:19, 20) but is directly tied to Christ and his cross, to the Spirit, and to God. This power is only connected to Paul as he is connected to Christ. Paul's power language creates a clear divine–human dichotomy throughout this section. This dichotomy is undergirded by an OT substructure. Paul utilizes six OT references (1 Cor 1:19; 1:31; 2:9; 2:16; 3:19; 3:20; cf. respectively LXX Isa 29:14; Jer 9:24/1 Sam 2:10; Isa 64:4; Isa 40:13; Job 5:13; Ps 94:11),[33] which are "all taken from passages that depict God as one who acts to judge and save his people in ways that defy human imagination."[34] These passages highlight God's divine sovereignty and grace in the midst of human disobedience, ignorance, and arrogance. They evidence the power struggle being advanced is not human versus human, as it might appear on the surface, but human versus divine, or more precisely human wisdom versus God's wisdom, flesh versus Spirit, and this age versus the coming age.

---

29. Kuck, *Judgment and Community Conflict*, 198–200. Although seeing it as secondary, Kuck also succumbs to a CCAA reading (197–99).

30. Fee, *First Corinthians*, 48.

31. *Pace*, Theissen, *Psychological Aspects*, 59.

32. Marshall, *Enmity in Corinth*.

33. Paul's reference in 1 Cor 4:6 is most likely pointing back to at least one of these OT texts. So also Hooker, "Beyond Things which are Written," 127–32; Wagner, "Not Beyond the Things," 279–87.

34. Hays, *Conversion of the Imagination*, 13.

Paul's OT citation in 1 Cor 1:31—Ὁ καυχώμενος ἐν κυρίῳ καυχάσθω—is significant, pointing back to either Jer 9:24, 1 Sam 2:10 LXX, or to both.[35] While most scholars primarily focus on the Jeremiah passage, citing contextual linguistic parallels,[36] J. Ross Wagner has made a strong argument for First Samuel based on thematic parallels.[37] Furthermore, Wagner shows verbal and thematic links between 1 Cor 1:18–31 and 4:6–13, which also echo 1 Sam 2:10 LXX, especially Paul's evoking of the triad in 1 Cor 4:10 (cf. 1 Cor 1:26). Wagner also argues, 1 Cor 4:6—"Nothing beyond what is written"—points back to the quotation in 1 Cor 1:31 and together these two sections provide an antithesis between the Corinthians' anthropocentric boasting (cf. 1 Cor 3:21–22) and the actions of Paul and Apollos who boast only in the Lord.

Paul's paternal language in 1 Cor 4:14–15 (τέκνα and πατήρ; cf. the maternal imagery of 3:1b–2) is often seen as a power play[38] in which Paul establish his dominance by invoking his status as *pater familias*.[39] Nevertheless, Thiselton's appeal for taking this language at face-value should not be quickly disregarded.[40] Paul's sternness throughout this epistle can just as easily represent his genuine love and compassion for those whom he considers his spiritual children. Additionally, if along with Ciampa and Rosner 1 Cor 4:18–21 is understood as belonging to the subsequent section (1 Cor 5:1–8), which deals with sexual immorality, then Paul's tone in these verses is appropriate considering the gravitas of the situation.[41]

Kathy Ehrensperger has argued Paul's parental language is part of a larger Jewish pedagogical discourse.[42] "[Paul] acts as a parent-teacher using power-over them to empower them and thus render himself, and the power-over exercised in this role, obsolete."[43] In essence, Paul sought to distribute power rather than wield it.[44] This claim is substantiated as

---

35. So Hays, *First Corinthians*, 34–35; Ciampa and Rosner, *First Corinthians*, 110–11.

36. See esp. Stanley, *Paul and the Language of Scripture*, 186–88.

37. Wagner, "Not Beyond the Things," 284.

38. See Castelli, *Imitating Paul*, 97–115; Polaski, *Paul and the Discourse of Power*, 31; Fiorenza, "Rhetorical Situation," 396–97.

39. White, "Paul and *Pater Familias*," 457–87.

40. Thiselton, *First Corinthians*, 369.

41. So Ciampa and Rosner, *First Corinthians*, 189–90.

42. Ehrensperger, *Paul and the Dynamics of Power*, 126–36.

43. Ehrensperger, *Paul and the Dynamics of Power*, 136.

44. This does not contradict Paul's "power in weakness" theme in 1 Cor 1–2 or in Second Corinthians. Ultimately, the power Paul distributes is God's power; this is the reason he cannot keep it to himself. Those possessing God's power recognize it is not

one remembers how Paul has already aligned his own calling with the Corinthians' calling (1 Cor 1:2). Paul's plea for imitation (1 Cor 4:16), echoing his plea for union of mind and purpose (1 Cor 1:10), is proof that he desires for the Corinthians to share in the power of God, which he possesses in Christ. This can only take place as the Corinthians realize the reversal which must happen in their own life as a result of their calling and participation in the eschatological age.

This evaluation has shown a CCAA reading of 1 Cor 1:10—4:21 is not necessary. Such a reading muddies the waters and makes it difficult to interpret the whole of Paul's argumentation, as well as the whole of the epistle. Rather than trying to defend, Paul primarily seeks to establish a new eschatological reality wherein the Corinthians understand the superiority of God's wisdom over their own. Paul posits his own life as an example of one who has submitted to this new reality and embraced a shared eschatological identity along with all other believers, the Corinthians notwithstanding. Paul invites the Corinthians to follow suit by encouraging them to embrace the same divine power and through it the same mind of Christ and same familial concern for one another which Paul has for them.

Before concluding this section, it is necessary to clearly state what the removal of a (primary) CCAA reading does *not* mean. First, it does *not* mean Paul sees his apostolic position as unimportant or ineffectual. Second, it does *not* mean Paul is unauthoritative. Paul speaks of apostleship more in this epistle than any other (ten times) and shows the importance of leadership in setting the example of transformation and Christ-like sacrifice. It is only through Paul's position and the authority it affords him that he can influence the Corinthians' thinking and actions.

The preliminary considerations addressed above provide a foundation for a more fruitful evaluation of Paul's Christophanic references in 1 Cor 9 and 15 below. Additional CCAA readings will be addressed as needed in these exegetical sections.

Exegesis of First Corinthians 9

The Context: First Corinthians 8:1–13 and 10:1—11:1

Paul's Christophanic reference in 1 Cor 9 is part of the larger argument of 8:1—11:1,[45] which deals with the surface issue of idol food. In 1 Cor 8:1–13

---

like the world's power. Instead, it is only evidenced in human weakness and thus in full reliance upon God.

45. The unity of this section is held by most modern scholars. Among the strongest

Paul employs the Corinthians' own words and their use of Deut 6 as part of his rebuttal. While Paul is in basic agreement with their monotheistic claims concerning God (1 Cor 8:4), their knowledge is based on the worldly wisdom of "authority/rights" rather than on the divine wisdom of "love." Paul's reshaped "Christianized *Shema*" (1 Cor 8:6)[46] places Christ and his example of love at center stage. Whereas the Corinthians' actions are a stumbling block and source of destruction to the weak (1 Cor 8:9, 11), Christ's actions have led to salvation for the weak and the strong, both of whom find existence in Christ (1 Cor 8:6).

Paul's reference to the "weak" who are being destroyed as ὁ ἀδελφὸς δι' ὃν Χριστὸς ἀπέθανεν (1 Cor 8:11), intentionally links those destroying and those being destroyed as part of the same body (cf. 1 Cor 5:11; 10:17; 12:12–31), adding that this sin is equally against Christ and the other (1 Cor 8:12). By linking the Corinthians' knowledge to sinning against Christ, Paul demonstrates they are on the wrong side of the divine–human divide (cf. 1 Cor 1:10—4:17). The Corinthians need to grasp the profound union which takes place not only between them and Christ (cf. 1 Cor 3:16, 23; 6:15–20) but also between one another as a result of the death of Christ (cf. 1 Cor 10:16). This single eschatological event, and the believers' connection to it, causes a shift in identity and eschatological location, which also means a shift in social location; they now reside "in Christ" as the body of Christ, and this should result in a shift in action toward one another. Paul's own actions are similar to the sacrificial actions of Christ and provide another opposing model (1 Cor 8:13) to their own.

A similar contrast takes place in 1 Cor 10:1—11:1, Paul employs Israel's story (now the Corinthians; 1 Cor 10:1; cf. 5:1) to emphasize the grace of God in his provisions to "all" Israel (1 Cor 10:1–4) against the actions of "some" who disobeyed and were destroyed (1 Cor 10:5–10). This warning serves to instruct the Corinthians, who are residing in the eschatological age (1 Cor 10:12). They have become part of Israel's story and are prone to the same shortcomings and outcomes as those who fell into sin in the wilderness. The only direct citation comes from Exod 32:6 (cf. 1 Cor 10:7), the golden calf episode. The context of the Exodus passage, with its emphasis on idol worship, fits well with the surface issue of idol food that Paul is addressing. The Corinthians, while thinking they are involved in authentic worship to God, are actually bordering on idolatry; their arrogance and ignorance toward one another, as well as their perceived rights, is leading them toward

---

arguments see, Willis, "Apostolic Apologia," 33–48.

46. Wright, *Climax of the Covenant*, 120–36.

the perishable rather than the imperishable (1 Cor 9:25),[47] and thus towards disqualification (1 Cor 9:27).

Paul reminds the Corinthians that they have entered into fellowship with Christ and his body (κοινωνία; 1 Cor 10:16; cf. 1:7) and have, therefore, become one body with each other (1 Cor 10:17; cf. 12:12–31). This eschatological union between Christ and each other means they cannot be partners (κοινωνός) with demons/idols (1 Cor 10:20) but are to imitate Paul in partnering with the gospel (συγκοινωνός; 1 Cor 9:23) by becoming slaves to all (1 Cor 9:19). The issue of idol food became almost superfluous. The eschatological people of God are not primarily marked by what or where they eat, but by their active participation in the body of Christ and the mission of Christ; they bring glory to God (1 Cor 10:31) by seeking the advantage of the other (1 Cor 10:24) and not giving offense to anyone (1 Cor 10:32). This brief analysis of 1 Cor 8:1–13 and 10:1—11:1 is brought to further clarity through Paul's antithetical example in 1 Cor 9.

Paul's Antithetical Example in First Corinthians 9

Many scholars posit CCAA as the primary purpose behind 1 Cor 9.[48] However, there are several difficulties with this position: First, Paul's "apologia" does not defend his authority but surrenders it;[49] second, it does not legitimize his apostleship but only differentiates it;[50] and third, it presupposes acceptance of his apostolic authority[51] arguing *from* this position not *for* it.[52] The last point is significant as it suggests that if Paul's apostolic status and authority were being questioned, Paul is either unaware of this "reality" or lacks significant concern to significantly address it.[53] Nevertheless, before

47. This language (perishable and imperishable) foreshadows Paul's resurrection discourse in 1 Cor 15:42, 53–54.

48. Barrett. *First Corinthians*, 200–202; Conzelmann, *First Corinthians*, 153; Theissen, *Social Setting of Pauline Christianity*, 40–55; Marshall, *Enmity in Corinth*, 282–317; Fitzmyer, *First Corinthians*, 352–75; Fee, *First Corinthians*, 392–441.

49. Willis, "Apostolic Apologia," 40.

50. Dodd, *Paul's Paradigmatic I*, 97.

51. Witherington, *Conflict & Community in Corinth*, 78–79, 136 n. 1. Witherington also argues that Paul's questions functions rhetorically "to anticipate possible arguments, not to answer actual arguments" (206).

52. Willis, "Apostolic Apologia," 40. So also Ciampa and Rosner, *First Corinthians*, 396, who write: "The series of rhetorical questions at the beginning of the chapter . . . depend upon the Corinthians' agreement for their rhetorical power in support of the argument that follows."

53. This too suggests limited opposition to Paul in Corinth at the time of this letter.

dismissing a CCAA position, one must seek to answer the following three questions. Why does Paul deem it necessary to reference his apostolic status at this point in the argument (1 Cor 9:1)? Why does Paul so intimately connect this status to the Corinthian community (1 Cor 9:2)? What does Paul mean by his use of ἀπολογία (1 Cor 9:3)?

It is best to begin with the final question as it provides clarity for addressing the other two questions. Margaret Mitchell is correct when she states that "[a]ny rhetorical analysis of 1 Cor 9 as an actual ἀπολογία must reconstruct the charge against which Paul defends himself here."[54] And in Mitchell's analysis, all attempts thus far have failed.[55] This is because Paul's argument appears to lack any real logic in terms of an actual ἀπολογία.[56] For example, Gordon Fee contends that Paul is defending himself against two charges. First, his refusal to take financial support from the Corinthians. Second, his vacillating views on marketplace food.[57]

Does Paul actually defend himself against these two charges? Regarding the first proposed charge, Paul begins by asserting his apostolic right to receive support and then gives a defense for not receiving this support. In Fee's own words, "That is unusual argumentation under any circumstance."[58] Concerning the second alleged charge, Paul's larger argument in 1 Cor 8:1—11:1 could easily have been construed by the Corinthians as additional vacillation rather than defense against such actions (e.g., 1 Cor 9:20-22;[59] and cf. 8:13 and 10:29).[60] Nevertheless, Paul's use of ἀπολογία[61] cannot be ignored. It would seem that he intentionally employs this language to represent a defense. The difficulty in deducing the charge/s or making sense of

---

54. Mitchell, *Rhetoric of Reconciliation*, 244–46.

55. Mitchell, *Rhetoric of Reconciliation*, 244 and n. 330.

56. Most scholars see 1 Cor 9:3 as pointing forward to the issues of freedom and rights (1 Cor 9:4–23) rather than backwards to the issue of apostolic status (1 Cor 9:1–2). So Ciampa and Rosner, *First Corinthians*, 400; Barrett, *First Corinthians*, 202; Hays, *First Corinthians*, 150; Fee, *First Corinthians*, 400–401; Witherington, *Conflict & Community in Corinth*, 207; contra Fitzmyer, *First Corinthians*, 357.

57. Fee, *First Corinthians*, 393, 424–25.

58. Fee, *First Corinthians*, 392, see also 398 and n. 9.

59. Fee, *First Corinthians*, 428, sees 1 Cor 9:20-22 as pertaining to the eating of certain foods.

60. I am not suggesting, as some have, that Paul is inconsistent here. Throughout 1 Cor 8:1–11:1, Paul consistently places the gospel mission and the good of the whole body of Christ as the criteria that must govern one's eating. However, if the Corinthians do not grasp or accept these limitations to their freedom, then they will likely only see Paul's vacillations.

61. So also in 2 Cor 7:11; Phil 1:7, 16; cf. ἀπολογέομαι in Rom 2:15; 2 Cor 12:19.

the argumentation may suggest that this is some type of mock or parodic defense.[62] Reason for such a strategy will be suggested below.

If Paul is not defending himself, then why does he introduce his apostleship as such? As noted above, Paul's apostolic status is stated rather than defended and assumes acceptance of this status and possibly even acceptance of the authority afforded by this status. Although seemingly trite, it can be assumed that Paul introduces his apostleship here because it is an important part of his ensuing argument. As Mitchell states: "In 9:1–3 he lays out the fundamental premises upon which his argument will build—that he is free, and that he is an apostle (because he has seen the Lord, and because he has founded churches such as the Corinthian church itself)."[63]

Additionally, Paul may introduce his apostleship in order to emphasize the intimate connection between himself and the Corinthians (1 Cor 9:2), which would then serve the goal of persuading them to imitate his actions and attitudes of always considering the other and the gospel mission (1 Cor 11:1; cf. 4:14–16). This would fit Paul's overall strategy in 1 Cor 8:1—11:1, where he goes to great lengths to intentionally show the intimacy that exists between Christ and his body as well as between the various members who make up this body, strong and weak together (e.g., 1 Cor 8:11–13; 10:16-17).

Another popular reading of 1 Cor 9:1–23 postulates that Paul establishes his apostolic position and rights (1 Cor 9:1–14) in order to relinquish these rights (1 Cor 9:15–23); in so doing, he provides an example for the Corinthians to emulate.[64] Michael Gorman writes: "Like Jesus, Paul possessed a particular status, and thus certain rights associated with that status, but rather than exploiting them for his own advantage, he took the form of a slave for the benefit of others."[65] Here, Gorman parallels Paul's example in 1 Cor 9 with Christ's example in Phil 2:6-8, which he refers to as the "although [x] not [y] but [z]" pattern.[66] As Gorman's argument develops, he suggests that the "although" is simultaneously "because." He writes: "It is not just *although* Christ, Paul, and all believers possess a certain identity ([x]) that their story has a certain shape (not [y] but [z]); it is also *because*

---

62. Mitchell, *Rhetoric of Reconciliation*, 130, and Witherington, *Conflict & Community in Corinth*, 207, call this a "mock" defense; and Wuellner, "Rhetorical Criticism," 150–56, calls it a "parodic" defense.

63. Mitchell, *Rhetoric of Reconciliation*, 247.

64. Gorman, *Apostle of the Crucified Lord*, 258–61; Mitchell, *Rhetoric of Reconciliation*, 247–50; Dodd, *Paul's Paradigmatic I*, 98–101; Garland, *First Corinthians*, 403; Ciampa and Rosner, *First Corinthians*, 397.

65. Gorman, *Apostle of the Crucified Lord*, 259.

66. Gorman, *Inhabiting the Cruciform God*, 22.

they possess that identity."[67] This hypothesis is compelling, especially as it relates to Phil 2. But it raises potential problems when applied to 1 Cor 9. The "because" suggests that the truest identity and action of apostleship, and by implication all believers, is *not* the possession and application of rights *but* the surrender of these rights.

Although this does appear to be the needed corrective to those in the Corinthian community who are abusing their rights, it creates a significant division between Paul and Barnabas on one side and James and Cephas on the other. By comparing James's and Cephas's actions to Barnabas's and his own (1 Cor 9:5–6) and then arguing the correct apostolic response is to lay down one's rights, Paul elevates his commitment to the gospel above the other apostolic leaders. This is odd considering Paul's multiple attempts to lessen the divisions presented in 1 Cor 1:12 and to provide a united front amongst the leaders (1 Cor 1:21–23; 2:6–7; 3:5–9; 4:1, 9–13; 15:1–11; 16:12). Is Paul creating unnecessary divisions in an epistle where he calls the Corinthians to unity? Before addressing this question, some additional inconsistencies, which present themselves within this reading of 1 Cor 9:1–14, will be highlighted and additional questions raised.

Brian Dodd argues Paul's words in 1 Cor 9:1–14 would be construed as self-praise by the Corinthians, and that this type of boasting was highly offensive.[68] Paul does not directly mention boasting in 1 Cor 9:1–14. However, there are several reasons why his words could be deemed boastful. First, Paul exalts himself above the Corinthians by highlighting his apostolic position and moreover his divine commission (1 Cor 9:1–2). Second, Paul appears to elevate himself above some of the other well-known apostles (1 Cor 9:5–6). Third, in light of his position Paul argues for his rights in such a way as to bring significant shame upon his audience (1 Cor 9:3–14). While self-praise was prized by some sophist,[69] who likely had influence in Corinth,[70] Paul had already gone to great lengths to stress the divine–human dichotomy in relation to boasting (1 Cor 1:26–31; 3:18–21; 4:6–7), which he reengages in 1 Cor 9:15–18. There is little doubt that Paul understood his many accomplishments as grace from God (cf. 1 Cor 15:10). There is no reason for him to boast in these accomplishments, since they are not primarily of his own doing. As Paul writes in 1 Cor 4:7: "What do you have that you did not receive? And if you received it, why do you boast as if it were not a gift?" Is Paul ignoring his own warning? Dodd's solution to this quandary is

---

67. Gorman, *Inhabiting the Cruciform God*, 25, emphasis his.

68. Dodd, *Paul's Paradigmatic I*, 103–6; cf. Quintilian, *Inst.* 11.1.15–17. See also Travis, "Paul's Boasting," 527–32, who has shown how human boasting was condemned throughout the OT; cf. 1 Kings 20:11; Prov 25:14; Judg 7:2; 1 Sam 2:2.

69. Plutarch, *Mor.* 7.547; Isocrates, *Soph.* 9–10, 19–20.

70. Winter, *Philo and Paul*, 7–9, 113–230.

to suggest that Paul is casting his boast in the form of a "fictitious" defense in keeping with Plutarch's rules "On Praising Oneself Inoffensively," which allows self-praise under certain conditions (*Mor.* 7.539-547).[71] Nevertheless, Dodd's explanation does not actually address the seeming contradiction of Paul's anthropocentric boast; it only makes it less offensive.

Another incongruity comes in Paul's employment of ἐλεύθερος in 1 Cor 9:1, which is unusual in comparison with his other uses (1 Cor 7:21, 22, 39; 9:1, 19; 12:13; cf. ἐλευθερία in 1 Cor 10:29), and especially 1 Cor 9:19. With the exception of 1 Cor 9:1 and 9:19, all the other references to ἐλεύθερος pertain to socio-economic and legal status. Nevertheless, Paul employs them to emphasize eschatological identity and more specifically the transfer of identities which takes place as a result of ones' union with Christ; "For whoever was called in the Lord as a slave is a freed person belonging to the Lord, just as whoever was free when called is a slave of Christ" (1 Cor 7:22). While Paul can speak of the freedom found in Christ (cf. Gal 2:4; 5:1), a more common self-designation is δοῦλος (Rom 1:1; Gal 1:10; Phil 1:1; cf. 1 Cor 3:5; 4:1, 2; 9:27).[72] In 1 Cor 9:16-17, Paul's use of the words "compulsion" (ἀνάγκη; cf. 1 Cor 7:26, 37) and "unwilling" (ἄκων) in correlation with "stewardship/commission" (οἰκονομίαν; 1 Cor 9:17; cf. 4:1, 2) implies a deportment of servitude on Paul's part, which shows him to be anything but free with regard to his eschatological calling. This focus is strengthened in 1 Cor 9:19—"For though I am free with respect to all, I have made myself a slave to all, so that I might win more of them." Paul understands himself first and foremost as being a slave to Christ. As Peter Marshall writes: "His argument is as simple as it is astounding. 'As an apostle I am a slave who has no rights at all.'"[73] Thus Paul's assertion in 1 Cor 9:19 carries a limitation 9:1 does not and raises the question of what Paul means by his claim to freedom in 9:1.

Finally, an irregularity can be seen between Paul Christophanic references in 1 Cor 9:1 and 15:8. Although ὁράω is employed in both, in 1 Cor 9:1 Paul uses the first person singular perfect active indicative (ἑόρακα) rather than the third person singular aorist passive indicative (ὤφθη). The passive voice is significant not only in resurrection appearances (1 Cor 15:5-8), but also in other revelatory episodes.[74] The LXX uses ὤφθη thirty-six times[75]

71. Dodd, *Paul's Paradigmatic I*, 103–6.

72. Martin, *Slavery as Salvation*, 82–83.

73. Marshall, *Enmity in Corinth*, 295.

74. Dunn, *Jesus and Spirit*, 108; cf. Witherington, *Conflict & Community in Corinth*, 301.

75. Wright, *Resurrection of the Son of God*, 323, surveys all eighty-five passive forms, forty-six of which "refer either to YHWH, or YHWH's glory, or an angel of YHWH, appearing to people."

with all but six[76] referring to theophanic events (or angelophanies)[77] or persons reporting about previous theophanies.[78] Likewise, of the eighteen occurrences of ὤφθη in the NT all but one[79] refer to supernatural appearances to people.[80] While there are some LXX uses of ὁράω in the active voice to report theophanies,[81] they are the exception, not the rule. Philo captures this when he writes of Gen 12:7: "For which reason it is said, not that the wise man saw (εἶδε, aorist active indicative) God but that God appeared (ὤφθη) to the wise man; for it was impossible for anyone to comprehend by his own unassisted power the true living God, unless he himself displayed and revealed himself to him" (*Abr.* 17.80). Furthermore, the passive voice of 1 Cor 15:8 parallels Paul's other Christophanic references; compare Gal 1:16 where God revealed his Son to Paul (cf. Gal 1:11) and Phil 3:12 where Christ took hold of Paul. Even in Second Corinthians, it is Christ who removes the veil that allows believers to behold the glory of the Lord (2 Cor 3:18) and God who takes the initiative to shine in our hearts (2 Cor 4:6). In each case but 1 Cor 9:1 the divine agency is made clear. However, in 1 Cor 9:16–17, Paul's use of the present passive ἐπίκειται and perfect passive πεπίστευμαι in connection to his apostolic calling assumes divine agency. Paul's nuancing of his Christophanic reference in 1 Cor 9:1 is regulated in 9:16–17.

It is intriguing that each of the inconsistencies highlighted in 1 Cor 9:1–14, apart from the division caused by Paul's words in 1 Cor 9:5–6, can be resolved by Paul's words in 1 Cor 9:15–23. Why is this? Interestingly, in a section (1 Cor 8:1—11:1) which addresses concerns raised by the Corinthians (1 Cor 8:1, Περὶ δὲ; cf. 7:1[82]), and in which Paul employed many of the Corinthians' own words and ideas (1 Cor 8:1, 4, 5, 6; 10:23[83]), it is always assumed chapter 9 represented only Paul's words and convictions.[84] Moving

76. Judg 19:30; Song 2:12; 1 Macc 4:6, 19; 9:27; 2 Macc 3:25.

77. Gen 12:7; 17:1; 18:1; 26:2, 24; 35:9; Exod 3:2; 16:10; Lev 9:23; Num 14:10; 16:19; 17:7; 20:6; Judg 6:12; 13:3; 1 Kgs 3:5; 9:2; 2 Chron 1:7; 7:12; Jer 38:3.

78. Gen 22:14; 48:3; 2 Sam 22:11; 2 Chron 3:1; Tob 12:2. Cf. Gen 1:9; Dan 8:1(bis); Baruch 3:22, 38.

79. Acts 7:26.

80. Matt 17:3; Mark 9:4; Luke 1:11; 22:43; 24:34; Acts 7:2, 30; 13:31; 16:9; 1 Cor 15:5, 6, 7, 8; 1 Tim 3:16; Rev 11:19; 12:1, 3.

81. E.g., Gen 32:2; Judg 6:22; Isa 6:1.

82. Thiselton, *First Corinthians*, 32–34, 483.

83. See Hurd, *Origin of 1 Corinthians*, 65–71; and Fotopoulos, "Arguments Concerning Food," 611–31, for an extensive list of proposed Corinthian' quotations and scholarly consensus.

84. A possible exception is, Jones, *Freiheit in des Apostels Paulus*, who believes Paul's use of ἐλεύθερος in 1 Cor 9:1 represents popular Hellenistic philosophical understandings, and is used by Paul in response to the Corinthians' use of the word in relation to idol food.

beyond this assumption opens up further possibilities for explaining the proposed discrepancies. Paul's "defense" in 1 Cor 9:1–14 could reflect the attitude (and possibly the jargon) of some of the Corinthians who believe their knowledge, and even their social-economic position, gives them the right to do as they please. Paul's use of ἐξουσία may be part of the Corinthians' language rather than his own. This is reflected in Paul's shift to the second person plural in 1 Cor 8:9 ("this liberty of yours"), which contains Paul's first use of ἐξουσία in this section. Additionally, if the sayings "all things are lawful" (1 Cor 6:12; 10:23) are correctly attributed to the Corinthians,[85] then the linguistic connection between ἔξεστιν and ἐξουσία[86] may signal Paul's play on words. There also appears to be a deliberate contrast between Paul's use of δύναμις in 1 Cor 1:10—4:21 and his use of ἐξουσία in 1 Cor 8:1—11:1. The former is always connected to God and the latter evidences human attitudes. This proposal might also explain Paul's reference to James and Cephas in 1 Cor 9:5–6. It seems at least conceivable that rather than Paul seeking to create division between the apostolic leadership, he is referencing an apostolic "right" the Corinthians have raised as a way of shaming Paul into accepting their patronage.

Paul's argument is based on the Corinthians' misconception of apostolic authority and is constructed as a way of showing the offensiveness of the Corinthians' own boastful attitudes and actions toward one another.[87] Paul accomplishes this by setting his perceived rights (ἐξουσία, 1 Cor 9:4,

85. So Thiselton, *First Corinthians*, 460–61; Hurd, *Origin of 1 Corinthians*, 68; Fee, *First Corinthians*, 251.

86. Foerster, "ἐξουσία," 2:562.

87. Although not necessarily agreeing with their conclusions, Mitchell's, Witherington's, and esp. Wuellner's suggestion of a "mock" or "parodic" defense appropriately represents what I am suggesting. Quintilian defined parody as: "a name drawn from songs sung in imitation of others, but employed by an abuse of language to designate imitation in verse or prose" (*Inst Orat* 9.2.35 [Butler, LCL]) and that it was most powerful when it imitated real sayings or documents (*Inst Orat* 9.2.34 [Butler, LCL]). Furthermore, irony, a trope, was common in parody, which was a figure of speech, "But in the *figurative* form of irony the speaker disguises his entire meaning, the disguise being apparent rather than confessed. For in the *trope* the conflict is purely verbal, while in the *figure* the meaning, and sometimes the whole aspect of our case, conflicts with the language and the tone of voice adopted." (*Inst Orat* 9.2.46 [Butler, LCL]). See also Sim, *A Relevant Way*, 53–70. Using Relevance Theory, Sim argues for the importance of recognizing verbal irony in Paul's letters, which is defined as "an utterance or representation with which the speaker disagrees, but which is believed by his hearers or other participants" (53–54). She also gives this important warning: "It has been said by some who are nervous about attributing an ironic statement to biblical authors that such attribution is an attempt to get out of 'hard' sayings. In response, I would claim that the sayings are 'hard' because we do *not* recognise the speaker's disassociating himself from such an opinion" (55, emphasis hers).

5, 6, 12, 18) up as a kind of straw-man argument (1 Cor 9:1–14) in order to provide the antithesis in 1 Cor 9:15–23. Paul's vehement retraction of authority in verses 12b, 15 makes the antithesis between these two sections clear. Even Fee, who argues strongly for a CCAA reading, "is somewhat taken aback that Paul, having so vigorously defended his rights to their support, now argues with similar emotion for his 'right' to give it up."[88] The interruption of verse 12b[89] within Paul's argument (1 Cor 9:1–14) speaks to the shear absurdity of Paul's boasting. Paul would rather die (1 Cor 9:15) than put an "obstacle in the way of the gospel of Christ" (cf. 1 Cor 1:17; 2:1–5).

There should be a clear distinction made between the language of "antithesis," used above, and what some scholars deem a restraint,[90] a refusal,[91] or a renunciation[92] of rights. Paul does not renounce certain rights for the sake of the body and the gospel. Instead, the antithetical nature of 1 Cor 9:15–23 shows that the boastful and selfish attitude of 1 Cor 9:1–14 is wrong, even while not denying the validity of some of the individual statements within. The first half of chapter 9 presents an anthropocentric attitude while the second half presents a Christ-centered attitude. By creating this contrast, Paul sets the example of moving from one sphere of reality to a new sphere; he models an eschatological reversal in attitude and action. This is similar to what Paul does in Phil 3:4–11. Therein Paul's shifts from a previous confidence in the flesh to the new source of his confidence in Christ. However, in Phil 3, Paul's list of previous confidences represents pre-Christophany understanding. Here, in 1 Cor 9, Paul speaks of apostolic rights, which appear to be post-Christophany perspectives, especially in light of his Christophanic reference in 1 Cor 9:1. Therefore, the parallel between 1 Cor 9 and Phil 3 only works if Paul is masking his apostolic rights in the human wisdom of some of the Corinthians. The active voice in Paul's Christophanic reference in 1 Cor 9:1 may, therefore, speak to human boasting and reveal that Paul references this experience ironically.[93]

---

88. Fee, *First Corinthians*, 414.

89. Nasuti, "The Woes of the Prophets," 246–64, explains the interruption of 1 Cor 9:12b by arguing vv. 13–14 carry a more personal connection to Paul's commission and serve to anticipate vv. 15ff. This argument is unconvincing in light of Paul's use of the more forceful conjunction ἀλλά in v. 12b.

90. Cf. Fee, *First Corinthians*, 414–22.

91. Ciampa and Rosner, *First Corinthians*, 415–33.

92. Hays, *First Corinthians*, 152–55

93. Cf. Sim, *A Relevant Way*, 56–57, 61–63, who argues 1 Cor 4:8 and 1 Cor 11:9 are cases of verbal irony.

Summary

I have tried to show that a CCAA reading of 1 Cor 9 is neither the only nor the most convincing reading of this passage. Instead, the "antithetical" reading set out above gives greater coherence to Paul's rhetorical strategy. Throughout 1 Cor 8:1—11:1, Paul seeks to enlarge the Corinthians' understanding of their union with Christ to include the body of Christ and the gospel mission. Only as they hold these three together are they embracing a correct eschatological identity. Paul's personal example models this union. His Christophanic reference is a small part of a much larger argument. Paul's claim to seeing the Lord in 1 Cor 9:1 uses irony as a negative example of human authority and freedom. Paul's antithetical reference in 1 Cor 9:16–17 emphasizes servitude to Christ through partnership with the gospel for the sake of the body of Christ. It advances a correct eschatological identity. Paul uses his own life to show the Corinthians the arrogance and offensiveness of their actions and attitudes toward one another and ultimately toward Christ (1 Cor 9:1–14). He then models an eschatological reversal (1 Cor 9:15–23), showing his own humility in imitating Christ's sacrificial death for the sake of others (1 Cor 8:11, 13) and encouraging them to do the same (1 Cor 11:1). Part of being the eschatological people of God means one is *not* free with regard to the other (cf. 1 Cor 6:19). Paul's attitude and actions sit in stark contrast to those of the Corinthians' (cf. 1 Cor 8:9–12), showing him to be on the correct side of the divine–human divide and providing them with a correct model of eschatological reversal. By focusing the discussion around his eschatological calling in correlation with his reversal, Paul brings forth the Corinthians' calling (1 Cor 1:2–9) and challenges them to this same eschatological reversal. In this way, Paul's Christophanic reference functions both paradigmatically and didactically.

Exegesis of First Corinthians 15[94]

The Context: First Corinthians 15:1–58

Paul's Christophanic reference in 1 Cor 15:1–11 stands together with all of chapter 15 and the important subject of resurrection of the dead. Paul's argument has been moving toward, foreshadowing this crescendo (cf. 1 Cor 6:13b–14)[95] wherein Paul addresses a vital element of the Corinthians' es-

---

94. Portions of this section were published earlier as: Fringer, "Dying to be the Church," 1–10.

95. See Wright, *Resurrection of the Son of God*, 277–97.

chatological reality and identity. As such, it flows tightly between a realized and future eschatology of resurrection[96] and integrates themes developed earlier, especially union between Christ and believers and between believers and one another. While containing vital theological themes, it serves a very pragmatic purpose addressing the fundamental issue of embodied faith, which is lacking in the Corinthians own secular-spiritualized and individualized actions. Their salvation is evidencing itself in outrageous acts of carnality rather than Spirit-led transformation and sanctification.[97] Paul concludes the entirety of his argument with his clearest expression of how the eschatological event of Christ's death and resurrection, and the believers' connection to Christ, has shaped and continues to shape both the present and the future, both their beliefs and their actions, both their dying and living.

The external impetus for Paul's immediate polemic is a group of Corinthians who denied ἀνάστασις νεκρῶν (1 Cor 15:12). Contextually, it may be concluded that the Corinthians have (at least at one time) accepted Christ's resurrection since Paul speaks of the Corinthians having "received" and "believed" the gospel message (1 Cor 15:1–3a), which would have included teaching about Christ's resurrection (1 Cor 15:3b–5) and general (believer) resurrection (1 Cor 15:12–14).[98] The main question is whether the Corinthians' initial acceptance of Paul's gospel included "bodily" resurrection or if they assumed a different conclusion based on their own cultural understanding of the term. Wright[99] and Alan Segal[100] demonstrate that most Greeks and Romans believed in an afterlife (cf. 1 Cor 15:29) and a dominant view consisted of some sort of immortality of the soul apart from the body. Wright argues that both Jews and non-Jews only understood the concept of resurrection in terms of a bodily phenomenon; although the majority of non-Jews would have rejected the possibility of resurrection, they nevertheless would have understood the (Jewish) Pauline meaning of it.[101] Paul's language of ἀνάστασις νεκρῶν and his polemic in 1 Cor 15:35–50 suggests an argument around the "bodily" aspect of resurrection, which

---

96. So Ciampa and Rosner, *First Corinthians*, 736. For an argument in favor of over-realized eschatology as well as survey of the literature see: Tuckett, "Corinthians Who Say," 245–75; and Thiselton, *First Corinthians*, 40.

97. See Brower, *Living as God's Holy People*, 80–85; Winter, "Carnal Conduct and Sanctification," 184–200.

98. *Pace*, Mitchell, "Rhetorical Shorthand," 74.

99. Wright, *Resurrection of the Son of God*, 32–84.

100. Segal, *Life After Death*, 204–47.

101. Wright, *Resurrection of the Son of God*, 82–83.

seems to assume an acceptance of the broad idea of resurrection apart from the specific element of corporealness (cf. 1 Cor 6:14; 15:1, 11).

It is more probable that the Corinthians either initially misunderstood Paul's teaching[102] or recently came to abandon the bodily aspect of resurrection[103] they formerly accepted.[104] Furthermore, since the thought of an embodied afterlife would be objectionable to most (cf. 1 Cor 15:50),[105] it stands to reason Jesus's bodily resurrection would be at least equally objectionable. If the Corinthians are abandoning the idea of their own bodily resurrection, they may also be abandoning this same element with regard to Christ's resurrection. Many scholars argue the latter while denying the former. They see the Corinthians denying their own bodily resurrection while fully accepting Christ's bodily resurrection.[106] But this does not adequately explain why Paul includes 1 Cor 15:1–11 and especially the extended "appearance" list (vv. 5–8).

Matthew Malcolm argues that besides a disregard for the body there is a general disregard for the dead.[107] This is not unique to the Corinthians but reflects wider Greco-Roman views about the inferior state of the dead. This disdain toward death and related concepts leads to significant misunderstandings related to Christ's death and the requirements of his followers and causes significant divisions among the body of Christ in Corinth. It is one thing to be conformed to Christ's resurrection, quite another to be conformed to his death. For Paul, these two phenomena are inseparable; a person cannot understand the significance of the resurrection if they do not understand and accept the significance of death, both Christ's and believers'.

Death and Resurrection: Dual Themes

The Corinthians' attitude toward death helps explain what otherwise appears to be a perplexing secondary focus to resurrection in 1 Cor 15, namely

---

102. Both Ciampa and Rosner, *First Corinthians*, 755 and Perkins, *First Corinthians*, 182, allude to the possibility of a misunderstanding about Christ's bodily resurrection.

103. Schmithals, *Gnosticism in Corinth*, 156–59.

104. Sider, "St. Paul's Understanding," 124–41.

105. Segal, *Life After Death*, 425.

106. So Hays, *First Corinthians*, 253; Martin, *The Corinthian Body*, 106; Nash, *First Corinthians*, 401; and Wright, *Resurrection of the Son of God*, 83, 322.

107. Malcolm, *Paul and Rhetoric of Reversal*, 231–66. See also Tuckett, "Corinthians Who Say," 261.

death.[108] Paul uses the adjective νεκρός thirteen times,[109] the verb ἀποθνῄσκω five times,[110] the noun θάνατος six times,[111] and the euphemism κοιμάω four times.[112] For comparison, in regard to resurrection, Paul uses the verb ἐγείρω nineteen times,[113] the noun ἀνάστασις four times,[114] and the euphemisms ζωοποιέω three times[115] and ἀλλάσσω twice.[116]

In order to understand the importance of Paul's "death" language, a brief analysis of how the language functions throughout the epistle becomes necessary. The adjective νεκρός is only found in chapter 15 and is always used in correlation with resurrection (e.g., ἀνάστασις νεκρῶν; νεκροὶ οὐκ ἐγείρονται), always referring to those who have physically died irrespective of their standing in Christ. Dale Martin argues for the translation "corpse," common in classical Greek.[117] As an adjective, it does appear to need a qualifier, which is likely either "person" or "body." Therefore, the translation "corpse" or "body" is justified. Paul uses νεκρός to stress the bodily aspect of the resurrection.

Paul's use of ἀποθνῄσκω is much more nuanced. It can refer to literal physical death for both believers and non-believers (1 Cor 9:15; 15:32), and is especially used for Christ's death (1 Cor 8:11; 15:3). Additionally, it can be used metaphorically, as when Paul says, "I die every day!" (1 Cor 15:31). These words are not a reference to physical death. Nor are they hyperbole, a way of saying his life is very difficult. Rather, Paul's ἀποθνῄσκω is because of and in line with Christ's ἀποθνῄσκω. The last two uses of ἀποθνῄσκω are more difficult to interpret: "for as all die in Adam, so all will be made alive in Christ" (1 Cor 15:22) and "What you sow does not come to life unless it dies" (1 Cor 15:36). The context does not warrant construing these as reference to physical death. The former is part of an Adam/Christ typology and the latter an elaborate metaphor concerning the "changed" resurrection body; both are making a similar point. Those in Adam are marked by death, in the present and in the future, both physically and spiritually. Nevertheless, those in Christ are made alive (ζωοποιέω) and freed from the finality

---

108. See Saw, *Paul's Rhetoric in 1 Corinthians*, 182–83.

109. 1 Cor 15:12(bis), 13, 15, 16, 20, 21, 29(bis), 32, 35, 42, 52

110. 1 Cor 15:3, 22, 31, 32, 36

111. 1 Cor 15:21, 26, 54, 55(bis), 56

112. 1 Cor 15:6, 18, 20, 51

113. 1 Cor 15:4, 12, 13, 14, 15(thrice), 16(bis), 17, 20, 29, 32, 35, 42, 43(bis), 44, 52

114. 1 Cor 15:12, 13, 21, 42

115. 1 Cor 15:22, 36, 45

116. 1 Cor 15:51, 52

117. Martin, *Corinthian Body*, 107–8 and see 271 n. 9 for a list of Greek sources.

of death both in the present and the future. Likewise, the seed which must die does so in order to be made alive (ζωοποιέω), changed from death to life both in the present and the future. This is an important point in Paul's elaborate argument. He is not arguing all believers must or will die a physical death; he says the exact opposite in 1 Cor 15:51. Instead, Paul alludes to another type of death which all believers must undergo; a death Paul has undergone and continues to experience daily (1 Cor 15:31), a death to his own carnal desires, whether noble or self-serving. It is a death to the constraints of the present evil age, which allows for the embrace of a new eschatological age and with it a new eschatological identity.

Paul's use of θάνατος is also quite versatile and closely aligns with ἀποθνήσκω in regard to physical death in general (1 Cor 3:22; 11:26). However, in chapter 15, θάνατος is personified, similarly to how Paul personifies "Sin" in Rom 5:12—8:3.[118] Paul describes "Death" in anthropomorphic terms as one who has come through Adam (1 Cor 15:21) and as an enemy waiting to be destroyed (1 Cor 15:26). Likewise, the poetic discourse of 1 Cor 15:54–56 (cf. Isa 25:8; Hos 13:14) is a mocking of Death, who has lost all power as a result of Christ's resurrection and the impending resurrection of believers. Just as death to self is a plausible reality in the present through Christ, so too is the power of resurrection in the life of the believer. In effect, believers defeat the finality of physical death in the present as they acknowledge and live out the Lordship of Christ. This too is part of the new eschatological reality brought about through Christ.

Paul uses the word κοιμάω, meaning to "fall asleep," as a euphemism for death. For Paul it is *not* synonymous with ἀποθνήσκω. The former is always used to refer to actual physical death, *but* only of believers in Christ. This is because κοιμάω "carries with it the expectation of *awaking to a new dawn and a new day,* i.e., the expectation of resurrection and the gift of renewed life and vigor."[119] It is to believers (ἀδελφοῖς)[120] that Christ appears, both those living and those who have fallen asleep (1 Cor 15:6). Paul speaks about those who κοιμάω "in Christ" (1 Cor 15:18) and refers to Christ as the first fruit of resurrection for those who κοιμάω (1 Cor 15:20). When speaking about marriage, Paul says that it is the woman "in the Lord" who is free to remarry only after her husband, also "in the Lord,"[121] falls asleep (κοιμάω), as long as her next marriage is "in the Lord" (1 Cor 7:39). There-

---

118. See Dunn, *Theology of Paul,* 111–14.

119. Thiselton, *First Corinthians,* 1220, emphasis his.

120. Paul regularly uses ἀδελφός as a reference to those who are in Christ. See Soden, "ἀδελφός," 1:143–46.

121. That the deceased husband is a believer is clear from the passage. So Fee, *First Corinthians,* 355 n. 37. Such is also the case in 1 Cor 11:30.

fore, when Paul says "we will not all die (κοιμάω), but we will all be changed" (1 Cor 15:51), he means that *not* all believers will face a physical death. This does not negate the need for believers to experience some type of death (ἀποθνῄσκω) in the present in order to be made alive in Christ (1 Cor 15:36), also in the present.

Paul's use of ἀπόλλυμι (to perish or destroy, used six times[122]) must also be evaluated. Similar to ἀποθνῄσκω and θάνατος, it can pertain to physical death or destruction (1 Cor 10:9, 10). It can also refer to the destruction of abstract phenomena such as wisdom (1 Cor 1:19). Unlike the others, it is exclusively reserved for unbelievers, those with no hope. Therefore, Paul can say the gospel is "foolishness to those who are perishing" (1 Cor 1:18), in reference to unbelievers. When he speaks of believers being destroyed by other believers (1 Cor 8:11), it is a reference to the shattering of their faith. The latter meaning helps clarify 1 Cor 15:18—"Then those who have died (κοιμηθέντες) in Christ have perished (ἀπώλοντο)." Paul argues if Christ has not been bodily raised, living believers remain in sin (1 Cor 15:17), no different from unbelievers. Furthermore, if Christ has not been bodily raised, then believers who have fallen asleep are actually dead, without hope.

Paul's Example in First Corinthians 15:1–11

The opening section of 1 Cor 15:1–11 is important in understanding how Paul employs death and resurrection to correct Corinthian misunderstandings of both. Unfortunately, many scholars read these verses, and especially verses 8–10, through a CCAA lens. For Kenneth Bailey,[123] Joseph Fitzmyer,[124] Fee,[125] and others, Paul's autobiographic insertion adds little to the current pericope, or to the chapter as a whole. But when CCAA is set aside, the importance of this pericope can be seen. It prepares Paul's audience for his discussion concerning death and resurrection and Paul's Christophanic reference provides an example for the Corinthians to emulate in the present. This is not an indictment of apostolic authority per se; Paul's apostleship provides him with a platform for shaping the Corinthians' understanding of human power and authority by stressing God's power over his own.

It has been recognized that the ὤφθη references (1 Cor 15:5–8) form a chiasm based on grammatical structure and lexical repetition. However, there is a larger chiasm encompassing the entire pericope (1 Cor 15:1–11)

---

122. 1 Cor 1:18, 19; 8:11; 10:9, 10; 15:18.

123. Bailey, *Paul Through Mediterranean Eyes*, 33–53.

124. Fitzmyer, *First Corinthians*, 551.

125. Fee, *First Corinthians*, 719.

and also based on thematic structure (see Appendix 1).[126] Verses 1 and 11 frame this section around the themes of proclamation and belief. Paul's use of γνωρίζω is meant to do more than "remind" the Corinthians of a previously accepted kerygma[127] or to introduce new information about the gospel and resurrection.[128] Paul begins this section by setting his argument in the form of a revelatory proclamation (cf. Gal 1:11). In so doing, Paul elevates the conversation and highlights the divine power behind the gospel he and others proclaim and behind the Corinthians' previous acceptance of this same gospel. He is able to remind the Corinthians τὸ εὐαγγέλιον ὃ εὐηγγελισάμην is a "demonstration of the Spirit and of power" and not a demonstration of "human wisdom" (1 Cor 2:4–5; cf. 1:17). Furthermore, γνωρίζω should be understood as introducing the whole of Paul's argument (1 Cor 15:1–58) and not just this pericope. While much of the information introduced in 1 Cor 15:12–58 (esp. 15:35–58) is new to the Corinthians, Paul presents it as a continuation of the revealed gospel they have already received.[129] It is part of the eschatological reality to which they now belong.

The focus on revelation does not negate the phenomena of tradition. Paul's passing on what he also received (ὃ καὶ παρέλαβον; 1 Cor 15:3a)[130] is a reference to the apostolic traditions handed down to him by other apostles.[131] Debate arises around this topic, some seeing 1 Cor 15:3 as a contradiction of Gal 1:12, 16.[132] But these statements are not at odds. Dunn shows that προσανατίθημι (Gal 1:16) carries the technical meaning of "consulting with someone who is recognized as a qualified interpreter about the significance of some sign—a dream, or omen, or portent."[133] Additionally, Dunn argues that ἱστορέω (Gal 1:18), which is usually translated simply "to visit," bears the intended purpose of the visit as "gaining information."[134] While Paul did not need to consult any human to understand his revelatory experience (cf. Gal 2:6), he did visit Cephas (and James) with the purpose of gaining information about Christ and about the Church's traditions.

126. Cf. Bailey, *Paul Through Mediterranean Eyes*, 422.

127. Pace, Fee, *First Corinthians*, 719; and Fitzmyer, *First Corinthians*, 540, 544.

128. Pace, Radl, "Der Sinn von *gnōrizō*," 243–45. Nor is it a "ceremonious introduction." Pace, Conzelmann, *First Corinthians*, 250.

129. Similarly Mitchell, "Rhetorical Shorthand," 74.

130. So Dunn, "How Are the Dead Raised," 5.

131. Pace, Churchill, *Divine Initiative and Christology*, 128.

132. Price, "Apocryphal Apparitions," 69–104, argues for 1 Cor 15:3–11 being an interpolation because he sees no resolution with the Galatians passage. Cf. Winger, "Tradition, Revelation and Gospel" 65–86.

133. Dunn, *Jesus, Paul and the Law*, 110.

134. Dunn, *Jesus, Paul and the Law*, 110–13.

Paul is not rejecting tradition, but rather elevating it to the level of revelation. Just as Paul received (παραλαμβάνω, 1 Cor 15:3) the traditions handed down to him from those in Christ before him and through the study of the Scriptures,[135] he in turn passes (παραδίδωμι, 1 Cor 15:3; cf. 11:23) these teachings to the Corinthians who both receive (παραλαμβάνω, 1 Cor 15:1) and believe (1 Cor 15:11). This reception is only made possible through the revelation of Christ to them by God through the Holy Spirit, which is part of the grace of God (1 Cor 1:4; 15:10). Both the transmission of tradition and the revelation from God occur simultaneously in the proclamation of the gospel (1 Cor 1:18; 2:4, 7; 4:1; 15:1, 11; cf. Gal 1:11–12; Rom 1:16–18). It is also clear that Paul sees both elements as continuous. The Corinthians continually need to receive revelation from God through the Spirit (1 Cor 1:7; 2:10) and/via the apostolic teaching (1 Cor 15:1, 11).

The Spirit plays a vital role in Paul's understanding of believers' salvation and transformation. It is the Spirit who reveals (ἀποκαλύπτω) God's wisdom to the believer, giving them the mind of Christ (1 Cor 2:10–16). Through the Spirit's indwelling, believers join one another in participating in a singular temple identity (1 Cor 3:16; 6:19), having been washed, sanctified, and justified (1 Cor 6:11). It is through the Spirit believers proclaim the lordship of Jesus and participate in the one body receiving a "manifestation of the Spirit for the common good" (1 Cor 12:3–13). In 1 Cor 15:45, Paul brings together Christ and the Spirit (cf. Rom 8:9; 2 Cor 3:17, 18; Gal 4:6; Phil 1:19); the risen Christ is in some way identified with the life-giving Spirit of God (cf. Gen 2:7).[136] This is not an amalgamation of the two but shows the ongoing work of the Spirit in the eschatological age, a work which includes the revelation of Christ.[137]

The kerygma and extended appearance list (1 Cor 15:3–10a), which includes Paul's Christophanic reference, form the climax of this section and begin the dual themes of death and resurrection which are explicated in 1 Cor 15:12–58. Argumentation over which phrases are Pauline and which

135. Ellis, "Traditions in 1 Corinthians," 481–502, reminds us Paul relied on both the early church and the exposition of the OT. Likewise, Bockmuehl, *Revelation and Mystery*, 174–75, 225–27, reminds us Paul had many revelations through inspired biblical interpretation.

136. Dunn, *Theology of Paul*, 262. Cf. Yates, *The Spirit and Creation*, 88–105, who does not believe Paul is identifying Christ and the Holy Spirit but is emphasizing Christ's divinity and noting the Spirit's role in the resurrection of the body for believers. Contra Fee, *God's Empowering Presence*, 266–67, who believes 1 Cor 15:45 is not a reference to the Holy Spirit but to Christ as the first spiritual being in a new spiritual realm.

137. Cf. Schweitzer, *The Mysticism of Paul*, 167. He writes: "For being in the Spirit is only a form of manifestation of the being-in-Christ. Both are descriptions of one and the same state."

are pre-Pauline creedal material is irrelevant to this reading.[138] Whatever the origins of this material, Paul is arguing from a common held belief as a platform for what follows in 1 Cor 15:6–10. This does not mean the pre-Pauline material is insignificant, quite the contrary. Reference to Christ's death and resurrection is of "first importance" (1 Cor 15:3).

Since Paul's audience is rejecting a bodily resurrection, not resurrection in general, it is odd that Paul does not include reference to Christ's body directly or via the empty tomb tradition.[139] However, this may be intentional in order to emphasize the dual themes of death and resurrection. This does not mean bodily resurrection is unimportant, but Paul's concern is not just in correcting the Corinthians' erroneous theology. Throughout the epistle, Paul tries to shape their identity in order to motivate them toward genuine and lasting transformation in the present. In essence, Paul is trying to help them embrace their new eschatological identity as those who have died to their old life and have been raised to new life. This necessitates Paul's theologically profound discussion concerning death and resurrection, of which Christ's example is the architype.

Many hypotheses are set forth concerning the six resurrection appearances and the order in which they appear.[140] Important here is the recognition that the list begins with Cephas and ends with Paul. Peter and his position are well-known in Corinth (cf. 1 Cor 1:12; 9:5) and Paul is the founder of this church (1 Cor 4:14–15). Since Paul's apostleship is not being significantly questioned, their unified testimony concerning Christ's resurrection is sufficient proof of this event (cf. Deut 17:6; 19:15). Additionally, Paul's mention of the 500 witnesses with the extended description "most of whom are still alive, though some have died" (1 Cor 15:6), occupies the climactic position in this chiasm. Murphy-O'Connor recognizes this climax, arguing that it best serves Paul's apologetic purpose, not in arguing for his apostleship but for the reality of resurrection.[141] He places the emphasis on the witnesses who are still living rather than on those who have died. This is a common reading for those arguing that Paul addresses the issue of bodily resurrection.[142] Those "still alive" are seen as

138. For further debate see, Murphy-O'Connor, "Tradition and Redaction," 582–89; Gerhardsson, "Evidence for Christ's Resurrection," 79–80; Eriksson, *Traditions and Rhetorical Proof*, 73–96.

139. Wright, *Resurrection of the Son of God*, 321, argues this is implicit with the resurrection language.

140. For detailed analysis see, Thiselton, *First Corinthians*, 1198–1208.

141. Murphy-O'Connor, "Tradition and Redaction," 588–89.

142. Fee, *First Corinthians*, 730–31; Hays, *First Corinthians*, 257; Thiselton, *First Corinthians*, 1205–206; Fitzmyer, *First Corinthians*, 550; Ciampa and Rosner, *First*

authoritative witnesses to the resurrection. Conversely, those arguing that Paul addresses denial of the futurity of resurrection[143] emphasize "some have died," and the reality that death precedes resurrection. In fact, this may not be an either/or but a both/and situation. Since the language of death and resurrection share equal footing, this reference provides Paul with another opportunity to stress both.

This explanation provides insight into Paul's extended autobiography and Christophanic reference. When 1 Cor 15:8–10a is examined closely there are striking parallels with 1 Cor 15:3–5a. Most notable is the paralleling of Christ's death and resurrection in Paul's story. Paul's description of himself as ἔκτρωμα (1 Cor 15:8) is difficult to interpret.[144] Arguably, it is part of his "death" language. In Scripture, it is only found here and three times in the LXX (Num 12:12; Eccl 6:3; Job 3:16), where it always refers to a still-born child, and thus to literal physical death. Outside of Scripture, its use is well attested in Greek literature in reference to miscarriages, abortions, and possibly "untimely births."[145] H. W. Hollander and G. E. van der Hout see Paul's reference as self-deprecating, referring to his deplorable (death-like) state prior to his conversion when he persecuted the church: his unworthiness to be an apostle thus highlights the grace of God in calling him.[146] David Garland, relying heavily on Hollander and van der Hout, but seeing Paul's self-abasement as sincere, writes: "Before his call and conversion he was dead, but he was miraculously given life through God's grace."[147] Paul's use of ἔκτρωμα to reference his own figurative death is not necessarily limited to his past life. After all, he writes, "I die every day!" (1 Cor 15:31); and from the immediate context, it can confidently be stated that Paul sees God's grace as continually working in and through him (1 Cor 15:10) and not just at the moment of his call/conversion. Paul uses his own situation to underscore the necessity of (spiritual) death prior to (present) resurrection. This does not negate the surface issue of bodily resurrection. However, this surface issue allows Paul to address the more pressing theological issue that is dividing the community. The answer to most of their problems is

---

Corinthians, 749–50.

143. Barth, *Resurrection of the Dead*, 151; Conzelmann, *First Corinthians*, 257–58; Tuckett, "Corinthians Who Say," 263; Lindemann, *Der erste Korintherbrief*, 333; Garland, *First Corinthians*, 689–90.

144. See Garland, *First Corinthians*, 691–93, for a survey of prominent views.

145. Schneider, "ἔκτρωμα," 2:465–66.

146. Hollander and van der Hout, "Paul Calling Himself an Abortion," 224–36. Yet they too see Paul as using this to defend his apostolic position.

147. Garland, *First Corinthians*, 693; see also Fitzmyer, *Frist Corinthians*, 552; Wright, *Resurrection of the Son of God*, 327–29.

a present death to self, to their own rights and positions. It is this action that allows them to fully participate in Christ and fully embrace their new eschatological identity.

In 1 Cor 15:3b, Paul refers to Christ's vicarious death for sin "in accordance with the scriptures" (cf. Gal 1:4; 2:20), which alludes to Isaiah and parallels Christ and Paul. While the plural γραφὰς shows a broad concern for the whole biblical narrative,[148] the most direct referent is Isa 53 (as argued above in chapter 3).[149] Paul subtly reveals his understanding of Christ as the Isaianic Servant who "died for our sins" and who was raised (1 Cor 15:4; cf. Isa 52:13). This interpretation may also provide a lens for reading Paul's Christophanic reference. While not as overt as those found in Gal 1, Paul's words in 1 Cor 15:8–10 evidence some echoes of Isa 49:1–7. First, there is the shared language of καλέω and κενός (cf. Isa 49:1, 4). Second, Paul's use of ἔκτρωμα is not a reference to just any kind of death but is specifically related to pregnancy, a death either in the womb or just outside the womb (cf. Isa 49:1, 5). Third, there is a divine emphasis in both passages; it is the work of God through the Servant which is highlighted. If Paul is echoing Isa 49 then it is ultimately governed by his allusion to Isa 53. Christ is the singular Servant who makes possible Paul's obedience as one of the servants of the Servant. Paul's own life, both his dying and rising as well as his divine calling, submission, and transformation is posited as a revelation of Christ's power and transformation; and it is a model for the Corinthians to emulate.

Paul's own example of a transforming grace both received and lived out provides a corrective to the Corinthians whose lives are marked by God's grace, and yet appear to lack the necessary transformation, which should serve as proof of God's grace in their lives. Paul reveals this contrast by stating that his faith is not in vain, while the Corinthians faith is dubious at best (1 Cor 15:2, 10b). Through his own example, Paul calls the Corinthians to the same Christ-centered death, a death which leads to resurrection. In Malcolm's words: "There can be no leaping ahead of present labour to manifest glory and immortality. Rather, the one pre-requisite for resurrection immortality is the inhabitation of death—Christ's death—in the present."[150] It is not enough for them to accept the gospel or to believe in the death and resurrection of Christ; they need to embody it and be transformed by it, both individually and corporately. This takes place as they die to themselves, to their own kind of wisdom, their own kind of power, their own

148. Wright, *Resurrection of the Son of God*, 320–21.

149. So also Ciampa and Rosner, *First Corinthians*, 747; Fee, *First Corinthians*, 724; Blomberg, *First Corinthians*, 296.

150. Malcolm, *Paul and Rhetoric of Reversal*, 235; cf. Ciampa and Rosner, *First Corinthians*, 746 n. 44.

kind of spirituality; as they die to the present evil age and as they presently live under the resurrection power of Christ as part of a new eschatological people of God. By embodying the death and resurrection of Christ in the present they assure their faith is not without result (1 Cor 15:14) and their labor in the Lord is not in vain (1 Cor 15:58).

Summary

Paul's Christophanic reference in chapter 15 reveals that both death and resurrection are part of the believers' present calling. It is only as the Corinthians embrace the sacrificial death of Christ in the present that they are also able to embrace the transforming resurrection of Christ in the present. Paul's own life, which is modelled after Christ's, is an example of both these realities and he invites the Corinthians to walk with him in death so as to walk with him in life, both in the present and in the future.

Conclusion

First Corinthians is written to address a multitude of issues taking place in the Corinthian church that are ultimately the result of a lack of understanding concerning the eschatological age and its impact upon the life of the believer. Paul's two Christophanic references sit within much larger arguments, which highlight this deficiency and provide the Corinthians with models of correct eschatological identity and action.

Paul employs 1 Cor 9:1–2, 16–17 as part of the larger argument of 1 Cor 8:1—11:1, which seeks to transform the Corinthians' thinking about their rights and freedoms in Christ. The first half of Paul's Christophanic reference (1 Cor 9:1–2) functions both ironically and negatively. This negative example is balanced by the continuation of his Christophanic reference in 1 Cor 9:16–17, which functions positively to demonstrate the servant attitude necessary for those belonging to Christ. When taken together, 1 Cor 9:1–2 and 9:16–17 serve a didactic and paradigmatic purpose. Didactically, it evidences a new eschatological reality and seeks to teach the Corinthians the difference between human and divine attitudes and actions toward one another and toward the gospel message and mission. Paradigmatically, it provides a practical example of the necessary reversal for those united in Christ. While Paul's calling is unique in its specific focus, nevertheless, all believers are called to glorify God by taking seriously their responsibility to the body of Christ and to the gospel of Christ.

Paul's second Christophanic reference is part of a larger discourse on death and resurrection (1 Cor 15:1–58) designed to emphasize Christ's actions as the norm for the Christian life; it too functions both paradigmatically and didactically. Just as Christ died and rose again, so too believers are called to die to their own anthropocentric desires in the present so as to experience resurrection life and power in the present. Paul's Christophanic reference (1 Cor 15:8–10) emulates Christ's actions by metaphorically portraying his own experience as one of dying and rising again by the grace of God. In so doing, Paul's Christophanic reference becomes another example for the Corinthians to emulate. A second model of emulation may be found in Paul's allusion to Isa 53 in regard to Christ and his echoing of Isa 49 in regard to his own experience. It is possible that Paul advances Christ as the suffering and exalted Isaianic Servant who ushers in a new eschatological reality and presents himself as one of the servants of this Servant. Didactically, Paul seeks to teach the Corinthians about the necessary transition from life to death to life, which must take place if they are truly to embrace their eschatological calling. Their previous lives, which include their socially conditioned ways of thinking and acting, need to be put to death so they can effectively live out of their new eschatological location and identity and in so doing love one another and Christ well.

Outside their wider literary contexts, both Christophanic references in 1 Corinthians are minor since they provide little historical data and lose their functionality. But when read in correlation with their larger sections and with the epistle as a whole, they strengthen Paul's arguments by assisting the Corinthians in their understanding of what Paul is trying to teach them and then providing a paradigm they can follow in order to embody this particular teaching. Paul's Christophanic references can, therefore, be said to be chiefly corporate in nature as they are not primarily concerned with gaining, maintaining, or asserting authority. Instead, Paul uses his own experience to shape the body of Christ and to further the Gospel.

5

Paul's Christophanic Reference in Philippians

PHILIPPIANS 3:4–14 IS THE first example of a secondary Christophanic reference. While it appears deliberate, recognition by the Philippians that this is a Christophanic reference is not necessary for their comprehension of Paul's meaning. As with the other references, Phil 3:4–14 is evaluated within its literary and socio-historical context in an attempt to better understand the purpose behind Paul's employment of it. Unlike Galatians and 1 Corinthians, Philippians has no direct OT quotations[1] and only a handful of allusions.[2] This absence does not necessarily imply the scriptural illiteracy of the Philippians.[3] While there is little evidence of a significant Jewish presence in Philippi (cf. Acts 16:13–14),[4] the scarcity of scriptural citations may be based on the lack of "controversial issues of scriptural interpretation"[5] in this community. Few details are known concerning the relationship between Paul and the Philippians, but it appears amicable as this group regularly supports Paul's gospel mission in various ways (e.g., Phil 1:7, 19; 2:25; 4:15–16). Therefore, at least limited teaching on the reading and study of the Jewish Scriptures by Paul to the Philippians may be assumed.[6]

1. Cf. Koch, *Die Schrift*, 22–23; Silva, "Old Testament in Paul," 631.

2. Ellis, *Paul's Use of Old Testament*, 154, lists eight allusions; Silva, "Philippians," 835–40, works with five possible allusions.

3. *Pace*, Stanley, *Arguing with Scripture*, 38–61.

4. Ascough, *Paul's Macedonian Association*, 191–212; Oakes, *Philippians*, 58–59, 87; Bockmuehl, *Philippians*, 9–10.

5. Hays, *Echoes of Scripture*, 21.

6. This may be evidenced in Polycarp's confidence in the Philippians being "well versed in the Scriptures" (Pol. *Phil* 12.1 [Lake, LCL]), a letter written only a few decades later.

Paul's Christophanic reference contains no OT allusions, which brings the validity of intertextual analysis in this chapter into question. Paul does, however, parallel Phil 3:4–14 (esp. vv. 7–11) with the Christological narrative[7] of Phil 2:6–11[8] and the latter contains multiple allusions to Isaiah.[9] This raises the question of whether these same allusions are meant to impact the interpretation of Paul's Christophanic reference; this will be addressed in the exegetical section below. In advance, a brief description of the theme of the epistle will provide the groundwork for a more fruitful evaluation of the Christophanic reference. This will include an analysis of how Paul utilizes the multiple oppositional references found within and the Christological narrative as part of his overall strategy.

Preliminary Considerations

The Occasion and Theme of Philippians

There are a variety of possible occasions for this "unified"[10] letter, some ascertainable with relative certainty and others purely speculative.[11] Based on the content and tenor of this letter, it is "fundamentally a progress-oriented, not a problem-solving discourse."[12] Paul desires for the Philippians' continued growth toward Christlikeness and for the continued spread of the gospel in Philippi.[13] The Philippians are experiencing a great deal of suffering, which is affecting their spiritual growth and their gospel effectiveness. Paul seeks to address these concerns by strengthening the Philippians' understanding of their eschatological identity in the hopes this will strengthen their

7. While Phil 2:6–11 is often referred to as a "Christological hymn," the term "Christological narrative" is used in this study to emphasize the larger Christ-story being posited by these verses.

8. Dodd, "The Story of Christ," 154–61; Williams, *Enemies of the Cross*, 236–41; Wright, *Climax of the Covenant*, 59; Gorman, *Apostle of the Crucified Lord*, 419–22; Hansen, *Philippians*, 231; Witherington, *Philippians*, 182, 205.

9. The most liberal intertextual analysis on this connection is found in Cerfaux, "L'hymne au Christ," 425–37.

10. *Pace*, Reumann, *Philippians*, 7–15. Concerning the unity of Philippians see: Garland, "Composition and Unity of Philippians," 141–73; Holloway, *Consolation in Philippians*, 7–33.

11. See Flemming, *Philippians*, 27–29, for a list of the more likely occasions.

12. Witherington, *Philippians*, 25. Cf. Flemming, *Philippians*, 29–30; similarly, Alexander, "Hellenistic Letter-Forms," 93–95.

13. This includes active evangelism and possibly even preaching the gospel. See: Keown, *Congregational Evangelism in Philippians*; Plummer, *Paul's Understanding of the Church's Mission*, 72–76, 134–35.

resolve. Paul's argument strategically revolves around a series of examples, with Christ's, then Paul's examples holding the pinnacle positions. These two examples are bracketed with antithetical references to the Philippians' opponents, which help distinguish eschatological identity from present-evil-age identity. Finally, the refrain of unity is seen throughout. Paul believes unity will help the Philippians overcome the spiritual impact of their suffering and will ultimately become part of their gospel witness.

The Philippian Opponents and Shaping Eschatological Identity[14]

Since Phil 2:6–11 and 3:4–11 form the heart of Paul's argument and of the epistle as a whole, it is no accident that Paul frames these two pericopae with the four references to Philippian opposition (Phil 1:28; 2:15; 3:2, 18–19). In this way, he is able to show a marked difference between the Philippians' new eschatological identity and the antithetical identity of their challengers. While various opponents have been suggested for each of the four references, the majority of scholars see at least two distinct parties with Phil 1:28 and 2:15 referring to one group and Phil 3:2 and 3:18–19 referring to another group. However, if Paul's oppositional references are functioning as antithetical examples of eschatological identity, then the actual identity of these opponents is somewhat insignificant.[15]

Paul's caricaturing of the opponents' faults over and against the Philippians' positive actions and attributes helps to unify them and to weakening the attraction of their opponents.[16] Furthermore, it provides additional information and affirmation about their new identity. Not only *are* they those who "stand firm in one spirit, striving side by side with one mind for the faith of the gospel" (Phil 1:27), "children of God without blemish"

14. An extended version of this section was published earlier as: Fringer, "Antithetical Identity," 112–24.

15. Cf. Bloomquist, *Function of Suffering*, 129–33, 196.

16. Cf. Koester, "Purpose of the Polemic," 319–20, who comes to a similar conclusion saying the aim "is not to describe the opponents, but to insult them." So also Saldarini, "Delegitimation of Leaders," 659–80. Also see, Brown, *Group Processes*, 315–21. Brown's sociological research on group dynamics may provide a lens for understanding the situation at Philippi. He argues that when a person who has entered a new social group continues to live among their old group, they must have a clear understanding of what makes them unique or the requisite for separation becomes untenable. The difficulty increases when there is no clear physical distinction (e.g., color, dress, markings). The risk of re-assimilation is high, since previous social pressures persist and many previous social norms remain part of one's new identity. Could it be that the Philippians find themselves in just such a situation?

who "shine like stars in the world . . . holding fast to the word of life" (Phil 2:15–16), and "the circumcision, who worship in the Spirit of God and boast in Christ Jesus and have no confidence in the flesh" (Phil 3:3), they are simultaneously *not* those set for destruction (Phil 1:28), *not* those who murmur and argue, *not* a "crooked and perverse generation" (Phil 2:14–15), *not* dogs, *not* evil workers, *not* the mutilation (Phil 3:2), and *not* enemies of the cross (Phil 3:18). In this way, the oppositional references continue to shape the Philippians' eschatological identity.

The Christological Narrative and Shaping Eschatological Identity

The volume of literature written on Phil 2:6–11 is witness to its importance within the epistle and to Christianity as a whole.[17] Much of the scholarly debate revolves around Christology.[18] However, Paul's primary aim[19] is to shape the Philippians' eschatological identity by reminding them of their eschatological foundations. This is similar to the reading put forth by Stephen Fowl who believes Paul employs the various hymns (i.e., Phil 2:6–11; Col 1:15–20; 1 Tim 3:16b) to remind and revise the corresponding community's story to move them toward right moral belief and ethical action.[20] Fowl's hypothesis is astute, although this thesis argues Paul is more concerned with identity formation than he is with ethical behavior,[21] since the former births the latter.[22]

These types of narrative genealogies are typical in the ancient world. Caroline Hodge shows how many influential people and even whole societies rewrote their foundation stories in order to bolster their identity.[23] For example, one of Rome's popular origin myths holds that her founders, twin brothers Romulus and Remus, were born of the god Mars and a royal Vestal

17. For extensive bibliography see O'Brien, *Philippians*, 186–88.

18. Wright, *Climax of the Covenant*, 56–98; Dunn, *Theology of Paul*, 245–52; Martin and Dodd, *Where Christology Began*; Fee, *Pauline Christology*, 370–400.

19. This reading does not depend on authorship of Phil 2:6–11. Although, the language and content of the pericope within the whole of the epistle seems to favor Pauline authorship. So Fowl, *The Story of Christ*, 31–45; Wright, *Resurrection of the Son of God*, 228; Oakes, *Philippians*, 210.

20. Similarly, Hellerman, *Reconstructing Honor*, 129–56; Oakes, *Philippians*, 188–90; Holloway, *Consolation*, 122; Peterman, *Paul's Gift from Philippi*, 114.

21. So Wortham, "Christology and Community Identity," 268–87.

22. Many of Fowl's conclusions lean in this direction. Cf. Fowl, *The Story of Christ*, 199–201.

23. Hodge, *If Sons, Then Heirs*, 31–36.

virgin.[24] Additionally, the Greek historian Dionysius rewrote Rome's history showing her to be descended from Greeks and not barbarians (*RomAnt* 1:9–70). In these various backstories, the importance of identity becomes evident. A significant Roman colony such as Philippi (cf. Acts 16:12) would have prided itself in its place and power within Macedonia and the Empire. This may further strengthen the many proposals postulating that the Christological narrative stands in antithesis to the Imperial Cult or the Emperor narrative;[25] "Christ, not the Emperor, was now the true figure of authority."[26] The church needed to be reminded of their new backstory,[27] which included unity in the face of suffering and ultimately hope in the midst of despair. Paul uses Phil 2:6–11 for this purpose and in so doing seeks to reshape the Philippians' eschatological identity. In the words of Hodge, "One way of describing Paul's task as an apostle to the Gentiles is to say that he is rewriting their genealogies. Gentile peoples who follow Christ become brothers of Christ and descendants of Abraham. They are adopted into a new lineage and granted a new heritage."[28]

Philippians 2:5 connects 2:1–4 and 2:6–11 with the underlying theme of unity. Debate revolves around how best to translate verse 5—Τοῦτο φρονεῖτε ἐν ὑμῖν ὃ καὶ ἐν Χριστῷ Ἰησοῦ. Walter Hansen shows how most translations fall into one of two categories, either emphasizing the ethical aspect of the hymn—"*Let this mind be in you that was in Christ Jesus*"—or the doctrinal aspect—"*Think this way among yourselves which also you think in Christ Jesus*."[29] As Gorman demonstrates, this is a false dichotomy. He translates verse 5: "Cultivate this mind-set in your community, which is in fact a community in Christ Jesus."[30] Gorman underscores how Christ's story ultimately defines the Philippians' story, who are called to recognize and embrace this new eschatological reality of being "in Christ."

While agreeing with most of Gorman's outcomes, the following translation maintains the parallelism of the two clauses: "*Each one of you should have this mindset in yourselves, which is the mindset you all already*

---

24. Wiseman, *Remus*, 1–17. Cf. *RomHist* 1.1.6–8.

25. Oakes, *Philippians*, 129–74; Fee, *Philippians*, 191–229; Hellerman, *Reconstructing Honor*, 129–63; Wright, "Paul's Gospel and Caesar's Empire," 160–83; Seeley, "Background of the Philippians Hymn," 49–72.

26. Oakes, *Philippians*, 170.

27. Gorman, *Cruciformity*, 88–92, argues that this pericope forms Paul's master story. See also Gorman, *Inhabiting the Cruciform God*, 9–39.

28. Hodge, *If Sons, Then Heirs*, 33.

29. Hansen, *Philippians*, 119–20.

30. Gorman, *Inhabiting the Cruciform God*, 11; see also Gorman, *Cruciformity*, 40–43; cf. Caird, *Paul's Letters from Prison*, 118–19.

have in Christ." The singular "each one" is garnered from the preceding context, which, while directed toward the whole community, speaks to the personal responsibility of each individual member. Paul's emphatic call to same-mindedness in Phil 2:1–5 (thrice) suggests that this group is still acting more individually minded than corporately. This becomes clear in Phil 2:3–4. Both verses are constructed of dual clauses with the "not . . . but" format emphatically positioned. In verse 4, the two clauses are divided by the participle, which governs both clauses. A similar configuration occurs in 2:5.[31]

Verse 3	Verse 4	Verse 5
Nothing (do) according to selfish ambition not even vain glory (individual/ negative)	Not (just) *each one* looking out for yourselves (individual/neutral)	Each one of you should have this mindset in yourselves (individual/ positive)
Rather in humility consider one another as surpassing yourselves (corporate/positive)	But also *every one* looking out for yourselves (corporate/positive)	Which is the mindset you all already have in Christ (corporate/positive)

Paul does not view the individual as being fully consumed within the corporate body of Christ; rather, the individual has a personal responsibility within the whole. These verses move from the negative to the positive with regard to the role of the individual. In verse 3, the double negative of the first clause reveals a concrete prohibition and thus the ἀλλά carries adversative force. The believer in Christ is never allowed to act out of selfishness but must always act out of humility. In verse 4, the first clause is neutral, the individual is not prohibited from caring for themselves but is reminded of the priority of caring for the other. In this case, the ἀλλά followed by καί has continuative force. Finally, in verse 5, both clauses are positive with no conjunction separating them. The first clause invites the believer to embrace the reality of the second clause. In Christ, they enter a community that already possesses this Christ mindset (cf. 1 Cor 2:16; Rom 12:2). However, the Philippians have not yet reached this goal (cf. Phil 3:12–13) because they have yet to recognize the importance of unity within their eschatological identity. The Christological narrative is another step in this recognition.

While various aspects of the Christological narrative have been emphasized, not many underscore the unity between the Father and Son. Verse 6 states that Jesus "exists in the form of God" (ἐν μορφῇ θεοῦ ὑπάρχων) and is

---

31. The following chart contains the author's interpretive translation.

"equal with God" (ἴσα θεῷ), although not wanting to exploit[32] this connection. The background[33] and meaning[34] of μορφῇ θεοῦ is hotly debated. Most scholars agree it is grammatically connected to ἴσα θεῷ[35] and both refer to Christ's divinity,[36] especially in light of the contrasting parallel of μορφὴν δούλου (v. 7).[37] Paul expresses the unity between the Father and Son, since "[b]eing equal with God has to do especially with Christ's sharing in God's eternal glory and divine status."[38]

Moreover, unity is displayed in the mission of the Son. Christ's *kenosis*, incarnation, slave-likeness, and death are all part of a divine mission of salvation. While soteriology is not explicit, or the primary purpose, it stands behind the description and reminds the Philippians what Christ accomplished and how this was accomplished. Paul's reference to Christ's exaltation (Phil 2:9–11) is not a reward or a promotion from the Father but confirmation of their shared mission and of the divine identity of the Father displayed through the Son.[39] Paul declares Christ's exaltation brings "glory to God the Father" (v. 11c). In this way, both are exalted since they each play an integral role within the divine mission.[40]

The only explicit reference to suffering comes in verse 8 with the mention of Jesus's death (*bis*) on a cross, viewed as a disgraceful form of death by Gentiles[41] and Jews[42] alike (cf. Deut 31:23). There are many other implicit references including Jesus's self-emptying (v. 7a). Joseph Hellerman articulates the social humiliation of Jesus's fall from "equal to God," to slave, to death on a cross, which he describes as utter degradation.[43] If social status is as impor-

32. For a defense of "exploit" and additional definitions of ἁρπαγμός see: Hoover, "The *HARPAGMOS* Enigma," 95–119.

33. Bockmuehl, "The Form of God," 1–23.

34. Jowers, "The Meaning of ΜΟΡΦΗ," 739–66.

35. Wright, *Climax of the Covenant*, 83; O'Brien, *Philippians*, 216; Fee, *Philippians*, 206. Contra Burk, "Articular Infinitive in Philippians," 253–73; Hellerman, "ΜΟΡΦΗ ΘΕΟΥ," 787–89.

36. Pace, Morgan, "Incarnation, Myth, and Theology," 43–73; Dunn, *Christology in the Making*, 114–21; cf. Dunn, *Theology of Paul*, 281–88, for a slight revision of his position.

37. Flemming, *Philippians*, 113; Bockmuehl, *Philippians*, 132; Habermann, *Präexistenzaussagen im Neuen Testament*, 115.

38. Flemming, *Philippians*, 114.

39. Gorman, *Inhabiting the Cruciform God*, 25–34, 122–23; Wright, *Climax of the Covenant*, 86–87; Park, *Submission within the Godhead*, 135–36.

40. Kreitzer, "When He at Last Is First," 121–22.

41. Hengel, *Crucifixion in the Ancient World*, 22–83.

42. Chapman, *Perceptions of Crucifixion*, esp. 41–222.

43. Hellerman, *Reconstructing Honor*, 130–48.

tant in Philippi as Hellerman purports,[44] then Jesus's humiliation would be viewed as a significant form of suffering, one in which followers of a crucified savior likely shared. There is also the suffering of separation from the Father as well as the Father's suffering, which stands behind the text.

The theme of suffering is enhanced through Paul's allusions to Isaiah (Phil 2:7–8 to Isa 53:12; Phil 2:9 to Isa 52:13; Phil 2:10–11 to Isa 45:23).[45] The first two allusions are a reversal of the bookends of the final so-called Servant Song, which form an intertextual inclusio. This inclusio provides an important picture of Paul's understanding of Christ as the Isaianic Servant[46] who suffered, died, was resurrected, and exalted. The reversal of order appears intentional as Paul emphasizes Christ's suffering and death prior to his resurrection and exaltation. For Christ-followers this is the natural progression (cf. 1 Cor 15).

Suffering is not, however, an end in itself. Both the Christological narrative of Phil 2:6–11 and the suffering Servant text of Isa 52:13—53:12 speak of a deeper purpose behind this suffering. The Isaianic Servant suffers to make "intercession for the transgressors" (Isa 53:12) and to "make many righteous" (Isa 53:11) and this is carried out in willing submission to the Lord. Similarly, Paul presents Christ as a willing participant in God's greater plan. While intercessory salvation and righteousness are not directly mentioned the allusion to Isa 45:23 in its literary context (Isa 45:22–25) carries these connotations:

> [22]Turn to me and be saved, all the ends of the earth! For I am God, and there is no other. [23]By myself I have sworn, from my mouth has gone forth in righteousness a word that shall not return: "To me every knee shall bow, every tongue shall swear." [24]Only in the Lord, it shall be said of me, are righteousness and strength; all who were incensed against him shall come to him and be ashamed. [25]In the Lord all the offspring of Israel shall triumph and glory. (NETS)

The work of the Servant of Isa 52:13—53:12 is the fulfillment of Isa 45:22–25.[47] Furthermore, the work of Yahweh through the Servant ul-

---

44. Hellerman, *Reconstructing Honor*, 88–109.

45. Cf. Bauckham, *Jesus and the God of Israel*, 201–10; Gorman, *Inhabiting the Cruciform God*, 31; Wright, *Faithfulness of God*, Book 2, 680–83; Ware, *Paul and the Mission*, 224–26; Cerfaux, "L'hymne au Christ," 425–37.

46. Cf. Bockmuehl, *Philippians*, 135–36; Bauckham, *Jesus and the God of Israel*, 205–6. Contra O'Brien, *Philippians*, 220, 268–71. For a reading of Phil 2:7a as reference to death rather than incarnation see: Jeremias, "Zu Phil ii 7," 182–88; Gundry, "Style and Substance," 290–93.

47. Cf. Bauckham, *Jesus and the God of Israel*, 208; Wright, *Faithfulness of God*,

timately leads to the triumph and glory of the offspring of Israel and the eventual shame of her enemies. This allusion would have brought hope to any Philippians who may have been educated by Paul in the Jewish Scriptures. Nevertheless, Paul leaves these concepts in the background. They are foundational but they are still secondary to what Paul is expressing through this Christological narrative. Paul emphasizes the unity in mission over the actual mission. Christ's suffering is seen as willing self-surrender for the sake of the mission. This is the mindset the Philippians are called to have both individually and corporately as they reside in Christ, the suffering Servant Savior who is united in mission with the Father.[48]

The Christological narrative reveals suffering is not *just* something the Philippians and Paul are experiencing. It is an important part of their backstory. They follow a suffering Servant Savior who was exalted by the God of "power-in-weakness." Yes, exaltation lies in their future (cf. Phil 3:10–11, 21), but suffering defines their present reality and their present identity, not as victim but as a privilege granted by a gracious God (Phil 1:29). Their suffering is not meaningless; its purpose is to bring glory to God (Phil 1:11, 20; 4:20). Likewise, unity is part of their identity as those who have been called together to unite with the Father and Son in their mission.[49] The example of Christ and the dual themes of unity and suffering, as modelled in the Christological narrative, provide a foundation for understanding Paul's Christophanic reference.

Shaping Eschatological Identity in Paul's Christophanic Reference

Like Phil 2:6–11, Paul's Christophanic reference in Phil 3:4–14 is primarily about identity and is intended to reorient the Philippians toward understanding Christ as the source of this identity. Like the accounts of Timothy and Epaphroditus (Phil 2:19–30), Paul is the third and major example of one who has embraced the backstory of a suffering Savior and who lives out of a new eschatological identity. Paul uses his own experiences as a way of revealing to the Philippians that Christ is also the primary source of their new identity. It is important they understand not only the correct

---

Book 2, 683.

48. Cf. Ware, *Paul and the Mission*, 229–33, who connects the Isaianic Servant, Christ, and Paul with regard to the eschatological mission to the Gentiles and argues Paul is encouraging the Philippians to join in this active (verbal) mission in spite of their suffering.

49. Gorman, *Inhabiting the Cruciform God*, 32.

source (Christ and not the flesh) but also the implications (transformation/ co-formation) and purpose (Gospel/mission) of this new identity. Whereas Timothy and Epaphroditus stand as examples of *what* the Philippians are to embrace (unity and sacrifice), Paul's autobiographical narrative aligns more closely to the backstory of Christ (Phil 2:6–11) and serves a much broader and important primary purpose—revealing the *how*.

This pericope is not about distinguishing the identities of Jews from Gentiles,[50] but rather Gentiles from other Gentiles.[51] Paul's autobiographical references are couched in Judaism because this is his starting point and not because issues of Judaism (e.g., law, covenant, circumcision) are the focus. This passage should not primarily be studied for an understanding of Paul's pre- or post-Christophanic beliefs about Judaism. Additionally, since Paul's Christophanic reference is secondary, it should not be overemphasized, as this too is not the primary focus.

Paul's Past Confidence in the Flesh (vv. 4–6)

Paul begins his autobiographical account with a select list of his previous reasons for confidence in the flesh (cf. 2 Cor 11:21–23). They are designed to reveal Paul's backstory and to bring the Philippians' own backstories to the surface. Paul's list, therefore, includes the important elements of "descent, geographic origins, and way of life,"[52] which are essential to such narratives. The Philippians are probably not fully aware of the significance of all of Paul's Jewish merits but could quickly relate them to their own fleshly markers, in which they too prided themselves, whether Greeks or Romans.[53]

Most scholars see Paul's seven-fold autobiographical catalogue (vv. 5–6) as unevenly divided between inherited (first four) and achieved (last three) merits, which climax in the final statement—"as to righteousness under the law, blameless." This interpretation tends to focus the argument around soteriology, and specifically a justification reading.[54] Within the flow of Paul's overall argument, this further isolates this chapter from the

---

50. *Pace*, Dunn, *New Perspective on Paul*, 470.

51. So Fringer, "Antithetical Identity," 117–23; Nanos, "Paul's Reversal," 448–82; Brawley, "From Reflex to Reflection," 128–46; Bateman, "Were the Opponents," 39–61; Grayston, "Opponents in Philippians," 170–72.

52. Hodge, *If Sons, Then Heirs*, 36.

53. Pilhofer, *Philippi*, 126, working off common Roman inscriptions makes the following comparison: *civis Romanus*—ἐκ γένους Ἰσραήλ; *tribu Voltinia*—φυλῆς Βενιαμίν; *Cai filius*—Ἑβραῖος ἐξ Ἑβραίων.

54. Wright, *What Saint Paul*, 119, 124–25, correctly argues this pericope is not about soteriology but ecclesiology.

rest of the epistle. However, it is possible to view Paul's fourth statement as the climactic declaration.[55]

The phrase Ἑβραῖος ἐξ Ἑβραίων is difficult to interpret having no parallels. Ἑβραῖος is only used two other times in the NT (2 Cor 11:22; Acts 6:1). The Acts reference makes a distinction between Ἑβραῖος and Ἑλληνιστής Jews,[56] which may have been the difference between native Palestinians and Diaspora Jews, or as Martin Hengel argues, between Greek speaking and Aramaic/Hebrew speaking Jews.[57] Many of Hengel conclusions rely on Luke's uses of Ἑβραΐδι (Acts 21:40; 22:2; 26:14),[58] which do pertain specifically to the Aramaic/Hebrew language. Nevertheless, this reading should not automatically be applied to Paul's statement in Phil 3:5.[59]

Ἑβραῖος is used forty-two times[60] in the LXX where it distinguishes Hebrews from other people groups, found both on the lips of foreigners and Israelites. It often focuses on the Hebrew's connection to their God (e.g., Exod 3:18; 5:3; 7:16; 9:1; 1 Sam 4:6; 2 Macc 7:31; 11:13) and to servitude (e.g., Gen 39:14; Exod 1:15; 21:2; Jer 41:9, 14; Jdt 14:18). The latter is best demonstrated by the fact the LXX translates עִבְרִי, found thirty-four times in the MT, with some form of Ἑβραῖος in all but six[61] instances and in three of these the LXX instead translates it with the word δοῦλος (1 Sam 13:3; 14:21; Jonah 1:9). Furthermore, Ἑβραῖος is similarly used in other Jewish literature[62] to distinguish Israelites from Gentiles and especially in the Diaspora.[63] A certain degree of nationalistic pride appears to be associated with this moniker. Their identity is tied to their service of the true God and this distinguishes them.

This fits the current context well where Paul thrice speaks about confidence in the flesh (Phil 3:3b–4). It also correlates to the same theme Paul has introduced thrice before (Phil 1:6, 14; 2:24), but which stands in opposition to the current context because therein confidence is solely grounded in Christ and not the flesh. Paul's use of Ἑβραῖος ἐξ Ἑβραίων is a prideful

---

55. Cf. deSilva, "No Confidence in the Flesh," 38, who views it as the climax of the first three. Cf. Ortlund, *Zeal without Knowledge*, 154, who regards it as the "hinge."

56. Moule, "Once More," 100–102.

57. Hengel, *Between Jesus and Paul*, 9–11, 142–43.

58. Cf. Ἑβραϊστί in John 5:2; 19:13, 17, 20; 20:16; Rev 9:11; 16:16.

59. So Bruce, *Philippians*, 108; Flemming, *Philippians*, 163; Witherington, *Philippians*, 198.

60. This includes nine variations of Ἑβραῖος (Exod 1:16, 19, 22; Deut 15:2; 1 Sam 4:9; 13:19; 14:11; 17:18; Jer 41:9).

61. Gen 14:13; 1 Sam 13:3, 7; 14:21; 29:3; Jonah 1:9.

62. E.g., it is found 310 times in Josephus and fifty-eight times in Philo.

63. Fee, *Philippians*, 307 and n. 14.

statement that emphasizes the previous source of his confidence. It is akin to saying a "man's man." Paul is a "Hebrew's Hebrew." From a Jewish worldly perspective, he is a step above the rest, *par excellence*.[64] This is similar to Paul's self-ascription in Gal 1:14—"I advanced in Judaism beyond many among my people of the same age, for I was far more zealous for the traditions of my ancestors." This fourth declaration helps balance and focus the interpretation of the other six merits; Paul is "boasting in the flesh."[65]

Dunn may be correct to emphasize that Paul's first three credentials focus on ethnic identity.[66] Additionally, although the final three badges are more individually focused, Paul's polemic is not primarily against "self-achieved righteousness."[67] Instead, Paul highlights both inherited (corporate) and achieved (individual) merits, which define identity. By climaxing this list in the fourth declaration, he illustrates how each is grounded in the same source, namely an overconfidence in the flesh. This does not necessarily mean Paul previously viewed his Jewish pedigree as a source of pride or as grounded in the flesh. The hyperbolic nature of Paul's argument (esp. Phil 3:8b) is designed to highlight the extremes between his past and present worldview and thus between "this age" and "coming age" realities; he sets up a divine–human dichotomy. From Paul's eschatological position in Christ, all "this age" realities appear to be grounded "in the flesh" and all sources of identity other than Christ are lacking, even Torah, even Roman citizenship. As Nijay Gupta's writes: "Paul does not condemn boasting in the flesh because it is inherently wrong, but because it has been exposed to be an outdated mode of operation."[68]

The New Source of Paul's Confidence (vv. 7–11)

Paul moves to speak of the effect of gaining Christ. Having entered into a new eschatological age, Paul embraced a different perspective by which to view his past life in the past age. Paul's shift to demoting his merits in light of his relationship to Christ would be both difficult and freeing to his Philippian audience. Paul's point is not that these fleshly gains were necessarily

64. Wallace, *Greek Grammar*, 103 n. 84, says this construction may be classified as "the genitive in relation to a *par excellence* noun."

65. Williams, *Enemies of the Cross*, 169; cf. Silva, *Philippians*, 146–54.

66. Dunn, *New Perspective on Paul*, 474–76.

67. Dunn, *Theology of Paul*, 370. Contra, Kim, *Paul and the New Perspective*, 75–81; Ortlund, *Zeal without Knowledge*, 154–62. Cf. Dunn, *New Perspective on Paul*, 480, where there is a semi-retraction of his previous statement.

68. Gupta, *Worship that Makes Sense*, 146, see also 141–48; Similarly, Donaldson, *Paul and the Gentiles*, 298.

bad; any of these could have value based on ones' starting point. Paul seeks
to shift their starting point from primarily being defined by previous backstories, which were grounded in the flesh, to being defined by their new
backstory, which is grounded in Christ.

Paul's opening statement (v. 7) frames the important categories of
"gains" (κέρδος) and "losses" (ζημία). Here, the merits of verses 5–6 are fully
in view. He does not deny their value, past or present (e.g., Rom 11:1–2;
2 Cor 11:22–23; cf. Rom 3:1–2, 9:1–5), only states that διὰ τὸν Χριστόν they
have now been transferred to the loss column. At this point, the comparison is not between Christ and flesh, but between earthly gains and losses.
Paul's wording places Christ and loss in the same column reminding the
Philippians that suffering is intrinsically tied to Christ (Phil 2:6–8) and thus
to all believers (Phil 1:29–30). This point is further underscored in verse 8
where Paul twice more credits Christ as the reason for his having suffered
loss (ἐζημιώθην; cf. 1 Cor 3:15; 2 Cor 7:9). This may cause the Philippians
to reflect on Paul's earlier statement in Phil 1:21 and to recognize its significance—to live in Christ means suffering, but to die (the ultimate loss) in
Christ means gain (κέρδος).

Verse 8a forms the climax of Paul's loss–gain metaphor as evidenced
by the emphatic construction (ἀλλὰ μενοῦνγε καί),[69] and the fact that the
rest of verses 8b–11 build off and further this statement. Paul's regarding
of "all things" as loss includes his ethnic merits and past achievements, but
it also includes all fleshly confidences, past, present, and future, including the Philippians' ethnic and achieved merits.[70] Judaism is "not the sole
target of Paul's rhetoric."[71] Instead, Paul seeks to draw his audience into an
understanding of how the "surpassing value of knowing Christ Jesus" renders all other criteria impotent. Christ has become the new source of their
identity and this identity is grounded in Christ's suffering and includes
their own suffering.

Suffering is but one aspect of their story with the other being the
"gain" that comes through their union with Christ. Paul's construction
places "knowing Christ Jesus" in the "gains" column as evidenced by the
parallel phrase "in order that I may gain Christ and be found in him" (v.
8b). While gaining Christ and knowing him are equal, the notion of being found in him takes this relationship to another level and expresses a
profound union (cf. Phil 2:5).[72] Even here, Paul makes union with Christ

---

69. O'Brien, *Philippians*, 386.

70. So W. Campbell, "I Rate All Things as Loss," 56–58.

71. Miller, "Paul and His Ethnicity," 47.

72. C. Campbell, *Paul and Union with Christ*, 233–34.

the goal behind the sacrifice of "all things" and the recognition of these things as rubbish (ἵνα Χριστὸν κερδήσω).[73] In this way, Paul is able to acknowledge the previous value of past confidences as well as the pains of present loss. Simultaneously, he reminds the Philippians that because of their union with Christ, their gain far surpasses their losses, and to the extent their losses may be regarded as σκύβαλα.

Paul's use of σκύβαλα is aimed at the source of his past confidence, namely "the flesh," and not specifically at the merits listed in Phil 3:5–6.[74] This is confirmed by verse 9 where the contrast is between righteousness sourced in Torah and righteousness sourced in the faithfulness of Christ[75] (cf. Gal 2:16). The fact verse 9 continues to articulate verse 8a shows how Paul's construction intentionally places the former in the "losses" column and the latter in the "gains" column. Torah functions as part of Paul's story of fleshly confidence as underscored by his use of the emphatic possessive pronoun ἐμὴν. Paul expects the Philippians to fill in the blank from their own contexts, e.g., "not having a righteousness of my own that comes from Roman citizenship." Therefore, "to know," "to gain," and "to be found" in Christ are all part of having a righteousness that comes through the faithfulness of Christ, which is based upon faith. This latter use of faith is a reference to human faith,[76] which derives from and correlates to Christ's faith, and distinguishes it from confidence in the flesh.[77]

It is now evident verses 8–9 forms a neatly presented pattern:

Segment	Gains	Losses
1	[Ἀλλὰ] ἅτινα ἦν μοι κέρδη,	ταῦτα ἥγημαι διὰ τὸν Χριστὸν ζημίαν.
2		ἀλλὰ μενοῦνγε καὶ ἡγοῦμαι πάντα ζημίαν εἶναι
3	διὰ τὸ ὑπερέχον τῆς γνώσεως Χριστοῦ Ἰησοῦ τοῦ κυρίου μου,	

73. Here, ἵνα plus the subjunctive denotes either purpose or purpose-result. For the latter see, Wallace, *Greek Grammar*, 473–74.

74. Cf. Flemming, *Philippians*, 167.

75. Bockmuehl, *Philippians*, 211–13; O'Brien, *Philippians*, 398–400; Foster, "Πίστις Χριστοῦ," 91–110. Cf. C. Campbell, *Paul and Union with Christ*, 187–88.

76. Bockmuehl, *Philippians*, 213; O'Brien, *Philippians*, 400; Foster, "Πίστις Χριστοῦ," 109.

77. Cf. Schenk, *Die Philipperbriefe*, 250–51, who argues the chiastic structure of verse 9 places ἐμὴν and ἐπὶ τῇ πίστει as contrasting corollaries.

Segment	Gains	Losses
4		δι' ὃν τὰ πάντα ἐζημιώθην, καὶ ἡγοῦμαι σκύβαλα,
5	ἵνα Χριστὸν κερδήσω καὶ εὑρεθῶ ἐν αὐτῷ,	
6		μὴ ἔχων ἐμὴν δικαιοσύνην τὴν ἐκ νόμου
7	ἀλλὰ τὴν διὰ πίστεως Χριστοῦ, τὴν ἐκ θεοῦ δικαιοσύνην ἐπὶ τῇ πίστει,	

Paul begins by framing the two categories, linking loss to Christ (Segment 1). He then develops the categories further, always beginning with loss (Segments 2, 4) and moving toward the source of this loss (Christ), while identifying it as a gain (Segments 3, 5). This seeming paradox models Christ's suffering and death prior to resurrection and exaltation. In the final two segments (6, 7), Paul reveals what ultimately is lost is confidence in the flesh (ἐμὴν δικαιοσύνην), which capitulates to confidence in Christ (διὰ πίστεως Χριστοῦ). While Paul is specifically speaking of his own story, he does so to move the Philippians toward viewing all things from the perspective of being in Christ and from this perspective toward recognizing that loss and suffering are proof of their union with Christ.[78] This does not mean all suffering demonstrates this union, only those losses patterned after Christ's willing obedience to the Father for the sake of the shared mission (cf. Phil 2:6–11).[79]

This understanding is solidified in verses 10–11, which more fully articulate the correlation between Christ and suffering, and advances the believers' relationship from union to participation. Paul's goal is to know (τοῦ γνῶναι)[80] Christ more fully, which means knowing both "the power of his resurrection" and the "sharing of his sufferings."[81] Fee is correct, these "two go together hand-in-glove"[82] and cannot be separated. Since Paul has already experienced this surpassing value (v. 8a), it must be possible for the Philippians to experience both of these phenomena in the present, through

78. Similarly, Bloomquist, *Function of Suffering*, 181.

79. Fowl, *Philippians*, 156.

80. Genitive articular infinitive denoting purpose. See Wallace, *Greek Grammar*, 590–91; O'Brien, *Philippians*, 400–401.

81. Bloomquist, *Function of Suffering*, 179, notes the reversal in Paul's current argument where we would expect suffering to come before resurrection.

82. Fee, *Philippians*, 331.

the Holy Spirit (cf. Phil 1:19; 3:3). This is what Paul tries to make clear to them. They have experienced Christ's suffering, but this also means they have experienced the power of his resurrection. That Paul and the Philippians can currently participate in these phenomena is further proof of the eschatological age and of their eschatological identity.

With the phrases "becoming like him in his death" and "if somehow I may attain the resurrection from the dead," both phenomena are recapitulated and advanced forming an important chiastic structure.[83] Paul frames suffering with resurrection,[84] both its present power and its future hope. The Philippians need assurance that suffering is not the end all (cf. Rom 8:17–18). Suffering is part of their eschatological calling but so is resurrection. Here the Philippians are reminded of their backstory, Christ was obedient to death but he was exalted to the glory of the Father (Phil 2:6–11). While this is an important truth, which the Philippians need to hear (cf. Phil 3:21), it is not the focus of this passage, or of this epistle.[85] Here the focus is the present, which needs to be shaped both by past realities and future hopes.

Paul's use of κοινωνίαν and συμμορφιζόμενος (Phil 3:10) in connection to Christ's suffering and death is powerful imagery that denies all earthly reasoning. It is hard to imagine Paul putting a more positive spin on suffering than he does in this beautifully articulated declaration. Suffering has purpose and meaning that can only be understood, experienced, and even desired as one resides in a new eschatological reality where Christ is the source of identity. Furthermore, being "formed together" in his death brings identity to a completely new level. Believers who embrace such transformation reflect not their own suffering, but the sufferings of Christ in their present life. This is reminiscent of Paul's words in 2 Cor 4:8–11. In this way, suffering is tied to the proclamation of the gospel. This gives greater depth to Paul's use of κοινωνία, linking it to the other uses of the κοινων-root, which highlight suffering for the sake of the gospel (Phil 1:5, 7; 4:14, 15; cf. 1 Cor 9:23). Paul's *pathos* is meant to move the Philippians toward a similar desire (Phil 3:17), which will further unite them together as the eschatological people of God (Phil 3:15) who are called to participate together in the proclamation of the gospel.

---

83. So Fee, *Philippians*, 329; Flemming, *Philippians*, 174; Hansen, *Philippians*, 243.

84. Cf. Rom 6:5; 1 Cor 15; Phil 2:8–9. Vincent, *Philippians*, 105, writes: "The order of arrangement here is the true one. The fellowship of the sufferings follows the experience of the power of the resurrection."

85. *Pace*, Bloomquist, *Function of Suffering*, 195.

The Impact of Christ-Identity (vv. 12–14)

Paul concludes his autobiographical retelling by underscoring his determination to live out the fullness of his eschatological calling. Paul's reference to not having fully taken hold of or arrived at the goal (τετελείωμαι; Phil 3:12) looks backwards (Οὐχ ὅτι)[86] to Phil 3:10–11 and does not just refer to resurrection[87] but equally to his being formed together with Christ in his death. Paul is not seeking martyrdom[88] or some fulfillment of "the pattern of Christ's suffering";[89] although, he is prepared for such an end (Phil 1:20–23; 2:17; cf. 2 Cor 1:8–9; 4:8–12; Col 1:24). Rather, verses 12–14, along with the εἴ πως[90] of verse 11, are a reminder of the ongoing commitment needed by follows of Christ (cf. Phil 2:12), and also of God's commitment to them (Phil 3:12b; cf. 2:13).

It is because God has "taken hold" (κατελήμφθην) of Paul that Paul is so determined to take hold (καταλάβω) of Christ (Phil 3:12). This is a reference to Paul's Christophanic experience and closely connects this section to Phil 3:5–11. Paul does not change subjects, only metaphors. He moves from the accounting language of κέρδος and ζημία to the athletic language of καταλαμβάνω, σκοπός, and βραβεῖον[91] (cf. Rom 9:30–32; 1 Cor 9:24–27). There may be a significant parallel between Paul's use of κερδαίνω and καταλαμβάνω. Just as Paul is willing to suffer the loss of all things in order to gain (κερδαίνω) Christ (Phil 3:8), so too he is willing to pursue (διώκω), to forget (ἐπιλανθάνομαι), and to strain (ἐπεκτείνομαι) in order to take hold of (καταλαμβάνω) Christ (Phil 3:12–13). Paul illustrates how continued union with Christ is not maintained through passivity, but through active participation, even with the same vigor one previously pursued past confidences (cf. Phil 3:6; διώκω) sourced in the flesh; this is the impact of being in Christ. Paul's striving provides the Philippians with a model for their own continued striving toward the goal and prize of fully knowing Christ Jesus.

Verse 15 is an important transition as Paul reveals all he has been sharing is connected to the Philippians' own situation and to their eschatological identity. Paul refers to them as the "mature" (τέλειοι), a play on the already/not yet reality of their identity; they are those who actively pursue Christ, but have yet to fully reach their goal (τετελείωμαι; Phil 3:12; cf. 2:5).

86. Fee, *Philippians*, 342 and n. 17.

87. *Pace*, Williams, *Enemies of the Cross*, 196–97.

88. *Pace*, Lohmeyer, *Die Philipper*.

89. Perriman, "Pattern of Christ's Sufferings," 62–79.

90. Flemming, *Philippians*, 176.

91. For Paul's use of athletic metaphors see Pfitzner, *Paul and the Agon Motif*, 139–53; and Arnold, "Re-envisioning the Olympic Games," 243–52.

Paul reminds them that this same-minded (τοῦτο φρονῶμεν) pursuit both unites them and distinguishes them from those who are different-minded (ἑτέρως φρονεῖτε; Phil 3:19). Just as Christ revealed himself to Paul in the Christophany, God continues to reveal (ἀποκαλύψει) himself to believers as they continue to "hold fast" to Christ (Phil 3:16), and as they join together in imitating Paul, Timothy, Epaphroditus, and all who reflect the story of Christ (Phil 3:17; cf. 1 Cor 4:6; 11:1; 1 Thess 1:6; 2:14). The Philippians have shown they are not enemies of the cross of Christ (Phil 3:18), but citizens of an eschatological kingdom and its suffering Savior Servant (Phil 3:20; 2:6–11). Christ is the source of their present identity, the one who is already beginning to form them together (σύμμορφον) as a unified body that reflects the gospel and Christ's glory (Phil 3:21), both in their suffering and in their constant striving together toward the goal of full union in Christ in their present resurrection living.

A Closer Look at Paul's Christophanic Reference

The verbal[92] and thematic[93] connections between the Christological narrative and Paul's own story are significant. Like Christ, Paul's privileged status (Phil 3:5–6; cf. 2:6) is surrendered for the sake of the mission (Phil 3:7–9; cf. 2:7–8) with a hope of future exaltation (Phil 3:10–14; cf. 2:9–11). Nevertheless, multiple differences exist. First, Paul's "privilege" is ultimately religious and is sourced in the flesh. Therefore, this "privilege" is actually part of a negative example.[94] Second, Paul's "loss" began involuntarily,[95] when Christ "took hold" of him (Phil 3:12), and only later moves toward a willing relinquishment of these fleshly benefits. Thus, Christ is truly the motivation for Paul's transformation. Third, Christ is also the source of Paul's righteousness and faith. This narrative is foremost about what Christ has done in and through Paul and only secondarily about what Paul has and is doing in light of this union. Fourth, Paul does not appear overly concerned with exaltation or even with future resurrection. His concern is for the present and for a deeper union with Christ in all things, including death and resurrection. The Philippians are reminded that Christ is the architype, and Paul, along with Timothy and Epaphroditus, merely an example, who is emulating Christ.

92. See Bloomquist, *Function of Suffering*, 165.

93. See Williams, *Enemies of the Cross*, 236–41.

94. Williams, *Enemies of the Cross*, 168.

95. Cf. Bloomquist, *Function of Suffering*, 166, 169, who insinuates that Christ's actions were involuntary.

Paul's example becomes an attainable model by which the Philippians can imitate Christ (cf. Phil 3:17; 4:9). Paul does not elevate himself to being equal with Christ (another difference). Instead, he descends from what might otherwise be seen as a lofty apostolic position to align himself with every other believer in Christ. This may account for Paul's lack of reference to his apostleship (ἀπόστολος) in this epistle, a rare omission, only here and in Philemon.[96]

Additionally, it may give explanation as to why the only use of ἀπόστολος in this epistle is targeted at Epaphroditus (Phil 2:25). Many downplay this epithet claiming it unequal to Paul's apostleship and instead referring to a messenger commissioned by a local congregation for a particular task (cf. 2 Cor 8:23).[97] However, Epaphroditus is also described by the term λειτουργός (cf. λειτουργία; Phil 2:17, 30), priestly language Paul uses to describe his own divine commission "to be a minister (λειτουργός) of Christ Jesus to the Gentiles in the priestly service (ἱερουργέω) of the gospel of God" (Rom 15:16).[98] It may be time to revisit Gerald Hawthorne's often dismissed claim:

> Paul, in harmony with the whole message to the Philippians, carefully chooses this word to stress again that relationships within the church must not be measured in terms of superiority or inferiority, but of equality. Epaphroditus is equally an "apostle" with Paul in that both were men commissioned and sent out with full authority to perform specific tasks of service.[99]

Paul elevates a member of the Philippian community, specifically commending him for modelling a Christ-like willingness to suffer and even die for the work of Christ (Phil 2:29–30). In one respect, this shows Paul's willingness to share the authority given to him through his Christophanic commissioning. In another sense, this reveals to the Philippians the significance of their eschatological position in Christ. They are neither limited by their worldly positions nor defined by their current physical situations. In Christ, they share a similar calling as Paul's to embrace unity in the midst of suffering as they participate in the *missio Dei*.

Paul makes a similar but more overt connection between Timothy and himself with regard to their shared status as δοῦλοι Χριστοῦ Ἰησοῦ (Phil

---

96. This includes the disputed Pauline epistles.

97. O'Brien, *Philippians*, 332; Bruce, *Philippians*, 95; Fee, *Philippians*, 226 and n. 18; Hooker, "Philippians," 520.

98. Flemming, *Philippians*, 148.

99. Hawthorne, *Philippians*, 116–17. In the revised edition, Ralph Martin's augments actually take away from Hawthorne's claim. See Hawthorne and Martin, *Philippians*, 163–64.

1:1; cf. 2:22).[100] The significance of this epithet in this epistle should not be overlooked as it provides an important link between the Christological narrative and Paul's Christophanic reference. Paul's identification as δοῦλος in a prescript is rare (i.e., Rom 1:1; Phil 1:1) and is only found here in the plural. This designation foreshadows Paul's reference to Christ in Phil 2:7, which alludes to the suffering Servant of Isaiah. While Phil 3:4–14 does not utilize the word δοῦλος, the concept of servitude to Christ is seen in Paul's use of κύριος (Phil 3:8), a correlative (cf. Matt 10:24–25; John 13:16; 15:15; 2 Cor 4:5; 2 Tim 2:24; Jas 1:1).[101] This is confirmed in the servile actions of Paul for Christ (Phil 3:7–8) and the phrase κατελήμφθην ὑπὸ Χριστοῦ [Ἰησοῦ] (Phil 3:12). The latter projects a vivid picture of Paul's involuntary seizure by Christ (cf. Mark 9:18; John 8:3; 1 Thess 5:4). Paul's Christophany subtly and briefly comes to the forefront to remind the Philippians of their own radical conversion experiences where Christ took hold of them through the proclamation of the Gospel by Paul and ultimately through the Holy Spirit, who "is the key to their unity"[102] (cf. Phil 2:1; 3:3). They too have been made slaves of Christ for the sake of the gospel (Phil 1:29; 2:5, 12–16; 3:17).

While no direct allusion to the Isaianic passage is found in Paul's Christophanic reference, the above link provides an indirect reference via the Christological narrative. If this connection is allowed, then a further, more direct echo of Isaiah may be found, which gives further clarity to Paul's self-understanding and how this identity encompasses all believers. A case can be argued for viewing Paul's words in Phil 3:9 as echoing Isa 53:11 (MT).[103] The Isaianic Servant, through his actions, extends his righteousness to the many. The Servant's vicarious suffering does more than atone for sin and provide salvation, it provides a means for transformation and then for participation in the Servant's mission. In Paul's understanding, the Servant provides a new eschatological realm of existence and identity. As Paul is found in Christ, he takes on God's righteousness, which comes through the faithfulness of Christ and which transforms his own identity and actions to align with the mission of Christ, the suffering Savior Servant. Paul's impassioned declaration in Phil 3:10–11, while linked directly to Christ's example in Phil 2:7–9, may also echo the intertextual allusions to Isa 52:13 and 53:12. It may be a way for Paul to evidence his having embraced the mission of the Servant.

100. Hawthorne and Martin, *Philippians*, 163; cf. O'Brien, *Philippians*, 44–45.

101. Harris, *Slave of Christ*, 90–91.

102. Fee, *God's Empowering Presence*, 754.

103. The LXX translates the MT in a way that does not emphasize the extension of the Servant's righteousness.

This depiction does not concern Paul alone. As Gregory Bloomquist writes: "Paul uses the Servant Song material to depict servants."[104] Like Paul and Timothy, the Philippians must embrace their identity as servants of the suffering Savior Servant Christ, and must embrace their calling to carry out the mission of the Servant, which, for them, begins with their deeper embrace of unity in the midst of their suffering. This extension of the "servants" status to the Philippians is at least partially evidenced in Phil 1:11, which references the Philippians preparedness for the "day of Christ." Paul's words parallel Phil 3:9 and thus Isa 53:11. The Philippians will be pure and blameless because they have been filled by Christ with the fruit of righteousness.

Additionally, Paul's command to be "imitators together" (συμμιμητής; Phil 3:17) of himself and others is a significant part of Paul's argument and is specifically geared at the "mature" (τέλειος) who are called to be of the "same mind" (τοῦτο φρονῶμεν; Phil 3:15; cf. 2:5). This message is difficult as the idea of being a slave would be unpopular. However, Paul is not asking them to do anything more or less than what Christ himself has done. In the Christological narrative δοῦλος is poetically paralleled with ἄνθρωπος implying being human is equal to being a slave.[105] Paul makes similar claims in other places with the result being that believers are called into servitude to God (cf. Rom 6:15–23; 1 Cor 7:21–23; Gal 4:3, 8–9). Christ is the architype, and Paul follows in his example inviting others to do the same. Paul, while further down the path than the Philippians, shows his maturity by his active pursuit toward the goal (τελειόω; Phil 3:12) of "same mindedness" (τοῦτο φρονεῖτε) with Christ (Phil 2:5; cf. 3:15), which has already been shown to include unity in the midst of suffering for the purpose of mission.

The level of maturity evidenced by the Philippians is a likely reason for Paul's secondary reference to his Christophany. Paul has no need to speak to this group about conversion as they have already shown their connection to Christ and his mission through their support of Paul and through their suffering for the gospel. This may also explain why soteriology is not the emphasis of the Christological narrative. Nevertheless, Paul does need to articulate a path toward greater union and participation with Christ and his mission, which begins with greater unity amongst the Philippians in their shared plight. Paul's Christophanic reference helps illustrate how they can more fully embrace their eschatological identity in Christ by continuing to die to themselves and by continuing to allow their lives, their being and doing, to be defined by their founder's story.

---

104. Bloomquist, *Function of Suffering*, 167.

105. Cf. Patte, *Paul's Faith*, 183, who goes so far as to argue "Christ by obedience to God made himself obedient and a slave to other powers."

Paul's statement in Phil 3:15b is intriguing in light of what is known about Paul's Christophany from other places (esp. Gal 1:11–17). He writes: καὶ εἴ τι ἑτέρως φρονεῖτε, καὶ τοῦτο ὁ θεὸς ὑμῖν ἀποκαλύψει. Paul recognizes there may be[106] some who will be of a "different mind" than him or Christ, but he assumes God's revelation will be the corrective. Since Paul's authority is not in question but is assumed in Philippi, Paul has no need to spiritualize his exhortation. That is to say, Paul does not need to say, "I have just told you what you need to do, but if you don't believe me then God will show you I am correct." Instead, Paul believes everything he has shared can only be grasped through a revelation from God through the Holy Spirit. Paul's proclamation only has power as God gives it power. In light of the current context and Paul's allusion to his Christophanic experience, this makes the words "this also" or "this too" (καὶ τοῦτο) important. What has God already revealed to the Philippians? Could Paul be speaking about their conversion? This idea is at least plausible if not probable. Chapter 3 has shown that Paul's own Christophanic experience shapes the way he understands all believers' conversion/call and continued transformation. Therefore, in Phil 3:15b, Paul may be alluding to the Philippians initial revelation of Christ, through the Holy Spirit, brought about by Paul's proclamation of the Gospel to them (cf. Phil 1:6).

Conclusion

Paul needs to help the Philippians embrace some of the deeper realities of their new identity and the mission that comes with it. He needs to help them understand how unity in the midst of suffering for the sake of the mission of God is part and parcel of this new identity, which has its foundation in a suffering Savior Servant. Paul carries out this agenda by way of multiple examples, some positive and others negative, which all inform the Philippians about the depths of their eschatological identity. The two primary examples are Christ's (Phil 2:6–11) then Paul's (Phil 3:4–14). To understand the latter one must first understand the former, upon which it is reliant. The Christological narrative provides a foundation story, which gives purpose to the Philippians' current situation. The suffering they are experiencing is neither unique to them nor is it something for which they should be ashamed. Christ's exaltation, which has provided them with salvation, was predicated on his willing humility, suffering, and death. However, this was

---

106. Fee, *Philippians*, 357 and n. 24, is correct that καὶ εἴ is conjunctive and should be translated "and if." Contra, Hawthorne, *Philippians*, 156, who views it as adversative and translates it "but since."

not carried out alone or aimlessly, it took place in unity with the Father for the sake of their shared mission in the world. Paul's intertextual allusions to Isa 52:13—53:12 in correlation with Isa 45:23 helps to reveal this shared mission and provides a picture of Paul's understanding of Christ as the suffering Savior Servant.

Paul's Christophanic reference, which sits in the background of Phil 3:4–14, primarily functions paradigmatically. Paul is an example of one who has embraced his eschatological identity and with it the shared mission of God through Christ. Moreover, his Christophanic reference provides a tangible and concrete model for the Philippians to emulate. He presents a journey from initial union with Christ to deeper transformation and participation. By means of his own experience, Paul reminds the Philippians of their conversion and their need to continue in the transformation process by refocusing on the source of their faith and identity. He helps them place their own losses and suffering into the category of gains for the sake of Christ. By showing parallels between his own experience and Christ's, Paul's Christophanic reference also makes subtle echoes of the Isaianic Servant in general and more specifically to Isa 53:11 and the concept of the extension of the singular Servant's righteousness and mission to his offspring. In so doing, Paul reveals a self-understanding as one of the servants of the suffering Savior Servant, Christ. Additionally, Paul extends this identity and calling to all believers through his invitation to imitation (Phil 3:17) and through the various ways he elevates others to the same status and calling. In essence, Paul's Christophanic reference teaches the Corinthians about their eschatological identity and calling in Christ and thus the reference also functions didactically, although to a somewhat lesser extent.

This Christophanic reference is secondary because Paul has no need to speak about conversion specifically. Instead, the reference is part of a larger purpose that takes the emphasis off himself and his Christophanic experience and places the focus on Christ and how he transforms identity and gives purpose. In this way, Paul's story becomes Christ's story even as Christ's story becomes Paul's. Additionally, Paul's story becomes the Philippians' story in part with an invitation to become the Philippians' story in full. In other words, Paul uses his Christophanic experience for the sake of the body of Christ; his Christophanic reference is at its core corporate. Paul is willing to emphasize previous actions and attitudes that show his erroneous focus in light of Christ for the purpose of helping the Philippians understand their own fleshly sourced backstories. He is willing to downplay the significance of his apostolic position and elevate Epaphroditus for the sake of helping the Philippians understand their eschatological potential. He is willing to invite the Philippians to share in elements of his same eschatological calling as one of the servants of the Servant. This does not mean that Paul is unaware of the uniqueness of his own apostolic calling, only that for the sake of this community and the sake of God's mission, Paul, like Christ, is willing to humble himself. Finally, Paul may be implying that the Philippians have shared in a similar revelation from Christ through the Holy Spirit as Paul experienced in his Christophanic experience (cf. Phil 3:15b). However, there is not enough evidence in this epistle to fully substantiate this claim.

6

Paul's Christophanic Reference in Second Corinthians

THIS CHAPTER CAREFULLY EVALUATES 2 Cor 3:1—4:6 giving evidence of its rightful place as a confirmed Christophanic reference and revealing how this reference functions within its literary and socio-historical context. Significant sections of Isaiah and Exodus form the foundation for interpreting this pericope and its larger literary context, which necessitates extended intertextual analysis. Likewise, the difficulty of understanding Paul's use of the *fpp* in this Christophanic reference is also explored and its complexity is found to be integral to Paul's overall epistolary purpose as well as to the functionality of the Christophanic reference. As the analysis unfolds, the importance of this Christophanic reference becomes increasingly evident.

Preliminary Considerations

Second Corinthians 2:14—7:4 and the Role of the First Person Plural

Second Corinthians 3:1—4:6 sits in the larger unit of 2:14—7:4. While the integrity of Second Corinthians has been disputed for nearly 250 years, with no clear end in sight,[1] present scholarship has tended to argue either for the

---

1. See Thrall, *Second Corinthians*, 3–49, for an analysis of the various arguments with strengths and weaknesses.

unity of the epistle[2] or for a two-letter composite, *viz.* chs. 1–9 and 10–13.[3] Neither of these hypotheses detours from the current focus since even the most imaginative and complex of the partition theories[4] holds 2 Cor 2:14—7:4 (minus 6:14—7:1[5]) to be a single unit.[6]

One of the greatest difficulties in determining the aim of 2 Cor 2:14—7:4 is the continuous change in person. The overwhelming majority of this section is in the *fpp*. Additionally, there are multiple uses of the second person plural and a handful of the first person singular.[7] The *fpp* is particularly problematic since the implied subject is hard to ascertain.[8] The majority of scholars interpret 2 Cor 2:14—7:4 as part of Paul's apostolic apologia and move through this section with the assumption that the bulk of the *fpp* refer to Paul alone,[9] the so-called "stylistic plural" or "literary plural."[10] Scott Hafemann, who argues for the primacy of the literary plural within this section,[11] provides a relatively standard reasoning for this position, namely, most of Paul's argument, while in the plural, expresses concrete personal experiences and concerns.[12] For example, Hafemann

2. Hughes, *Second Corinthians*; Danker, *Second Corinthians*; Barnett, *Second Corinthians*, 137–45; Scott, *Second Corinthians*; Lambrecht, *Second Corinthians*; Hafemann, *Second Corinthians*; Matera, *Second Corinthians*; Long, *Ancient Rhetoric and Paul's Apology*; Harris, *Second Corinthians*; Seifrid, *Second Corinthians*.

3. Bruce, *First and Second Corinthians*; Barrett, *Second Corinthians*; Martin, *Second Corinthians*; Furnish, *Second Corinthians*; Murphy-O'Connor, *Theology of Second Corinthians*; Thrall, *Second Corinthians*; Talbert, *Reading Corinthians*.

4. Schmithals, *Die Briefe des Paulus*, 19–85; Bornkamm, "Die Vorgeschichte des sogennanten," 162–94.

5. For discussions on the authenticity of this pericope see: Harris, *Second Corinthians*, 14–25; Thrall, *Second Corinthians*, 25–36; Murphy-O'Connor, "Philo and 2 Cor 6:14—7:1," 55–69; Adewuya, *Holiness and Community*, 13–42; Beale, "Background of Reconciliation," 550–81; Contra Fitzmyer, "Qumrân and the Interpolated Paragraph," 271–80.

6. Also cf. Harris, *Second Corinthians*, 240–41; Barnett, *Second Corinthians*, 58 n. 7, 137–45; Thrall, *Second Corinthians*, 188.

7. See Carrez, "Le 'nous' en 2 Corinthiens," 475, for a statistical chart of uses.

8. Wallace, *Greek Grammar*, 393–99.

9. Kim, *Origin of Paul's Gospel*, 231–35; Belleville, "Letter of Apologetic Self-Commendation," 142–63, esp. 153–56; Thrall, *Second Corinthians*, 107; Barnett, *Second Corinthians*, 140–41, see also n. 6; Matera, *Second Corinthians*, 70 n. 12.

10. Also known as "epistolary plural" and "editorial we." For debate over if, when, and how often Paul uses the literary plural see: Thrall, *Second Corinthians*, 105–7; Cranfield, "Changes of Person and Number," 283–87; Byrskog, "Co-Senders, Co-Authors," 230–50; Verhoef, "The Senders of the Letters," 417–25. Cf. Lightfoot, *Colossians and to Philemon*, 229, who says Paul never uses the "epistolary" plural.

11. Hafemann, *Suffering and Ministry*, 15–18.

12. Cf. Baumert, *Täglich Sterben und Auferstehen*, 25–36; Thrall, *Second Corinthians*,

believes Paul has in mind his founding of the Corinthian church in 2 Cor 3:1–6 and his conversion/call in 2 Cor 4:1–6.[13]

While these allusions to Paul's personal experiences may be accurate, this does not necessitate Paul's employment of the literary plural. There are several reasons to take many of Paul's *fpp* in 2 Cor 2:14—7:4 as genuine plurals that include others. Maurice Carrez has designated four "we" categories used by Paul in Second Corinthians: We-Community; We-Ministers; We-Apostles; We-I.[14] The importance of determining how Paul is using the *fpp* will prove invaluable in knowing how best to interpret this section.

Paul's letters are riddled with references to his co-workers and companions. All of the undisputed epistle, except Romans, include mention of a "co-sender" (1 Cor 1:1; 2 Cor 1:1; Gal 1:2; Phil 1:1; 1 Thess 1:1; Phlm 1).[15] There is often an unnamed (cf. Gal 6:11; 1 Cor 16:21; Phlm 19) or named amanuensis (Rom 16:23).[16] Paul sends greetings from co-workers, many likely present during composition (Rom 16:21–23; 1 Cor 16:19; 2 Cor 7:6–15; Phil 2:19–30; Phlm 23–24). While none of this proves Paul's *fpp* are genuine plurals, it is a reminder that Paul writes in dialogue with others.[17] Regarding co-senders, it is improbable Paul would include these names without their knowledge and consent of the content[18]—especially the We-statements. It may also be assumed that Paul's audience would take the *fpp* at face value, particularly in light of the multiple uses of the first person singular.[19]

In Second Corinthians, there are several clues that Paul employs *fpp* in the sense of We-Ministers/We-Apostles.[20] First, Timothy is named co-sender (2 Cor 1:1; cf. 1:13). Second, Timothy and Silvanus are named, along with Paul, as those who proclaimed Jesus Christ among the Corinthians (2 Cor 1:19; cf. 6:11), possibly a reference to the church's founding (cf. Acts

---

195–96; Kim, *Origin of Paul's Gospel*, 5 n. 7, 235; Bruce, *First and Second Corinthians*, 194.

13. Hafemann, *Suffering and Ministry*, 15–16.

14. Carrez, "Le 'nous' en 2 Corinthiens," 476.

15. See Byrskog, "Co-Senders, Co-Authors"; Murphy-O'Connor, *Paul the Letter-Writer*, 16–33; Prior, *Paul the Letter-Writer*, 37–45.

16. For various roles of the amanuensis see: Richards, *Paul and First-Century Letter*.

17. Becker, *Schreiben und Verstehen*, 152, writes: "[Paulus] präsentiert sich den Adressaten als Briefeschreiber, der selbst in einem Dialog steht." Cf. Byrskog, "Co-Senders, Co-Authors," 249; Ehrensperger, *Paul and the Dynamics of Power*, 46–57.

18. Gorman, *Apostle of the Crucified Lord*, 87.

19. Murphy-O'Connor, *Paul the Letter-Writer*, 19.

20. I have chosen to group We-Ministers and We-Apostles because the differences are insignificant to this study. For the differences, see, Carrez, "Le 'nous' en 2 Corinthiens," 478–81.

18:5). Third, Paul mentions the arrival of Titus and his positive report concerning the Corinthians (2 Cor 7:6–7, 13–15). Fourth, Paul mentions Titus's eagerness to return to Corinth to take up the collection (2 Cor 8:16–17, 23), along with two other brothers (2 Cor 8:18, 22). With so many of these references occurring directly before and after 2 Cor 2:14—7:4, it is hard *not* to see many of Paul's *fpp* in this section as including his co-workers.

Paul's multiple references to suffering and affliction (2 Cor 1:4–10; 4:7–12; 4:16—5:5; 6:3–12; 7:5–6; 11:23—12:10; cf. 2:14–16) may strengthen this conclusion. Many scholars assume that these references pertain to Paul's experience alone.[21] Nevertheless, all but the final large unit of 2 Cor 11:23—12:10 are written in the *fpp*. While this latter list has some similarities with the earlier lists, this does not necessitate equivalence. Most scholars highlight the more aggressive tone and polemic of chapters 10–13 and the general shift to predominately first person singulars, whereas chapters 1–9, a section some believe Timothy co-authored (cf. 2 Cor 1:13),[22] are dominated by use of the *fpp*. That Paul is comfortable speaking about his own suffering in the first person singular (2 Cor 11:23—12:10; cf. 2:2–4) should be a caution against automatically assuming use of the literary plural in Paul's other hardship accounts. Paul is not alone in his affliction; in other places, he mentions co-workers who have suffered physically and been imprisoned with him (Rom 16:3, 7; Phil 2:25–30; Phlm 24).

Most scholars see limited use of the We-Community statements in 2 Cor 2:14—7:4, especially in light of the multiple uses of the second person plural. Furthermore, since there are certainly places where Paul is utilizing the *fpp* as We-Minsters/We-Apostles (and possibly as We-I), the interpreter is left trying to look for contextual clues as to when (or if[23]) Paul shifts to the We-Community. Hafemann argues that Paul attaches the adjective πᾶς to the *fpp* when he intends to include the whole community of believers (2 Cor 3:18, 5:10), thus signaling a clear shift from

---

21. See especially the full-length works on suffering in 2 Corinthians by: Harvey, *Renewal through Suffering*; Lim, *The Sufferings of Christ*; Fitzgerald, *Cracks in an Earthen Vessel*. See also related passages in Barnett, *Second Corinthians*; Harris, *Second Corinthians*; Hafemann, *Second Corinthians*, and 34–35. Cf. Furnish, *Second Corinthians*, 120, who says: "*us* refers, first and certainly, to Paul, and perhaps secondarily to his associates."

22. Richards, *Paul and First-Century Letter*, 156–57; Murphy-O'Connor, *Paul the Letter-Writer*, 24–30; Murphy-O'Connor, "Co-Authorship in the Corinthian Correspondence," 570–79; Collins, *Second Corinthians*, 23. Cf. Byrskog, "Co-Sender, Co-Authors," 246, who views at least 2 Cor 1:1–14 as co-authored by Timothy.

23. Belleville, *Reflections of Glory*, 275–76, believes even passages such as 2 Cor 3:18 and 5:21 refer only to Paul and the other ministers.

his more widely used literary plural.[24] But even Hafemann does not abide by this principle as he correctly argues 2 Cor 1:22, 5:21, 6:16 and 7:1 are We-Community references.[25] It appears rather than indicating a shift in subject, the πᾶς of 2 Cor 3:18 and 5:10 provides emphasis at certain climactic points in Paul's argument (cf. 2 Cor 5:14–15).

Carrez sees Paul offering a possible segue between the apostolic ministry and the Corinthians. He writes, "Ce NOUS/VOUS exprime la participation possible de la communauté au ministère qu'exerce Paul. S'il en est le porteur, elle en est le champ d'extension."[26] Carrez accurately exposes, at least in part, the reason for Paul's rather convoluted discourse. Paul sees his apostolic ministry as an important factor in helping people move from their present reality into the new eschatological reality, and thus to assume a new identity. However, the emphasis is not so much on Paul's ministry as it is on the ministry of the new covenant, of which Paul and his associates are included. Paul invites the Corinthians to join the We-Minister/We-Apostles through their recognition and acceptance of this new ministry and new eschatological identity.

In this way, one can understand many of Paul's "we" statements as paradigmatic.[27] This explains why these statements are inclusive of other ministers and other apostles. Even statements which appear to be references to Paul's unique experiences, such as his founding of the Corinthian church or his conversion/call, are stripped of their particulars in order to show the universal elements of these events. This is because Paul seeks to use this argument as a way of shaping the Corinthians' eschatological identity, especially toward unity, and the ambiguity in person is an important strategic element.

Intertextual Reliance upon Isaiah 40–66 in Second Corinthians 1–7

There are multiple connections between 2 Cor 2:14—7:4 and Isa 40–66. The most obvious is found in 2 Cor 6:2, which is a verbatim quotation of Isa 49:8 (LXX). Two additional paraphrastic quotations are found in 2 Cor 6:17 (Isa 52:11) and 6:18b (Isa 43:6), which are part of a concatenation of

---

24. Hafemann, *Suffering and Ministry*, 13 n. 24; Hafemann, *Second Corinthians*, 161, 216.

25. Hafemann, *Second Corinthians*, 244–45, 282–88.

26. Carrez, "Le 'nous' en 2 Corinthiens," 478.

27. Gupta, *Worship that Makes Sense*, 89, reaches a similar conclusion.

seven OT citations.[28] Still, most scholars give little attention to the larger Isaianic context from whence these quotations derive.[29] Jan Lambrecht goes so far as to say, "Paul does not seem to take into account the rich theological ideas present in the Isaian [sic] context."[30] This conclusion does not appear to account for the multiple allusions and echoes between these two texts.[31] Most commentators correctly acknowledge an allusion to Isa 43:18–19 and 65:17–25 in 2 Cor 5:17.[32] Additionally, Otfried Hofius makes a strong argument for seeing 2 Cor 5:18–21 (esp. 5:21) as finding its only parallel in Isa 53 (esp. 53:5).[33] Florian Wilk notes a direct allusion to Isa 53:12 in 2 Cor 4:11 and sees parallels between the Isaianic context and Paul's argumentation in 2 Cor 4:1–15 giving the following examples: "2 Cor. 4:3 (Isa. 53:1), 4:4 (Isa. 52.14), 4:5 (Isa. 52:11, 15), 4:6 (Isa. 52:13), 4:9 (Isa. 54:6)."[34] Wilk also argues for an echo of Isa 49:13 in 2 Cor 7:6.[35] G. K. Beale contends the most probable text behind 2 Cor 6:11b is Isa 60:5 rather than Ps 118:32 (LXX; 119:32 MT) or Deut 11:16.[36] Finally, Paul Barnett briefly notes the association between Paul's multiple use of παράκλησις and παρακαλέω, which open this epistle (esp. 2 Cor 1:3–7; cf. 7:4–13), and the opening words of Isa 40:1 (cf. Isa 51:3, 12, 19).[37]

28. See Lambrecht, *Second Corinthians*, 123–25.

29. Furnish, *Second Corinthians*, 353; McCant, *Second Corinthians*, 55; Martin, *Second Corinthians*, 168–69.

30. Lambrecht, *Second Corinthians*, 108; similarly Stanley, *Arguing with Scripture*, 98–105.

31. Limited space prevents me from arguing the validity of the various allusions that have been postulated; I will simply list those that seem most probable as well as the scholars who have made the strongest arguments for them.

32. Carver, *Second Corinthians*, 191; Hays, *Echoes of Scripture*, 159; Hafemann, *Second Corinthians*, 243–44; Matera, *Second Corinthians*, 136–37.

33. Hofius, "Erwägungen zur Gestalt und Herkunft," 186–99; so also Furnish, *Second Corinthians*, 351. Cf. Beale, "OT Background," 553–58; and Barnett, *Second Corinthians*, 46, who connect 2 Cor 5:14–21 to multiple themes found in Isa 40–66. Also see Hafemann, *Second Corinthians*, 249, who makes a connection between 2 Cor 5:20 and Isa 40:1. Kim, *Paul and the New Perspective*, 214–38, sees the Isaianic background as secondary and places far too much weight on Paul's Christophany for his conception of reconciliation. Additionally, Marshall, "The Meaning of 'Reconciliation,'" 117–32, proposes a *MMT* behind this concept. However, the Isaianic context seems more likely and is probably the origin for the Maccabean understanding.

34. Wilk, "Isaiah in 1 and 2 Corinthians," 149, and n. 67.

35. Wilk, "Isaiah in 1 and 2 Corinthians," 153; also Beale, "OT Background," 576.

36. Beale, "OT Background," 576–77.

37. Barnett, *Second Corinthians*, 72. Cf. Hafemann, *Second Corinthians*, 249, who makes a connection between 2 Cor 5:20 and Isa 40:1 based on the same lexeme. Also Webb, *Returning Home*, 79–84, argues the background for 2 Cor 2:14–16 is not Roman

Based solely on linguistic connections, many of these intertextual links may appear suspect. However, if thematic parallels between Isa 40–66 and 2 Cor 2:14—7:4 are included, the relationship becomes more evident. Three dominant themes emerge out of a study of Isa 40–66: (1) an eschatological shift,[38] especially evidenced in terms of an everlasting covenant, new things, and new heaven and earth (Isa 42:6–9; 43:18–19; 48:6–7; 49:8; 54:10; 55:3; 56:1–8; 59:20–21; 61:8; 62:2, 11–12; 65:17; 66:22–23); which involves (2) deliverance, restoration, and forgiveness of sin for Israel and the nations (Isa 40:1–5; 43:1–28; 44:22; 45:22; 46:12–13; 48:20; 49:6; 51:1–8; 52:1–11; 53:4–6, 10–12; 56:1–8; 61:1–11; 65:17–25; 66:18–24);[39] and is made possible through (3) the role of the Servant and ongoing role of the servants (Isa 41:8–9; 42:1–4; 19; 43:10; 44:1–2, 21; 45:4; 48; 48:20; 49:1–7; 50:4–11; 52:13—53:12; 54:17; 56:6; 63:17; 65:8–9, 13–15; 66:14).[40]

Many of the same themes are strongly represented and even central to 2 Cor 1–7. Paul's words are bursting with the eschatological language of "newness." He speaks of the resurrection (2 Cor 1:9; 4:14; 5:1–8), the ministry and reception of God's Spirit (2 Cor 1:22; 3:3–18; 5:5), the coming day of judgment (2 Cor 1:13–14; 5:10), and about new covenant (2 Cor 3:6) and new creation (2 Cor 5:17). Paul's quotation of Isa 49:8 brings together God's promised salvation and the eschatological reality of the present—"See, now is the acceptable time; see, now is the day of salvation!" (2 Cor 6:2).[41] Paul goes to great lengths to encompass the Corinthians in this new eschatological reality that is present in Christ, which is meant to shape their present identity.

The Isaianic themes of deliverance, restoration, and forgiveness of sins are also evidenced in Paul's argument. Deliverance is demonstrated in the imagery of comfort and salvation (2 Cor 1:3–6; 2:15–16; 6:1–2; 7:6–11). Restoration is recast in terms of transformation into the image of God (2 Cor 3:18; 4:6, 16; 5:21; 6:14—7:1; cf. 4:4) and sharing in his

---

triumphal procession but OT triumphal procession, which is seen in Isa 40:3–5; Cf. Westermann, *Isaiah*, 36–39; Gupta, *Worship that Makes Sense*, 88, suggests a connection between the offering metaphor in 2 Cor 2:15–16 and Israel becoming an eschatological offering to the Lord in Isa 66:20.

38. Examples of those favoring an eschatological reading of Isaiah 40–66 include: Seitz, "Isaiah 40–66," 321, 328; Childs, *Isaiah*, 303; Childs, "Retrospective Reading," 376–77; Gignilliat, *Paul and Isaiah's Servants*, 64–67; Bauckham, *Jesus and the God of Israel*, 33–34.

39. Bauckham, *Jesus and the God of Israel*, 34, focuses on the importance of these first two themes for early Christians and sees this as the impetus for their copious references to this section of Isaiah.

40. So Gignilliat, *Paul and Isaiah's Servants*, 68–86; cf. McKenzie, *Second Isaiah*, lvii.

41. Cf. Westermann, *Isaiah 40–66*, 215; Furnish, *Second Corinthians*, 353.

mission (2 Cor 1:5–6, 21–22; 2:14–17; 3:1, 6; 4:1–11; 5:14–20; 6:4–10). Forgiveness is found in the Pauline metaphor of reconciliation (2 Cor 5:18–20; cf. 6:14—7:1[42]). While these concepts have been divided, they are interconnected, in both Paul and Isaiah. Furthermore, all these concepts are thoroughly eschatological in Paul. Paul sees God's promises in Isa 40–66 coming to fruition in the "now."[43]

The final Isaianic theme, which focuses on the role of the Servant and ongoing role of the servants (see chapter 3), is especially intriguing when brought into connection with Paul's uses of the *fpp*. Beale, in evaluating 2 Cor 5–7, argues that Paul applies the Isa 49 prophecy about himself— "He is in some way the fulfilment of the righteous 'Servant, Israel.'"[44] Beale reaches this conclusion in part because he focuses on Paul's apostolic defense and ignores the fact that all of the pertinent Isaianic quotations and allusions take place in sections where Paul is speaking in the *fpp*. But if Paul's *fpp* are genuine plurals which, at the very least, include We-Ministers/We-Apostles, then Beale's reading is unnecessary. It would be more accurate to speak of Paul's identification with the plural servants rather than with the singular Servant.

Mark Gignilliat, evaluating 2 Cor 5:14—6:10, comes to a similar conclusion that Paul views Christ as the singular Servant (cf. Rom 4:25; 1 Cor 15:1–4; Phil 2:5–11) and himself as the "servant of the Servant."[45] Gignilliat connects Christ and the Servant in 2 Cor 5:14–21 arguing verse 19—"God was reconciling the world to himself through Christ"[46]—signals a link between God's redemptive work and Christ's reconciling actions. Reconciliation assumes an estrangement between humanity and God and Christ's actions have provided a means of atonement and thus forgiveness of sin (cf. Isa 53:4–12).[47] Comparing 2 Cor 5:21 and Isa 53:11, Gignilliat claims

42. The link between 2 Cor 6:14—7:1 and the reconciliation spoken of in 5:18–20 has been seen and argued by many. E.g., Lane, "Covenant," 24–25; Martin, *Second Corinthians*, 195; Beale, "OT Background," 567–77.

43. Beale, "OT Background," 579.

44. Beale, "OT Background," 562. While Beale doesn't necessarily mean that Paul self-identifies as the Servant, not only in Christ, his argument leaves this possibility open. See also Stanley, "Servant of Yahweh," 412–25; Webb, *Returning Home*, 128–31; Donaldson, *Paul and the Gentiles*, 254. For an examination of the confusion around this subject see: Gignilliat, *Paul and Isaiah's Servants*, 51–54.

45. Gignilliat, *Paul and Isaiah's Servants*, 132–42; cf. Hughes, *Second Corinthians*, 220.

46. This follows the reading of 2 Cor 5:19 by Porter, Καταλλάσσω *in Ancient Greek*, 131–35, who argues the main clause should be taken periphrastically and also denoting means. Thus, Christ was the means by which God reconciled the world to himself.

47. Gignilliat, *Paul and Isaiah's Servants*, 100–103. Similarly, Dunn, *Theology of*

that just as the Servant's sacrificial actions led to making many righteous, so Christ's actions result in humanity becoming the righteousness of God.[48] If Gignilliat's reading is correct and Paul does view Christ as the singular Servant of Isaiah, then the multiple other allusions to Isaiah may be emphasizing the new eschatological reality made possible by God through Christ. For Gignilliat, this means that Paul views himself not as the singular Servant but as an eschatological servant of the Servant (cf. 2 Cor 6:4; 11:23) who continues to herald God's redemptive message in the world and who shares in the Servant's suffering and righteousness.

Gignilliat's reading of 2 Cor 5:14—6:10 is helpful in moving the reader toward a deeper consideration of the various OT Scriptures that shape Paul's identity and thought. However, like so many, Gignilliat's emphasis lies on Paul and his apostolic role within Second Corinthians.[49] He fails to take seriously the role of Paul's *fpp* and ultimately re-singularizes the plural servants of Isaiah. In this way, Gignilliat's reading is not significantly different from Beale's. Likewise, Gignilliat's reading is not markedly different from Hafemann's; whereas Gignilliat is concerned with 2 Cor 5:14—6:10 and the undergirding Isaianic passages, Hafemann concentrates on 2 Cor 3 and the underlying narrative of Exod 32-34.[50] Hafemann views Paul's argumentation through an apologetic lens and his reading of Second Corinthians as a whole bears this weight. This narrow reading, like Gignilliat's, tends to skip over other important aspects of the text which need to be considered and even emphasized.

Intertextual Reliance upon Exodus 32–34 in Second Corinthians 3:1—4:6

Paul makes multiple references to Moses and his ministry in 2 Cor 3:1—4:6. There are no verbatim quotations in this section; however, most scholars hold 2 Cor 3:16 to be an altered quotation of Exod 34:34a (LXX).

Paul, 228–30.

48. Gignilliat, *Paul and Isaiah's Servants*, 104.

49. See esp. Gignilliat, *Paul and Isaiah's Servants*, 132–42.

50. Hafemann, *Paul, Moses*; cf. Aernie, *Is Paul also among the Prophets?*, 114–57, who makes similar assertion about how Paul uses Exodus and Isaiah.

2 Corinthians 3:16	Exodus 34:34a
ἡνίκα δὲ ἐὰν ἐπιστρέψῃ πρὸς κύριον, περιαιρεῖται τὸ κάλυμμα	ἡνίκα δ' ἂν εἰσεπορεύετο Μωυσῆς ἔναντι κυρίου λαλεῖν αὐτῷ, περιῃρεῖτο τὸ κάλυμμα ἕως τοῦ ἐκπορεύεσθαι.

This view is substantiated by the context of Paul's argument, which relies heavily on Exod 34:29–35. Therein, Moses descends Mount Sinai with the second set of stone tablets (Exod 34:29—πλάξ, [referred to as πλάκας λιθίνας in Exod 31:18]; cf. 2 Cor 3:3) of the covenant (διαθήκη[51]; cf. 2 Cor 3:6, 13) and with a glorified (Exod 34:29, 30, 35—δοξάζω in the LXX; קרן in the MT; cf. 2 Cor 3:10[bis][52]) face, which he veils (Exod 34:33, 34, 35—κάλυμμα; cf. 2 Cor 3:13–16[four times]) because of the people's fear. This account sits within the larger infamous golden calf narrative (Exod 32–34), which is a story of covenant violation and covenant renewal[53] and highlights Yahweh's mercy and Moses's intercessory role amidst Israel's disobedience and idolatry.[54]

Hafemann contends that Exod 32–34 functions paradigmatically within the OT canon to demonstrate the limitation of the Sinai covenant.[55] This is not a limitation on the part of Yahweh or on the part of Torah; it is a limitation on the part of the people. "The problem with Israel is not their occasional disobedience, but their moral turpitude. The gross idolatry with the golden calf serves primarily to reveal this fact."[56] Israel is no longer able to bear the full weight of God's glory and, therefore, Moses must be the mediatory of God's presence. In consequence, argues Hafemann, Moses's veiling is an act of mercy safeguarding the people from being fully overwhelmed by Yahweh's reflected glory.[57]

With this interpretation in hand, Hafemann views Paul as giving a straightforward reading of the Exodus narrative in its context. Paul is not making a negative comparison between Moses and himself[58] but between Moses's ministry and his own. The former was deficient because of Israel's

---

51. The LXX does not use διαθήκη in Exod 34:29; although it does in Exod 34:27, 28. Cf. MT, which uses עֵדוּת in Exod 34:29 (cf. 31:18) and בְּרִית in 34:27, 28.

52. See also δόξα, used thirteen times in 2 Cor 3:1–4:6.

53. So Meyers, *Exodus*, 253–67.

54. Fretheim, *Exodus*, 279, appropriately titles this section "The Fall and Restoration of Israel."

55. Hafemann, *Paul, Moses*, 230–31, 446–47.

56. Hafemann, *Paul, Moses*, 226; similarly, Childs, *Exodus*, 564–65, 579.

57. Hafemann, *Paul, Moses*, 222–27.

58. Pace, Kim, *Origin of Paul's Gospel*, 233–39; Stockhausen, *Moses' Veil*, 123–25.

"stiff-necked" condition, their lack of God's Spirit, and thus their inability to encounter the glory of God face to face. The latter is sufficient because of the eschatological reality brought through Christ, in which the Spirit is now being poured out, so believers can, like Moses, experience the transforming glory. It is the difference between being under the old covenant and being under the new covenant.[59]

Hafemann's emphasis on Paul's apologetic purpose also moves him to argue for multiple connections between Paul's (2 Cor 2:16b, 3:4–18) and Moses's calls (Exod 3–4),[60] viewing the primary function to highlight Paul's role as God's spokesperson. This connection establishes Paul's legitimacy and authority despite his insufficiency, a theme common in the prophets.[61] Hafemann maintains that Paul does not view himself as a second or new Moses,[62] but views himself in line with the prophets, which carries with it "an *implicit* claim to speak with divinely sanctioned authority to the people of God."[63] Nevertheless, the prominence Hafemann places on Paul's divine calling and apostolic role, implicitly if not explicitly, elevates Paul to "second Moses" status. For example, Hafemann writes:

> [A]s the "Spirit-giver" with the gospel, Paul's role is parallel to that of Moses', the mediator *par excellence* between YHWH and Israel, whose task it was to give the law . . . [A]s the "Spirit-giver," Paul is the intermediary agent of the eschatological reality of the new age characterized by the work of the Spirit in the hearts of flesh prophesied by Ezekiel. It thus seems almost impossible to over exaggerate the significance which Paul attributed to his apostolic ministry in II Cor. 2:4—3:3.[64]

Hafemann, contrary to his claims, does appear to make a strong comparison between the persons of Moses and Paul and not just between their different ministries. Paul is presented as the prophet *par excellence* of this

---

59. Hafemann, *Paul, Moses*, 450. For Hafemann, this should not be confused with a contrast between the two Covenants, but rather as a contrast between two dispensations. Similarly, Cranfield, "Paul and the Law," 160. Contra, Harris, *Second Corinthians*, 280.

60. So also Stockhausen, *Moses' Veil*, 82–85.

61. Hafemann, *Paul, Moses*, 92–186; Hafemann, *Second Corinthians*, 126–33.

62. *Pace*, Stockhausen, *Moses' Veil*, 172–75; Jones, "The Apostle Paul," 219–41.

63. Hafemann, *Paul, Moses*, 104, emphasis his. Similarly, Aernie, *Is Paul also among the Prophets?*, 72–184; Sandnes, *Paul—One of the Prophets*.

64. Hafemann, *Suffering and Ministry*, 220. However, Hafemann, *Paul, Moses*, 102–3 n. 32, later notes the difficulty with associating the language of "Spirit-giver" to Paul and says it is ultimately tied to Christ. Nevertheless, his language does not change much (cf. 400).

new covenant and can be understood as greater than Moses because he does not just provide the Torah, he gives the Spirit, which frees people to see the glory of the Lord with unveiled face.

Hafemann's reading raises the question of Paul's role within 2 Cor 3:1—4:6. Is it, as Hafemann believes, central? Or is it secondary? To answer this question, Moses's role within the Exodus narrative must be analyzed. Therein, Moses appears to be elevated beyond mere prophet status to god-like status. In Exod 4:16, as part of Moses call, he is told Aaron would be his mouthpiece to the people and Moses would be as god/s to Aaron (תִּהְיֶה־לֹּו לֵאלֹהִים). In Exod 7:1, Yahweh tells Moses he has made him a god/s to Pharaoh (נְתַתִּיךָ אֱלֹהִים לְפַרְעֹה). Exod 32–34 also has several god-like references to Moses. In Exod 32:1, the people petition Aaron to make a god/s (אֱלֹהִים) for them who will go before them, not to replace Yahweh, but to replace Moses, who is credited as being the one who brought them out of Egypt,[65] a role Yahweh is happy to relinquish to Moses (Exod 32:7). Moses also shoulders the role of divine judge by carrying out Yahweh's wrath; a wrath Moses has just extinguished (Exod 32:10, 11). In Exod 32:19, Moses descends the mountain and his "wrath burned hot" (וַיִּחַר־אַף). Throughout Exodus, this phrase is always attributed to Yahweh alone (cf. Exod 4:14; 22:23–24; 32:10, 11, 22). In Exod 34:28, Moses writes the words of the covenant on the stone tablets, an action previously performed by the finger of God (Exod 31:18; 32:16). Finally, the shining face of Moses (Exod 34:29–35) may signal some type of divine transfiguration as he now begins to reflect physically the glory of God.[66]

A type of apotheosis of Moses is also attested in STJL. Sirach 45:2 says, "[Yahweh] made [Moses] equal in glory to the holy ones" (cf. *As. Mos.* 10:2; 11:17; *1 En.* 89:36). This angelification is directly connected to Exod 33–34 in Sir 45:3, "[Yahweh] gave him commandments for his people, and revealed to him his glory." In 4Q374 2 ii:6–8, a connection is made between Exod 7:1 and 34:29–35, "[6]and he made him like a God over the powerful ones, and a cause of reel[ing] (?) for Pharaoh . . . [. . .] [7]melted, and their hearts trembled, and [th]eir entrails dissolved. [But] he had pity with [. . .] [8]and when he let his face shine for them for healing,

---

65. So Coats, *Moses: Heroic Man*, 174. Fretheim, *Exodus*, 281–82, argues the people are not trying to replace Yahweh or Moses but want a visible image of the "messenger of God," who is a physical representation of Yahweh in their midst, which ultimately makes them more independent from Yahweh.

66. While we are told of others on the mountain with Moses (e.g., the seventy elders of Israel), nevertheless, Exodus reports "God did not lay his hand on the chief men of the people of Israel" (Exod 24:11). Numbers 11:16–30 reports another episode where some of the spirit (Moses's or Yahweh's?) was taken from Moses and put on the seventy elders. Still, it is interesting God does not give the spirit directly to the elders but it comes from Moses.

they strengthened [their] hearts again, and at the time [. . .]" (cf. 4Q377 1 ii:6–12). Whether this text signals Moses's deification or angelification is debatable.[67] At the very least, Moses is elevated to a god-like status.[68] In Philo, the apotheosis appears more solidified.[69] Philo says of Moses: "Has he not also enjoyed an even greater communion with the Father and Creator of the universe . . . For he also was called the god and king of the whole nation . . . he established himself as a most beautiful and Godlike (θεοειδής) work, to be a model for all those who were inclined to imitate him" (Mos. 1:158).[70] Moses is said to have gradually been transformed into the divine (Virt. 76; Sacr. 9), until "transforming him wholly and entirely into a most sun-like mind" (Mos. 2:288). Similarly, in his exposition of Exod 24:2, Philo say Moses's mind was filled with God, having given up all mortal things, "he is changed into the divine, so that such men become kin to God and truly divine" (QE 2:29; cf. 2:40).

Nevertheless, even for Philo, this type of language concerning Moses, or any human figure, would not constitute a movement away from monotheism. In the words of Philo, "For there is in truth no created Lord, not even a king shall have extended his authority . . . but only the uncreated God, the real governor" (Mut. 22). Thus, Moses's god-like status is delegated rather than essential.[71] Moses's elevated status, born out of the Exodus narrative, is grounded in his unique role as intercessory between the people and Yahweh.[72] Exodus 32–34 paints a picture of Moses as indispensable to Yahweh's continued presence among Israel; "with Moses gone, access to Yahweh is cut off."[73] This may account for Deut 18:15–18 and the concept of a second or new Moses, which was important within Judaism as evidenced

67. Fletcher-Louis, "4Q374," 247–52. Lierman, NT Moses, 246, says that in Jewish understanding these two ideas, in relation to a human figure, amount to the same thing.

68. Foster, "Communal Participation in the Spirit," 89–95. Also see As. Mos. 11:16, which describes Moses as "the sacred spirit who was worthy of the Lord, manifold and incomprehensible, the lord of the word, who was faithful in all things, God's chief prophet throughout the earth, the most perfect teacher in the world."

69. See esp. Litwa, We are Being Transformed, 106–9. Cf. Bauckham, "Moses in Philo," 246–65.

70. Bauckham, "Moses in Philo," 263–64, argues that Philo's descriptions of Moses usually refer to his virtuosity and this language carries a Stoic "figurative-ethical meaning." However, in Mos. 1:158, Philo refers to Moses's unique role as ruler of Israel but there is still no understanding of divine-like transformation.

71. Lierman, NT Moses, 231–32, 246–47; cf. Dunn, Christology in the Making, 19.

72. See Hafemann, "Moses in the Apocrypha," 79–104, who shows that Moses as mediator/intercessor, more than as prophet, lawgiver, and deliverer, is emphasized in the apocryphal and pseudepigraphal literature.

73. Durham, Exodus, 419.

by the Mosaic characteristics prevalent in the OT texts and especially the various depictions of the prophets.[74]

There may also be connections between the phrase "man of God" (אִישׁ־הָאֱלֹהִים) and the continuation of a Moses-like leader. The phrase is used six times in correlation to Moses (Deut 33:1; Josh 14:6; Ps 90:1; 1 Chron 23:14; 2 Chron 30:10; Ezra 3:2) and denotes not only a special relationship between Moses and Yahweh but moreover a remembrance of this relationship within Judaism. George Coats argues it becomes an epithet for Moses and when used of other OT figures (e.g., Elijah, Elisha, Samuel, and David),[75] it functions to connect these figures to Moses's heroic saga and thus to his mediatory role therein.[76]

Coats also believes "Servant of the LORD" (עֶבֶד־יְהוָה)[77] is an epithet connected to Moses (cf. Exod 14:31; Num 12:7–8; Deut 34:5).[78] This idea is most clearly seen in Joshua, which begins with a dual reference to Moses's servant position and to his death (Josh 2:1, 2), and which points back to Deut 34:5. Here the reader is reminded of Moses's selection of Joshua as Israel's new leader (Deut 34:9; 31:1–8) and simultaneously reminded, "Never since has there arisen a prophet in Israel like Moses, whom the Lord knew face to face" (Deut 34:10). Yahweh commissions Joshua, saying he is to remember the deeds of Moses and to "act in accordance with all the law that my servant Moses commanded you" (Josh 1:7), and Joshua directs the people to "remember the words that Moses the servant of the Lord commanded" (Josh 1:13; cf. 8:31, 33; 11:12, 15; 22:2, 5). The people's response is also telling: "Just as we obeyed Moses in all things, so we will obey you. Only may the Lord your God be with you, as he was with Moses!" (Josh 1:17). The proof of Joshua's Moses-like connection to Yahweh is symbolized in his being called a Servant of the Lord at his death (Josh 24:29; cf. Judg 2:8). Outside Joshua, there are multiple other references to Moses as Servant of the Lord, usually tied to his Sanai actions of spokesperson (1 Kgs 8:56; cf. Ps 105:26), tent-maker (2 Chron 1:3; 24:6, 9), and especially law-giver (2 Kgs 18:12; 21:8; Neh 1:8; 9:14; Dan 9:11; Mal 3:22).

---

74. See, Allison, *The New Moses*, 11–95. E.g., Clements, "Jeremiah 1–25," 94–113; McKeating, "Ezekiel 'Prophet Like Moses,'" 97–109; O'Kane, "Isaiah a Prophet," 29–51. See esp. Coats, *Moses: Heroic Man*, 205–11, who argues the new Moses is not limited to a prophetic character.

75. E.g., Judg 13:6–8; 1 Kgs 13; 17:18; 20:28; 2 Kgs 1:9–13; 4:7–42; 1 Sam 9:6–10; Neh 12:24–26.

76. Coats, *Moses: Heroic Man*, 179–82.

77. Cf. הָאֱלֹהִים עֶבֶד in 1 Chron 6:34; Dan 9:11; Neh 10:30.

78. Coats, *Moses: Heroic Man*, 182–85. So also Blenkinsopp, *A History of Prophecy*, 189.

These images, Moses as god-like figure, man of God, and Servant of the Lord, attest to his importance within Judaism and most have a strong connection to Exod 32–34. It is hard to imagine a devout and studied Jew such as Paul being ignorant of the significance of Exod 32–34 and related traditions that branch from it. This raises the question of whether Paul is seeking to elevate his own apostolic position to this legendary status. Such a claim would have been tantamount to self-praise[79] and would have been highly offensive to Paul's Greco-Roman audience.[80] Thrall notes this danger and, therefore, argues Paul's reference to Moses is in response to the comparison being made by his critics, a hypothesis which is nearly impossible to substantiate.[81]

There is of course another option available, namely, that Paul is not claiming to be a new or second Moses figure but making a connection between Moses and Christ[82] and presenting himself and his associates as servants of this new Moses (i.e., Christ). This is similar to the reading argued above concerning Paul's use of Isaiah and his self-understanding as one of many servants of the Servant. This suggestion is strengthened if a link can be shown between Moses and Christ and if a connection between Isaiah's Servant and Moses can be established.

Attempts to show early connections between a second Moses figure and an eschatological messianic figure rely heavily on latter rabbinic and Samaritan writings, with only a few arguing for the concept within the Qumran texts.[83] This casts doubts on whether Paul would make such a connection. Nevertheless, the NT articulates a link between Moses and Christ, which is clearest in Act 3:17–26 and 7:20–53, where both Peter and Stephen quote Deut 18:15, 18 (Acts 3:22; 7:37) in correlation to Jesus. Likewise, all four gospel accounts draw Moses and Jesus together, making an implied, and sometimes overt, link (Matt 17:1–13; Mark 8:27–30; 9:2–8; Luke 24:26–27; John 1:45; 5:39–47; 6:14; 7:40–41; cf. Heb 3:1–6). John Lierman shows strong connections between the way early Christ-followers spoke about Christ and the way Jews were accustomed to speak about Moses.[84] He writes: "The similarity is so extensive that it is difficult to resist the implication that early Christians in thinking about Christ must consciously have

79. See chapter 4.

80. Pace, Damgaard, *Recasting Moses*, 105–11.

81. Thrall, *Second Corinthians*, 227–48. Similarly, Kooten, "Why Did Paul," 149–81; Georgi, *The Opponents of Paul*, 265–300.

82. Bockmuehl, *Revelation and Mystery*, 149.

83. See esp., Fabry, "Mose, der 'Gesalbte JHWHs,'" 129–42. Contra Banks, "The Eschatological Role of Law," 182–85.

84. Lierman, *NT Moses*, 279.

drawn on the figure of Moses in a fuller, more coherent way than has hereto-fore been acknowledged."[85] While a pre-Jesus connection between a second Moses figure and an eschatological messianic figure is inconclusive, the fact that first and second-century C.E. Christ-followers, Jews, and Samaritans all made this association means it was not a difficult leap. The elevated status of Moses throughout Israel's history made him an ideal messianic prototype. It is highly probable Paul could have come to this same conclusion. Neverthe-less, the question remains whether Paul is suggesting, either implicitly or explicitly, this connection in 2 Cor 3–4.

The answer is partial found in the connection between the Servant of Isaiah and Moses. Many scholars argue for a new exodus motif in Isaiah. Bernhard Anderson, contending an Exodus typology in Isa 40–55, lists ten passages where this theme is especially prevalent (Isa 40:3–5; 41:17–20; 42:14–16; 43:1–3; 43:14–21; 48:20–21; 49:8–12; 51:9–10; 52:11–12; 55:12–13).[86] While the emphasis is strongest in Isa 40–55, it is also found in both the earlier (Isa 4:5–6; 10:24–27; 11:16–18; 14:19, 24; 19:19–25; 35:8–10)[87] and later sections of Isaiah (Isa 58:8–11; 63:7–14). However, Moses is only mentioned twice in the MT (Isa 63:11, 12) and once in the LXX (Isa 63:12). These citations sit within a corporate lament (Isa 63:7—64:11; cf. Neh 9), which begins with a remembrance of Yahweh's gracious character as revealed in his deliverance of a rebellious people from Egypt and simultaneously en-quires about the whereabouts of this great deliver (Isa 63:7–14).

There are several connections between this pericope and Exod 32–34. In the MT, Isa 63:9 makes reference to Yahweh's salvation by way of an "an-gel of his presence" (וּמַלְאַךְ פָּנָיו). While this exact phrase is unattested else-where in the OT, it has parallels in Exod 33:2, 14–15 (cf. Exod 23:20–23),[88] which highlights Yahweh's continued presence despite Israel's disobedience. The role of Moses is also highlighted, especially in the LXX. Whereas in the MT God's glorious arm is said to go at the right hand of Moses (Isa 63:12), the LXX reads: ὁ ἀγαγὼν τῇ δεξιᾷ Μωυσῆν, ὁ βραχίων τῆς δόξης αὐτοῦ. The participle ὁ ἀγαγών points back to Yahweh as the one who leads Moses. However, the antecedent of ὁ βραχίων is more ambiguous. It could func-

---

85. Lierman, NT Moses, 287. Cf. Hafemann, Paul, Moses, 102 n. 32, 103.

86. Anderson, "Exodus Typology in Second Isaiah," 181–82.

87. See O'Kane, "Isaiah a Prophet," 46–47; Beaulieu, "Egypt as God's People," 207–18; Watts, Isaiah 34–66, 81. Watts also believes the twenty-three uses of "redeem/redeemer" and thirty-one uses of "save/savior" are related to the Exodus narrative (106–7).

88. Cf. Childs, Isaiah, 523; Oswalt, Isaiah 40–66, 607. The LXX alters the MT to place the focus directly on Yahweh. This alteration is likely in keeping with the altered LXX version of Exod 33:14–15, which omits the word "presence."

tion with ὁ ἀγαγών as an attributive construction, which would make the translation similar to the MT—"the arm of his glory which led Moses by the right hand." Nevertheless, the distance of ὁ βραχίων from the participle does not make this a straightforward reading. Furthermore, ὁ βραχίων appears to begin a subordinate clause, which makes the NETS rendering unlikely ("Where is his glorious arm?"). Instead, the word order in the Greek, with Μωυσῆν directly followed by ὁ βραχίων, may signal an appositional construction.[89] A more verbatim translation would then read: "the one who led by the right hand Moses, the arm of his glory."

Reference to Moses as an extension of Yahweh's glory is an allusion to Exod 34:29–35. This reading is strengthened by the LXX's alteration of Isa 63:11, which singularizes the Hebrew רֹעֵי, and replaces "sea" with "land." It, therefore, points back to Moses's call—"the one who brought up from the land the shepherd of the sheep" (cf. Exod 3–4). Both in the MT and moreover in the LXX, the author/redactor invites the readers to join in calling Yahweh to a particular action, that of raising up another servant[90] like Moses, through whom Yahweh's glory might shine once more, so the people might again experience the Holy Spirit in their midst.[91]

When this Mosaic reference is combined with the pervasive new Exodus motif and the OT understanding of Servant of the Lord as an epithet for Moses, the probability of construing a second Moses backdrop for the Isaianic Servant increases substantially.[92] The Isaianic Servant's role, like Moses's, is to allow Yahweh to be glorified through him (Isa 49:3; cf. 40:5) by drawing together and delivering the tribes of Jacob and the survivors of Israel (cf. Jer 31:31–34; Ezek 37:15–28) and by being a light to the nations (Isa 49:6). This is not a resurrected Moses but a new mediator, whose connection to Yahweh and intercessory role both models the Moses tradition and surpasses it (esp. Isa 52:13—53:12).[93]

Summary

The foundation for a more fruitful interpretation of 2 Cor 3:1—4:6 has now been laid through this brief literary analysis, both grammatical and

89. See, Wallace, *Greek Grammar*, 62.

90. The Syr. reads "Moses his servant" rather than "Moses his people."

91. Similarly, Oswalt, *Isaiah 40–66*, 608; Oswalt, *Isaiah*, 666. Cf. Clifford, "Narrative and Lament in Isaiah," 94–100, who argues Moses is the hypothetical speaker of vv. 11–12, who intercedes on behalf of Israel as he did in Exod 32:30–44 and 33:13–16.

92. So Coats, *Moses: Heroic Man*, 207–11.

93. Coats, *Moses: Heroic Man*, 208.

intertextual. It has been argued that Paul's *fpp* are best understood as genuine plurals which include We-Ministers and We-Apostles. The proposal for understanding Paul's *fpp* as invitations to We-Community has also been posited. Paul's language is intentionally nuanced with the hopes the Corinthians will feel included and begin to participate in the We-Minister/We-Apostles. In this way, they function paradigmatically. This reading allows for an alternate motive for Paul's argumentation. Rather than primarily being concerned with defense of his apostleship, Paul seeks to move the Corinthians toward embracing their new eschatological identity in Christ.

It has also been argued that Isa 40–66 sits behind Paul's discourse in 2 Cor 2:14—7:4 and therein Paul develops an understanding of Christ as the singular Servant and all believers, himself included, as servants of the Servant. Important aspects of Gignilliat's and Hafemann's readings have been brought together, apart from their narrowed apostolic-centricities. It has been discovered that 2 Cor 3:1—4:6 is greatly enriched when the Exod 32–34 narrative is read through the lens of Isa 40–66. Paul's comparison in 2 Cor 3:1—4:6 is not between Paul and Moses or even between Paul's ministry and Moses's ministry but between Christ and Moses. Christ is developed as a second Moses figure, which parallels Paul's understanding of the singular Isaianic Servant. When viewed from this perspective, Paul's argument takes on an entirely new shape. Rather than trying to assert his apostolic authority, Paul's self-understanding as one of the servants of the Servant is intentionally extended to his Corinthian audience. Here the beauty and brilliance of Paul's nuanced use of the *fpp* is revealed. Paul calls the Corinthians to embrace their new eschatological identity as servants of the Servant by extending God's forgiveness and reconciliation to them through the covenant renewal imagery of Exod 32–34 and through an allusion to his own Christophany. These proposals will be substantiated in the detailed exegesis of 2 Cor 3:1—4:6 below.

Exegesis of Second Corinthians 3:1—4:6

Second Corinthians 3:1–6

Paul begins 2 Cor 3:1a with a rhetorical question concerning commendation. Mention of "epistles of commendation" (συστατικῶν ἐπιστολῶν) is in response to the current negative situation created by the "super apostles" (cf. 2 Cor 10:12, 18; 12:11), and possibly due to misunderstanding brought about by Paul's first letter (1 Corinthians).[94] The adverb πάλιν creates some

---

94. Damgaard, *Recasting Moses*, 104–11.

confusion as to when Paul and the others previously commended themselves (cf. 2 Cor 5:12). Nevertheless, the focus is currently on the negative aspects of such a self-commendation. Paul moves the Corinthians toward an understanding of their own importance within the ministry of the new covenant, of which Paul and his associates are servants. Second Corinthians 3:2–3 forms an AB–AB pattern with the first tier (3:2) providing a transition from the plural "epistles of commendation" (3:1) to the singular "epistle of Christ" (3:3). The diagrammed translation[95] is as follows:

    (A) ²You yourselves are our epistle

        (B) [an epistle] having been engraved[96] on our hearts, being known and being read by all people

    (A₁) ³You yourselves are manifesting[97] that you are an epistle from Christ, ministered to by us

        (B₁) [an epistle] having been engraved[98] not with ink but with the Spirit of the living God, not on tablets of stone but on tablets of hearts of flesh.

By moving from the plural *epistles* to the singular *epistle* (A), Paul is able to stress the unity he desires for the Corinthians, both amongst themselves and between them and the Pauline cohort; the former is evidenced in the emphatic ὑμεῖς ἐστε and the latter by the ἡμῶν. The Corinthians have become one with Paul and his associates by way of God's engraving action (B; B1), of which Paul and his associates played a significant role (A1). Paul is adamant that the focus should be placed firmly on God (2 Cor 3:5–6). Paul does not claim authorship of this letter; Christ is the author (ἐπιστολὴ Χριστοῦ[99]). The role of Paul and his associates is that of ministers or servants (διακονηθεῖσα). The reason they do not need letters of commendation is because God is the one who has done these things and the evidence of his work is "being made known" through the Pauline cohort and "being manifest" by the Corinthians. Both of these groups together form a single epistle of commendation attesting to the sufficiency of Christ.

---

95. Author's translation.

96. Attributive participle, modifying ἡ ἐπιστολή in (A).

97. Participle is translated as a middle because of its correlation to (A).

98. Attributive participle, modifying ἡ ἐπιστολή in (A1).

99. Taken as a subjective genitive. So Martin, *Second Corinthians*, 51; Furnish, *Second Corinthians*, 182. Cf. Harris, *Second Corinthians*, 263, who views Paul as the amanuensis.

A proper understanding of Christ's authority and work is the safeguard against self-praise, both for the Pauline cohort and for the Corinthians (2 Cor 3:4). Verse 4 may signal a shift from Paul's use of the *fpp* as We-Ministers/ We-Apostles in verses 1–3 to We-Community in verses 4–6, at least in a paradigmatic sense. While hard to prove, it does fit the flow of Paul's purpose of unification presented in verses 1–3 and in the rest of Paul's argument in 2 Cor 3:7–18, which climaxes in a definite We-Community statement (3:18). The difficulty with this reading comes in verse 6a with the reference to "ministers of a new covenant" (διακόνους καινῆς διαθήκης), which many commentators believe is part of a We-I statement pointing back to Paul's Damascus encounter.[100] This reading ignores the *fpp* and focuses strictly on the comparison between Moses's and Paul's servant roles. However, διάκονος is widely used by Paul to designate *not* himself alone but also fellow servants (Rom 16:1; 1 Cor 3:5; Phil 1:1; 1 Thess 3:2[101]), other authorities (Rom 13:4), false-servants (2 Cor 11:15, 23), and Christ (Rom 15:8; Gal 2:17). Apart from Phil 1:1, it appears to be a general term referring to Christian service rather than to a particular office or position;[102] thus it may also include the Corinthians. Even as Paul's Christophanic experience sits behind these words, his pluralization of them is designed to disseminate the focus.

Reference to "new covenant" would immediately bring forward imagery of the Lord's Supper (1 Cor 11:25), which for Paul's audience is connected to Paul's plea for unification amongst the Corinthians (1 Cor 11:17–22; 27–34). Here, Paul re-contextualizes the concept for a similar purpose. The language of new covenant has been linked to Jer 31:31 (LXX Jer 38:31).[103] Therein, the prophet proclaims a future day when God will establish a "new covenant" with the houses of Israel and Judah. God will place his laws in their minds and write them upon their hearts (cf. Ezek 36:26–27). The prophet also contrasts this new covenant to the previous covenant made with those God brought out of Egypt, a covenant they broke (Jer 31:32).

Jeremiah 31:32–33 is often seen as a reference to Exod 19:1—24:11.[104] But mention of Israel's covenant disobedience makes Exod 32–34 another possibility.[105] If so, mention of the new covenant may actually be an allusion

---

100. So Hafemann, *Paul, Moses,* 100–106; Kim, *Origin of Paul's Gospel,* 11; Harris, *Second Corinthians,* 270; Hughes, *Second Corinthians,* 93; Furnish, *Second Corinthians,* 184; Thrall, *Second Corinthians,* 231.

101. The reading καὶ διάκονον τοῦ θεοῦ is well attested: e.g., ℵ A P Ψ 81 629* 1739.

102. So Dunn, *Jesus and the Spirit,* 288; cf. Hafemann, *Paul, Moses,* 110–14.

103. See esp. Hafemann, *Paul, Moses,* 119–40.

104. E.g., Thompson, *Jeremiah,* 580.

105. So Dearman, *Jeremiah and Lamentations,* 287.

to the covenant renewal of Exod 34:10–28.[106] Terence Fretheim argues that Exod 34:10–28 actually depicts a *"new* covenant grounded in a new act of God on behalf of Israel."[107] This may mean that Paul is already grounding his argument in the Exodus narrative and echoes of Jer 31 and Ezek 36 are secondary.[108] They sit in the back of Paul's mind but the Exodus narrative is still front and center as it has been since 2 Cor 3:3.

Paul concludes 2 Cor 3:6 with a contrast between the letter (γράμμα) which kills and the Spirit (πνεῦμα) which gives life. The latter points back to verse 3b (ἐγγεγραμμένη . . . πνεύματι θεοῦ ζῶντος) and makes a direct link between "ministers of a new covenant" and "epistle of Christ." The singular epistle, which represents all believers, is aligned with the plural minsters, which currently represents Paul and his associates. Paul's purpose in making this connection is to invite his readers to realize they are already included by way of being connected to the new covenant, which is connected to Christ. This foreshadows Paul's words in 2 Cor 5:17.

The former, γράμμα, points forward to Moses and the "old covenant" (2 Cor 3:14; cf. Gal 4:21—5:1). Paul consciously constructs a comparison between Christ and Moses, not between Moses and himself. Paul make a deliberate shift from ἐπιστολή to γράμμα so there is no confusion between the continued comparisons in 2 Cor 3:7–18. Γράμμα is not equivalent to Torah just as πνεῦμα is not equivalent to Gospel (cf. Rom 2:29; 7:6).[109] Paul is careful in his wording. Both γράμμα and πνεῦμα in verse 6b are connected to διακόνους rather than to καινῆς διαθήκης.[110] Grammatically, this reading is more difficult. Nevertheless, in light of the subsequent verses, this reading is preferred;[111] otherwise, the antithesis between new covenant and old covenant is lost and letter/Spirit is easily misunderstood as pertaining to two different new covenants.[112] Worse still, this reading may (mis)interpret Paul as equating life with new covenant and death with old covenant.

Paul's point is that as servants of the new covenant, he and his associates are servants of Spirit and life rather than servants of letter and death (cf. 2 Cor 3:7–8; Rom 7:6). Stated differently, they are servants of the

---

106. Kaiser, "The Old Promise," 17, writes: "Both Hebrew *hadas* and Greek *kainos* frequently mean 'to renew' or 'to restore.'" Cf. Fretheim, *Exodus*, 308.

107. Fretheim, *Exodus*, 308, emphasis his.

108. Similarly, Watson, *Paul and Hermeneutics*, 288 and n. 33.

109. So correctly, Hafemann, *Second Corinthians*, 130–33.

110. *Pace*, Harris, *Second Corinthians*, 271; Thrall, *Second Corinthians*, 234; Stock-hausen, *Moses' Veil*, 34, 62.

111. So also Hafemann, *Paul, Moses*, 157; Westerholm, "'Letter' and 'Spirit'," 240; cf. Barnett, *Second Corinthians*, 175 n. 23; Carver, *Second Corinthians*, 128–29.

112. Murphy-O'Connor, *Theology of Second Corinthians*, 32–33.

Servant Christ rather than servants of the servant Moses. It is a seemingly minor difference but with major implications. If death is connected to covenant then God himself is found deficient. However, if death is connected to Moses's ministry and construed through the lens of *Heilsgeschichte*, it does not automatically indict Moses or the old covenant. Rather than attacking Moses, Paul's words are a *qal wāḥômer* comparison. This technique requires the audience to have a proper understanding and respect for Moses, who serves as a starting place for understanding the surpassing greatness of Christ (cf. Phil 3:8).[113] In a predominately Gentile church, it is safe to assume some of their positive estimation of Moses can be accredited to Paul's earlier teaching (cf. Acts 18:9–11).

Second Corinthians 3:7–11

In 2 Cor 3:7–11, Paul continues his Moses/letter, Christ/Spirit comparison as he brings his audience deeper into the Exod 32–34 narrative. Key to interpretation is a clear understanding of glory language as Paul employs δόξα thirteen times (out of nineteen) and δοξάζω two times (out of three) in 2 Cor 3:7—4:6. This concept unites the two correlating sides of Paul's *synkrisis* as both share in the divine glory, which should be interpreted in line with the Hebrew כָּבוֹד, and thus with Yahweh's powerful presence (cf. Exod 33:18–23; Isa 6:1–5).[114]

This explains Paul's reading of Exod 34:30 (LXX) in 2 Cor 3:7. Moses's "ministry of death" came with the full weight of God's powerful presence, which prevented the people from gazing at his face. The Exodus narrative says the people were afraid to approach Moses, which echoes Exod 20:18–19 where the people were afraid to approach Yahweh because of the spectacular manifestation they witnessed upon Mount Sinai. While "glory" is not employed in Exod 20:18–19 LXX (although cf. Exod 24:16–17 LXX), the powerful presence of Yahweh is evident—a presence now manifest on the face of Moses (Exod 34:29–35) as a result of his extraordinary encounter with Yahweh in Exod 33:18–23. One is immediately reminded of Isa 63:12 LXX and the understanding of Moses as an extension of God's glory. Since Moses is Yahweh's selected, and Israel's elected, spokesperson, they cannot remove themselves from his presence and, therefore, the veil

---

113. Duff, "Glory in the Ministry of Death," 319–20.

114. Contra Garrett, "Veiled Hearts," 747, who believes Paul is speaking about Yahweh's goodness (טוֹב) as displayed in Exod 33:19.

provides a barrier protecting the people from their valid fear of death (cf. Exod 19:9b–25).[115]

Paul's use of the participle τὴν καταργουμένην should not be translated adverbially since it is articular and stands in an attributive relationship with τὴν δόξαν. Therefore, translations showing concession (NIV) or causality (ISV) should be avoided. This does not lessen the difficulty in understanding the intended meaning of καταργέω and of the continuous aspect of the present tense. Hafemann argues καταργέω is never used with the sense of "fading away" and this interpretation by others is based solely on 2 Cor 3. In light of Paul's other passive uses of καταργέω and the Exod 32–34 backdrop, Hafemann believes it carries the meaning of being rendered inoperative in regard to effects.[116] This interpretation alleviates problems caused by translations such as "fading away"[117] or "being abolished."[118] For example, neither the Exodus narrative[119] nor subsequent traditions speak of such an event. Rather, most allude to the opposite effect, the permanent glory of Moses's face.[120]

Moses's glory, which is God's reflective glory, is often directly or indirectly equated with the old covenant. This becomes problematic if the old covenant is abolished by God. Paul does not believe God eradicates his own glory because God had a greater glory prepared as part of the new covenant. Instead, it is Moses who, acting on God's behalf, renders the effects of God's glory inoperative by way of the veil, while still providing an accessible Yahwistic presence for Israel.[121] The glory Moses possessed is Yahweh's glory

115. Similarly, Hafemann, *Paul, Moses*, 312, believes that Moses's veiling himself was an act of grace and mercy.

116. Hafemann, *Paul, Moses*, 301–9; Hafemann, *Second Corinthians*, 147–48; so also Baker, "Glory of Moses' Face," 1–15; Garrett, "Veiled Hearts," 739–45; cf. Hays, *Echoes of Scripture*, 134.

117. Harris, *Second Corinthians*, 284–85; Hughes, *Second Corinthians*, 102. Cf. Collins, *Second Corinthians*, 83.

118. Barrett, *Second Corinthians*, 116; Matera, *Second Corinthians*, 82–83; Furnish, *Second Corinthians*, 203. Cf. Thrall, *Second Corinthians*, 244.

119. *Pace*, Childs, *Isaiah*, 621, who argues that Midrashic exegesis could have deduced from Exod 34 in correlation with Exod 40:35 that Moses's glory was not permanent.

120. Belleville, *Reflections of Glory*, 26–72, lists a variety of references on this subject including: *S. Eli. Rab.* 18; *L.A.B.* 19:16; *Pesiq. Rab.* 21:6; *Tg. Onq.* on Deut 34:7. She also lists some rabbinic texts she interprets as showing a transitory view of Moses's glory (67).

121. There may be a parallel between Yahweh's actions in Exod 33:20–33 and Moses's actions in Exod 34:33–35. As Yahweh protects Moses from the full weight of his glory by covering him with his hand, so Moses protects the people by covering his face with the veil.

and is the same glory which is part of the new covenant.[122] What changes is not the glory, but the need for a veil to pacify the powerful presence of this glory; what changes is the greater presence of the Spirit, which is the hallmark of the new covenant (2 Cor 1:22; 3:8; 5:5; cf. Isa 44:1–5; 59:20–21; Ezek 36:26–27; Joel 2:28–32).

The ministry of the Spirit particularly equates with the ministry of righteousness (2 Cor 3:9). For Paul, the latter is closely related to the ministry of reconciliation (2 Cor 5:18–21) and both are closely related to the role of the Servant in Isaiah, whom Paul understands to be Christ (cf. Isa 53:4–12). Second Corinthians 5:16–21 provides other parallels to 2 Cor 3:7–18, which prove helpful. First, Paul understands Christ as providing the means for reconciliation between God and humanity by way of being made sin (2 Cor 5:21). This is, for Paul, the deficiency in the ministry of Moses and the old covenant. While Moses is able to mediate an outward peace between Yahweh and Israel (Exod 34:7–14) and secure Yahweh's sustained presence (Exod 33:12–17), he is unable to provide a means for internal cleansing (cf. 2 Cor 7:1; Ezek 36:25), which would allow the relationship to become internal and everlasting. Moses's ministry is one of the external letter rather than of the internal Spirit. This is why Moses's ministry is ultimately one of condemnation and death. This is not a condemnation of Moses or of God's old covenant. It is a declaration of the supremacy of the Spirit (2 Cor 3:10), which is ultimately the supremacy of Christ (2 Cor 3:14).

Second, Paul can speak of believers becoming the righteousness of God only because the ministry of righteousness, which abounds in glory, has had and is having its desired effect. The righteousness of the Servant Christ (cf. Phil 2:6–11) has made many righteous (Isa 53:11; cf. 1 Cor 1:30; Gal 2:16–17; 3:24; Phil 3:9); and since the "ministry of righteousness" is equal to the "ministry of the Spirit," then Paul and his associates by way of being "servants of the life-giving Spirit" are servant of the Servant Christ (contra 2 Cor 11:15). Paul is continuing to bring together the connection between Christ and the Spirit, which began in 2 Cor 3:3. Ironically, this life-giving Spirit, which is given to all believers (2 Cor 1:22: 5:5), results in death to self for all those who follow in the footsteps of the Servant (2 Cor 5:14–16; cf. 4:10–11).

The capstone of Paul's *qal wāḥômer* comes in 2 Cor 3:10–11. To understand verse 10 one must determine the antecedent of the neuter articular participle τὸ δεδοξασμένον. Hafemann correctly disqualifies the masculine νόμος, the feminine δόξα, and the feminine διακονία.[123] How-

---

122. So Hafemann, *Paul, Moses*, 322–23.

123. *Pace*, Furnish, *Second Corinthians*, 204; Matera, *Second Corinthians*, 89; Harris,

ever, he and others see the neuter as a reference "to the ministry of the old covenant *as a whole*, especially its theological purpose (v. 9a) and result (v. 7)."[124] But διαθήκη is also feminine. Therefore, it is better to take τὸ πρόσωπον from 2 Cor 3:7 as the antecedent, which aligns with Exod 34:30, 35.[125] Rather than speaking broadly about the entire old covenant, Paul is here speaking specifically about the face of Moses (τὸ πρόσωπον Μωϋσέως) in comparison to the "surpassing glory," which is representative of Christ. The use of "surpassing" (ὑπερβάλλω/ὑπερβολή) appears multiple time in this letter usually juxtaposing suffering and God's glorious power (2 Cor 4:7, 17; 12:7; cf. 1:8; 9:14). Paul reminds the Corinthians that God's glory is intrinsically tied to suffering, for both Christ and his followers. Thus a paraphrase of verse 10 is as follows: "For indeed, [the face of Moses] which has been glorified has not been glorified in this respect, on account of the surpassing glory [of Christ]."

This interpretation is strengthened when taken together with verse 11. Like τὸ δεδοξασμένον, the neuter articular participle τὸ καταργούμενον also points back to the face of Moses, rather than to the feminine δόξα as it had in verse 7. Paul's focus sharpens and rather than the glory itself being rendered inoperative by the veil, the face of Moses is rendered inoperative by glory. Many translations interpret the preposition διά as "with" (ESV, NIV, NASB, RSV) or drop the preposition and translate the noun adjectivally—"was glorious" (KJV; NKJV; HCSB). However, διά followed by the genitive (δόξης) is more generally translated as "through" or "by." Moreover, when following a passive verb such as τὸ καταργούμενον, it expresses intermediate agency and therefore "by" is the preferred meaning. The answer to how the face of Moses is being rendered inoperative *by* glory is found in verse 11b. Again, the neuter articular participle τὸ μένον points back to the neuter πρόσωπον, but rather than a reference to Moses's face, it is a reference to Christ's face, which is said to remain in glory. The face that remains in glory is equated with the "surpassing glory" of Christ, which is the same glory which renders Moses's face inoperative. This is not meant to degrade the glorious face of Moses, but rather to elevate the glorious face of Christ. The ministry of the

Second Corinthians, 288; Belleville, *Reflections of Glory*, 202–3. Stockhausen, *Moses' Veil*, 121, argues for this view saying that the neuter in Greek can be used to emphasis "a general quality rather than an individual reality."

124. Hafemann, *Paul, Moses*, 323, emphasis his; similarly, Harris, *Second Corinthians*, 288; Barnett, *Second Corinthians*, 186 and n. 34. Hafemann makes a distinction between the old covenant and ministry of death, which he believes has been abolished in Christ, and the glory of God that is revealed in the old covenant and remains in the new covenant (324 n. 213). Contra Dumbrell, "Paul's Use of Exodus 34," 186–87, who believes the old covenant is not abolished but built upon (cf. Jer 31:31–34).

125. Thrall, *Second Corinthians*, 250.

Servant Christ is superior to the ministry of the Servant Moses to the extent the latter is eclipsed by the former. This eclipsing is partially in terms of effectiveness. The glory of Moses's face was rendered ineffective for all but Moses whereas the glory of Christ's face is able to be experienced and even extended to all (2 Cor 3:18).[126]

This comparison is important to Paul because his argument relies on an acceptance of Christ as the central Servant rather than Moses. The theme of Exod 32–34 is not Moses's shining face but the story of covenant violation and covenant renewal. Paul's desire is to emphasis the new eschatological covenant made possible through Christ and to invite the Corinthians to renew their covenant commitment to God, to Paul and his associates, and to the body of Christ as a whole.

Second Corinthians 3:12–18

A slight shift in Paul's argument takes place in 2 Cor 3:12 as he returns to the *fpp* (cf. 2 Cor 3:7–11). Having shown the amelioration of Christ and the new covenant, Paul, for the first time, makes a comparison between Moses and himself. However, this comparison is not to himself alone but to all believers; Paul is using the *fpp* in the sense of We-Community throughout 2 Cor 3:12–18.[127] "This hope," which Paul refers to in verse 12a, points back to verses 10–11, to the surpassing glory which remains, and thus to Christ himself.[128] It is because[129] of this hope in Christ that believers are able to employ great boldness (v. 12b). While the type of boldness cannot be confidently determined, if understood in the context of Exod 34:29–35, it may be a reference to the action[130] of approaching the glory of God without fear, thus inviting the Corinthians to fully engage the covenant (cf. Exod 20:20; Wis 4:20—5:1). It is also possible that Paul's use of πολλῇ παρρησίᾳ is meant to echo the πολλῷ μᾶλλον of verses 9 and 11 (cf. v. 8), which points to the surpassing glory of Christ. By connecting πολλῇ παρρησίᾳ with χρώμεθα, which typically means "make use of" (cf. 1 Cor 7:21, 31; 9:12, 15; 2 Cor

126. Cf. Garrett, "Veiled Hearts," 747.

127. So also Barnett, *Second Corinthians*, 190 and n. 4.

128. *Pace*, Hafemann, *Paul, Moses*, 336–37, who believes "this hope" points back to 2 Cor 3:8. See Hughes, *Second Corinthians*, 107, for a list of 5 options for the referent of hope.

129. Ἔχοντες should be understood causatively.

130. The addition of "speech" to παρρησία is unwarranted here (contra NASB, KJV, NKJV). While παρρησία can pertain to speech, it can also pertain to action, which fits the context better (cf. 2 Cor 7:4; Phil 1:20; Philem 8). Also see Belleville, *Reflections of Glory*, 194–98.

1:17; 13:10), Paul claims those who have the hope of Christ are able to make use of Christ's glory. "Great boldness" is only possible for those living in the eschatological new covenant/new creation sphere. This is what differentiates believers from those residing under the old covenant.

This boldness is often compared to Moses's apparent lack of boldness, even impropriety, in veiling his face (v. 13).[131] However, the οὐ καθάπερ ("not just as") does not contrast believers' boldness versus Moses's cowardice. Instead, Paul focuses on the manner in which believers carry out their boldness in contrast to the manner in which Moses was forced to carry out his boldness. Paul's positive depiction of Moses, as one who was able to withstand the glory of God's powerful presence, means Moses is illustrative of the new covenant, although still tied to the old covenant. Moses, like believers, had the same hope that allowed him to employ great boldness. Yet, because of Israel's disobedience and deficiency of Spirit (2 Cor 3:14; 4:4; cf. Exod 33:5), Moses's act of great boldness came in the form of veiling his face. It was an act of selfless grace and mercy so that the Israelites would not be destroyed by the full weight of Yahweh's glory (cf. Exod 32:7–14, 32; 33:12–17). Paul's point is that because the new covenant has been inaugurated through Christ, believers no longer have veiled face (2 Cor 3:16, 18) and thus may more freely utilize their boldness to reveal this new reality.

As in verse 10, Paul's use of τοῦ καταργουμένου in verse 13 takes τὸ πρόσωπον as its referent. Verse 13 is best read through the lens of verses 10–11 in correlation with Exod 34:33. In Exodus, Moses's giving of the commandment was done with unveiled face. It was only after this point that Moses covered his face for the dual reasons of protecting the people from the full weight of Yahweh's powerful presence (cf. 2 Cor 3:7) and also to assure that the people did not worship him instead of the source of his glory.[132] In verse 13, Paul argues that part of the reason Moses veiled his face was so that the people would stop gazing at him, so as to recognize the surpassing glory of God, proleptically, Christ. The τέλος should be rendered "end"[133] rather than "goal,"[134] as Paul is making a hyperbolic comparison similar to

131. Esp. Watson, *Paul and Hermeneutics*, 291–96; cf. Thrall, *Second Corinthians*, 255; Matera, *Second Corinthians*, 90; Barrett, *Second Corinthians*, 119; Belleville, *Reflections of Glory*, 198.

132. Similarly, Harris, *Second Corinthians*, 300, who says it was to "prevent preoccupation with outward δόξα."

133. Cf. Belleville, *Reflections of Glory*, 201–2; Martin, *Second Corinthians*, 68; Stockhausen, *Moses' Veil*, 126, although all with different reasons and conclusions than here. Stockhausen says Paul intended the ambiguity and thus the word carries both ideas, though in other places she argues more for "end" (120).

134. Thrall, *Second Corinthians*, 257; Barrett, *Second Corinthians*, 119–20; Wright, *Climax of the Covenant*, 181.

the one made in verses 10–11. Moses's face is coming to an end in the light of Christ's surpassing glory.

Verse 14a is still wrapped in the Exodus narrative as it refers to Israel's idolatry with the golden calf (Exod 32:9; 33:3, 5),[135] possibly through the interpretation of Isa 63:17—"Why, O Lord, do you make us stray from your ways and harden our heart, so that we do not fear you?"[136] (cf. Isa 29:10; 42:17–20; Deut 29:2–4). The ἀλλά is a reference to the negative outcome of Moses's positive attempt to help the people see the surpassing glory. Isaiah 63:17 may also be in Paul's purview in 2 Cor 3:15 when the veil moves from being over "their minds" to being over "their heart" as the MT uses the singular לֵב (cf. the LXX's τὰς καρδίας).[137]

Verse 14b makes a shift to the present tense, which is meant to engage Paul's audience[138] with an eschatological quandary. The phrase ἄχρι (γὰρ) τῆς σήμερον ἡμέρας may be an allusion to Deut 29:3 LXX—ἕως τῆς ἡμέρας ταύτης, which is also part of a Mosaic covenant renewal narrative. Paul's use of ἡμέρα usually carries eschatological significance,[139] and here and in verse 15, Paul juxtaposes the past and the present. Paul reminds the Corinthians that although they are living in the eschatological now, as part of the new covenant people, there are still those who continue to exist under the constraints of the old covenant (παλαιᾶς διαθήκης) age, who continue to hear and read Moses and the Torah he represents through the "same veil" (τὸ αὐτὸ κάλυμμα). Like the Israelites of Moses's day, they too are unable to see beyond Moses's glorious face[140] to the surpassing glory, now revealed to be Christ. In verse 14c, Paul employs his fourth and final use of καταργέω. Here, however, the present passive verb (καταργεῖται) refers to the "not unveiled" (μὴ ἀνακαλυπτόμενον)[141] veil rather than to Moses's face, and certainly not to παλαιᾶς διαθήκης.[142] Thus, the veil itself is being rendered inoperative in

---

135. Note Paul's use of the aorist ἐπωρώθη.

136. Goldingay, *Isaiah*, 360, writes: "'Why do you harden our hearts?' implies that Yahweh has treated Israel and Pharaoh in the same way and that Yahweh lies behind the recalcitrance that Israel begins to show even at Sinai."

137. The difference between plural "minds" and singular "heart" should not be overemphasized, nor should the difference between mind and heart; they are more likely complementary. Cf. the NRSV translation of v. 15.

138. So Baker, "Glory of Moses' Face," 13.

139. Rom 2:5, 16; 13:12, 13; 1 Cor 1:14; 6:2; 2 Cor 1:8; 5:5; Phil 1:6, 10; 2:16; 1 Thess 5:2, 4, 5, 8; cf. Rom 11:8; 2 Cor 4:3.

140. *Pace*, Thrall, *Second Corinthians*, 263–64, who thinks the veil lies over the old covenant and not over Moses's face.

141. See Harris, *Second Corinthians*, 303, for four options on how to deal with this participle.

142. Contra Dunn, *Christ and Spirit*, 117 n. 10; Garrett, "Veiled Hearts," 758; cf.

Christ. The present tense is imperfective as Paul focuses on the already and not yet effects of Christ's actions.

Verses 15–16 both parallel and advance Paul's point from verse 14.[143]

14b For until the day of today this same veil remains at the reading of the old covenant, not being unveiled,	14c because in Christ it is being rendered inoperative.
15 But as far as today whenever Moses is being read, a veil lies over their heart;	16 now whenever a person turns to the Lord, the veil is being removed.

Moses is likely a metonym for old covenant.[144] Christ and Moses are juxtaposed in such a way as to highlight the superiority of Christ and the new covenant over Moses and the old covenant. The parallel between verses 14c and 16 also suggests Lord and Christ are synonymous.[145] But this conclusion is greatly contested. Since, verse 16 is an altered quotation of Exod 34:34a LXX,[146] it appears Paul is inviting his readers to do as Moses has done, to go to the Lord and have their veils removed. Within the Exodus narrative, κύριος is undoubtedly Yahweh, making many deduce Paul must also be referring to Yahweh.[147] Thus, the continued narratological reading of Exodus alone is the strongest argument for this position.[148]

Mehrdad Fatehi makes an argument for κύριος as a reference to Christ and not Yahweh. The following six points are among his strongest: (1) the connection between Christ, the Spirit, and the new covenant in 2 Cor 3:3 shows Christ to be the new covenant counterpart of Yahweh; (2) the emphasis is on the veil in 2 Cor 3:13–18 and 3:14c clearly states this veil is removed in Christ; (3) the parallelism between ἐν Χριστῷ in 2 Cor 3:14c and κύριος in 3:16; (4) the multiple connections between 2 Cor 3:16–18 and 4:1–6, which favors a Christological interpretation of the former; (5) the fact Paul refers

Furnish, *Second Corinthians*, 210.

143. Author's translation. Cf. Fatehi, *Spirit's Relation*, 294.

144. Harris, *Second Corinthians*, 305

145. So Fatehi, *Spirit's Relation*, 294; Hooker, "Beyond Things which are Written," 301.

146. *Pace*, Emily Wong, "The Lord is the Spirit," 48–72.

147. So Dunn, *Christ and Spirit*, 123–24; Furnish, *Second Corinthians*, 212; Belleville, *Reflections of Glory*, 255; Harris, *Second Corinthians*, 308–9; Thrall, *Second Corinthians*, 272–73; Fee, *God's Empowering Presence*, 312.

148. Thrall, *Second Corinthians*, 271–72, while arguing in favor of κύριος referring to Yahweh, notes Paul does sometimes use κύριος in an OT quotation to refer to Christ (e.g., Rom 10:13; 1 Cor 10:22; cf. 1 Cor 2:16; 10:26: 2 Cor 8:21) and that κύριος without the definite article often refers to Christ (e.g., Rom 1:7; 10:9; 1 Cor 1:3; 4:5; Phil 2:11), especially with a prepositional phrase. For example, Paul's use of ἐν κυρίῳ, used thirty-four times in the undisputed Pauline letters and almost all in reference to Christ.

to Christ as "the Lord of glory" in 1 Cor 2:8; and (6) since all the main verbs from 2 Cor 3:14b forward change from the past tense to the present, Paul has already made a switch to speaking about the application of the Exodus narrative in his current situation.[149]

Additionally, throughout this large pericope (2 Cor 3:1—4:6), Paul utilizes θεός and not κύριος to refer to Yahweh (2 Cor 3:3, 4, 5; 4:2, 4, 6, 7). Paul's use of the phrase Ἰησοῦν Χριστὸν κύριον in 2 Cor 4:5 makes it unlikely Paul is referring to Yahweh as κύριος in 2 Cor 3:16–18. Furthermore, most scholars correctly see Paul's use of the articular ὁ κύριος in 2 Cor 3:17 as anaphoric, pointing back to the κύριος of 2 Cor 3:16. However, by itself, 2 Cor 3:17 seems to point to κύριος as Christ, since the act of spiritual liberation (ἐλευθερία and its cognates) is usually connected to Christ (cf. Rom 8:2; 1 Cor 9:1; Gal 2:4; 5:1).[150] The implicit connection between Christ and Spirit in 2 Cor 3:3, 6, 8 foreshadows the more explicit statement of 2 Cor 3:17. Taken together, all of these arguments solidify the conclusion that κύριος in 2 Cor 3:16–18 is a reference to Christ and not Yahweh.

It is only after this debate is settled that the context can be reengaged. If 2 Cor 3:14–16 is read together with old covenant/Moses and Christ/Lord acting as contrasting parallels, then the contrasting parallel between verses 15 and 16 must also be taken seriously.

| Verse 15 | whenever [a person] reads Moses | veil lies over their heart |
| Verse 16 | whenever a person turns to the Lord | veil is taken away |

Although verse 16 is a paraphrased quotation of Exod 34:34 LXX, Paul makes significant changes for the sake of his current argument. Instead of speaking about turning to Yahweh, Paul is contrasting the present situation of people turning to Moses and the old covenant versus those turning to Christ and the new covenant. Once again, this is not a negative statement about Moses or the old covenant. Moses's veil has been removed because of the new eschatological reality brought about by Christ. Moreover, the need for the veil has also been removed. The people are able to look upon the glory of God because Christ has mediated an everlasting covenant with the Father, which removes sin and allows for true reconciliation. For Paul, the people are to look upon this glory via Christ's glorious face rather than Moses's. However, even those who look upon Moses's glorious face, by way of the reading of the old covenant, should still be redirected toward the surpassing

---

149. Fatehi, *Spirit's Relation*, 289–302.

150. There may be a strong parallel between 2 Cor 3:16b and Rom 8:2, where Christ and the Spirit participate in the act of liberation (ἐλευθερόω).

glory of Christ, who is proleptically foreshadowed in Israel's narratives, and Torah (cf. 1 Cor 10:4). In Paul's understanding, those who refuse to recognize Christ, whether through the hearing of the gospel or through the reading of the old covenant, place a veil over their own heart.[151]

Paul's repositioning of the veil over the heart of unbelievers in verse 15 may implicitly highlight the spiritual depths of Israel's blindness. However, the Corinthians, in hearing Paul's allusions to Exod 32–34 would quickly have remembered similar references to Israel's desert narrative, which Paul used in First Corinthians (10:1–11), writing the Corinthians into Israel's story. Israel's ancestors are now referred to as "our ancestors" (1 Cor 10:1; οἱ πατέρες ἡμῶν) in relation to the Corinthians, and Paul speaks of their *previous* Gentile state (1 Cor 12:2; ὅτε ἔθνη ἦτε; cf. 1 Cor 5:1; 10:20). As was shown in chapter 5, Paul used various methods for shaping eschatological identity, including rewriting Gentile's narrative genealogies (Phil 2:5–11; cf. Rom 11:17–24; 1 Thess 4:5).[152] Therefore, one should not automatically interpret 2 Cor 3:1—4:6, or any part therein, as a polemic against Judaism.[153] Nor should the assumption be that the Corinthians would have come to this conclusion. Instead, the Corinthians are reminded of their propensity toward disobedience and the historic consequence of these acts. They are reminded of the prophetic promises of a new covenant and of the invitation before them for covenant renewal.

Paul's apparent equating of κύριος and πνεῦμα in 3:17–18 is unique. In other places Paul is able to speak of the Spirit in connection to both Christ (Rom 8:9c; 1 Cor 15:45; Gal 4:6; Phil 1:19; cf. Rom 1:3–4) and God (Rom 8:9b, 11[*bis*], 14; 15:19; 1 Cor 2:11, 14; 3:16; 6:11; 7:40; 12:3; 2 Cor 3:3; Phil 3:3). While the latter is more prevalent, the former is not out of the question, especially when Paul's argument necessitates such a connection. Fatehi, in evaluating the role of the Spirit in correlation to both Yahweh and Christ, speaks of "dynamic identification." In connection to Christ, this means the Spirit "does not refer to the risen Lord as he is in himself, but as he communicates his power, his life, his will, his very presence, to his people."[154] In the current pericope, Paul needs to shift his argument from speaking about what God has done through Moses to what God has done through Christ. Still more, Paul's goal is to move the people toward covenant renewal and thus toward greater unity. This necessitates their understanding of what God is doing in them through the Spirit. The dynamic presence of the Spirit

---

151. Taking κεῖται as middle not passive.

152. Cf. Donaldson, *Paul and the Gentiles*, 236–38; Hodge, *If Sons, Then Heirs*, 33.

153. Cf. Duff, "Glory in the Ministry of Death."

154. Fatehi, *Spirit's Relation*, 304.

in the life of the believer has already been noted in 2 Cor 3:3—believers are letters of Christ engraved by the Spirit. This verse is given new meaning in light of 2 Cor 3:16. When believers turn to Christ, the Spirit eliminates the heart of stone and engraves God's law on their hearts.[155] The Spirit is instrumental in the removing of the veil.[156] Likewise, since Paul and his associates are servants of a new covenant (i.e., servants of Christ), they are simultaneously servants of the life-giving Spirit (2 Cor 3:6), who carries out the ministry of this new covenant (2 Cor 3:8). The Spirit is Christ in action bringing freedom in the life of the believer.

This freedom exemplifies itself in terms of unification and transformation. Paul begins 2 Cor 3:18 with the all-inclusive ἡμεῖς πάντες,[157] which is meant to draw the Corinthians fully and explicitly into the narrative just constructed. What Paul has articulated is not limited to him or a select few. If this were the case, then Christ's glory would not surpass Moses's in term of effectiveness. Paul is not the mediator of the Spirit or of the new covenant;[158] he is one of the servants,[159] a servant of the surpassing glory, a servant of the Spirit, a servant of the Servant Christ, the new Moses. As one of the servants, Paul joins with all believers who together form a singular unveiled face (ἀνακεκαλυμμένῳ προσώπῳ).[160] The singularity of this participial phrase is instrumental in Paul's argument and parallels the singular epistle of Christ in 2 Cor 3:3. Paul's words have eliminated the distance between him and the Corinthians and between themselves. Those in Christ form a glorious unified body (cf. Rom 12:1–5; 1 Cor 12:12–13, 27) with an unveiled face and unveiled heart. This stands in contrast to the veiled minds and heart of

155. Garland, *Second Corinthians*, 195.

156. Similarly, Philip, *Origins of Pauline Pneumatology*, 187–88. Although he argues for the Spirit of Yahweh and not Christ.

157. Hafemann, *Suffering and Ministry*, 13 n. 24; Thrall, *Second Corinthians*, 282; Barrett, *Second Corinthians*, 124. Contra, Belleville, *Reflections of Glory*, 275–76; cf. Wallace, *Snatched into Paradise*, 179. Furthermore, while Paul would include both Jew and Gentile in his understanding of "we all," here, his focus is on the unity of the Corinthians with each other and with him and his associates.

158. Pace, Hafemann, *Paul, Moses*, 400; Hafemann, *Suffering and Ministry*, 220.

159. Cf. Crafton, *The Agency of the Apostle*, 61, who utilizes the contrasting language of "agent" and "agency," which aligns with the difference suggested here between "mediator" and "servant." Crafton, however, incorrectly sees a contrast between Moses's role as agent and Paul's role of agency (82–93). I would argue that both Moses and Christ are agents and Paul, along with all believers, takes on the role of agency.

160. Many translations pluralize this participial phrase (NIV, NRSV, CEV, HCSB, ISV); although some maintain the singular (NASB, KJV, NKJV, LEB, ESV). Cf. Harris, *Second Corinthians*, 313, who pluralizes it calling it a "distributive singular."

Israel (2 Cor 3:14–15), who continues to turn to Moses and experience the limitation and even constraint of the old covenant.

Paul's use of "face" rather than "heart" is curious since the connection between verses 15 and 16 suggests the veil removed in Christ resides over the heart. Like in verse 12, Paul's return to the *fpp* marks only the second time Paul makes a comparison between Moses and believers. Again, Moses is presented positively. Like Moses before Yahweh, believers before Christ share an unveiled face.[161] Nevertheless, the controlling contrast is still between those turning to Christ and those turning to Moses. The latter are unable to experience the full weight of the glory and thus unable to be transformed. The former, through the Spirit, have the freedom to gaze intently into Christ's face and be transformed by the glory. The "unveiled-ness" of those in Christ is comprehensive, including face, mind, and heart. Furthermore, the use of face more appropriately fits Paul's illustrative language of κατοπτριζόμενοι and εἰκόνα.

Κατοπτριζόμενοι, a *hapax legomenon* in the NT, can mean "behold as in a mirror"[162] or "reflect like a mirror."[163] The former has stronger linguistic support in Hellenistic sources[164] and when read in connection with its controlling verb (μεταμορφόω), the concept of transformation by beholding[165] is preferable to transformation by reflecting (cf. Ezek 1:28; Wis 7:26–27; 1 John 3:2). The real query concerns the "mirror" through which believers behold. Since it is the glory of the Lord (i.e., Christ[166]) believers behold, it is unlikely Christ is the mirror.[167] Additionally, since Paul is here

---

161. Martin, *Second Corinthians*, 71, says the believer becomes like Moses by turning to the Lord. Contra, Belleville, *Reflections of Glory*, 278, who believes the contrast is between Moses's veiled face and the apostles' unveiled face.

162. Lambrecht, "Transformation in 2 Corinthians," 246–51; Hafemann, *Paul, Moses*, 409 and n. 231; Wong, "The Lord is the Spirit," 65; Fee, *God's Empowering Presence*, 316–17; Thrall, *Second Corinthians*, 282, 290–92; Garland, *Second Corinthians*, 199. Cf. Matera, *Second Corinthians*, 96–97, who argues for "contemplating."

163. Belleville, *Reflections of Glory*, 278–82; Hooker, "Beyond Things which are Written," 301; Stockhausen, *Moses' Veil*, 89–90; Dunn, *Christology in the Making*, 143–44. Cf. Garrett, "Veiled Hearts," 762–66, who argues the middle voice means both to reflect and to become what we reflect. Also see, Bruce, *First and Second Corinthians*, 193, who holds the dual meanings of behold and reflect.

164. Furnish, *Second Corinthians*, 214.

165. This doesn't necessarily denote a solely visionary experience but may also include a mental contemplation. Cf. Rabens, "*Pneuma* and the Beholding of God," 313–14, who argues for both ideas but translates 2 Cor 3:18 as "transformation through contemplation."

166. Contra, Harris, *Second Corinthians*, 314.

167. Contra, Garland, *Second Corinthians*, 200 and n. 473; Barrett, *Second Corinthians*, 125; Rabens, "*Pneuma* and the Beholding of God," 314.

including all believers, he is not referring solely to himself and/or other ministers/apostles as the mirror.[168] More probable is Lambrecht's proposal of the gospel as mirror[169] or Wright's proposal of all believers as mirror.[170] However, the fact the believers are experiencing transformation as a result of beholding the glory of the Lord through this mirror suggests it is neither the gospel nor the believers themselves but rather the dynamic power behind them both—the Spirit.[171] This brings clarity to Paul's final clause in 2 Cor 3:18—καθάπερ ἀπὸ[172] κυρίου πνεύματος—and helps strengthen the above reading of 2 Cor 3:17. In the absence of the physical presence of Christ, the Spirit becomes the mediator of the divine glory, which leads to transformation. This is not a comparison between those who saw Christ directly and those who experience him via the Spirit.[173] Paul has gone to great lengths to equate these two experiences. Again, the glory referenced is still God's, here evidenced on the face of Christ (cf. 2 Cor 4:6), through the Spirit, for all believers to directly experience,[174] rather than on the face of Moses. The face-to-face beholding of God's glory has thus far been for the mediators (Moses and Christ). Furthermore, the surpassing glory of Christ and the new covenant suggests that whereas Moses only experienced the backside of God's glory, Christ reflects the fullness of God's glory. The servants of the Servant must await the consummation of the new age to experience a direct beholding (cf. 1 Cor 13:12).

The "same image" (τὴν αὐτὴν εἰκόνα) refers back to Lord (i.e., Christ; cf. 2 Cor 4:4). In Paul's understanding, believers do not simply gaze upon the glory. This continual gazing leads to continual transformation.[175] Believers reflect the same image and thus the same glory through their connection with the Spirit. This may be an exposition on the surpassing-ness of Christ who is able to extend glory. Furthermore, when read in correlation with 2 Cor 3:2–3, Paul may be alluding to the Isaianic offspring of the Servant and especially Isa 61:9—"Their offspring will be known among the nations, and their offspring among the peoples. All who see them will acknowledge them, that they are the offspring which Yahweh has blessed." Paul

---

168. Contra, Belleville, *Reflections of Glory*, 281 n. 1.

169. Lambrecht, "Transformation in 2 Corinthians," 302–3, stresses gospel but also includes the Christian life.

170. Wright, *Climax of the Covenant*, 185–89.

171. So also Philip, *Pneumatology*, 189–90; cf. Dunn, *Theology of Paul*, 422.

172. Καθάπερ ἀπό denotes agency. See Philip, *Pneumatology*, 190.

173. *Pace*, Lambrecht, "Transformation in 2 Corinthians," 301–2; Thrall, *Second Corinthians*, 284.

174. So correctly, Garland, *Second Corinthians*, 199–200.

175. Wright, *Resurrection of the Son of God*, 384.

makes clear that this transformation and subsequent reflecting takes place communally with a singular unveiled face. Their continued transformation into glory requires them to be reconciled to Christ but also to his body, which includes Paul and his associates (cf. 2 Cor 5:18–20).

Herein, the importance of the Exodus covenant renewal imagery emerges as Paul invites the Corinthians to turn to Christ, who mediates a new covenant by way of the Spirit. His words serve as a speech-act calling the people to a specific action. Their acceptance of this invitation to covenant renewal will be evidenced primarily in their transformation, which first requires their full acceptance of the Spirit and which will thus lead to their full acceptance of all believers. The *fpp* has allowed Paul to include the Corinthians in the very transformation to which he is calling them. It is both paradigmatic and proleptic, the former as it points to Paul and his associates and the latter as it points to the Corinthians who are both already and not yet the eschatological people of God (cf. 2 Cor 1:13–14).

Second Corinthians 4:1–6

There is a notable focus on the proclamation of the gospel in 2 Cor 4:1–6. When read in correlation with the second person plural in 2 Cor 4:5 (cf. 2 Cor 4:12, 14–15), there is a tendency to see the *fpp* as strictly We-Ministers/We-Apostles or We-I references. Nevertheless, Paul is reinforcing his previous argument by presenting a picture of those who presently live as part of the eschatological people of God over and against those living in the present evil age, more specifically his opponents (*not* the Corinthians). The διά οὗτος, which begins this section, points backwards to the preceding section and most directly to 2 Cor 3:18, which includes all believers.[176] Likewise, Paul's reference to τὴν διακονίαν ταύτην (2 Cor 4:1) should be read with 2 Cor 3:8–9 and the ministry of the Spirit/righteousness (cf. 2 Cor 5:18; 6:3; 8:4: 9:1, 12, 13).[177] The focus is on the work of the Spirit in and through the eschatological people of God; it is on God's mercy and its tangible impact in the life of believers in general and here specifically in the life of Paul and his associates. God's transforming work has led them to act with great boldness (2 Cor 3:12), to persevere (οὐκ ἐγκακοῦμεν, 2 Cor 4:1) in the midst of trial (cf. 2 Cor 4:16), to renounce the hidden things of shame, and not to walk in craftiness nor adulterate God's word (2 Cor 4:2a). These are not

---

176. *Pace*, Thrall, *Second Corinthians*, 298; Martin, *Second Corinthians*, 76. Correctly, Harris, *Second Corinthians*, 322.

177. *Pace*, Kim, *Origin of Paul's Gospel*, 5, who believes it points to "the apostolic ministry of the new covenant"; see also Aernie, *Is Paul also among the Prophets?*, 196–97.

words of defense. They are a concrete example of those who live as part of the unveiled community of Christ.

The use of συνίστημι in 2 Cor 4:2b brings the argument full circle to 2 Cor 3:1 and signals an important difference between correct and incorrect commendation. The opponents' commendation comes in the form of letters (2 Cor 3:2) or as self-commendation (2 Cor 10:12, 18); it is external rather than internal (cf. 2 Cor 5:12) and human rather than divine. For Paul and his associates, commendation is tied to τῇ φανερώσει τῆς ἀληθείας. Paul is not speaking about human words that demonstrate his gospel is superior to others. Instead, Paul is speaking about the ministry of the Spirit at work in and through him and his associates (cf. 1 Cor 12:7), the Spirit who manifests the truth of the gospel "to the conscience of everyone in the sight of God."

The revelatory language of 2 Cor 4:2b is riddled throughout 2 Cor 2:14—7:4 and is often connected to divine agency, though usually through an indirect human agent. God manifests (φανεροῦντι) himself through the fragrance of those led in triumphal procession (2 Cor 2:14). The Corinthians bear witness (φανερούμενοι) to being a letter written by Christ via the Spirit ministered to by Paul and his associates (2 Cor 3:3) as well as written on their hearts to be known and read by all (2 Cor 3:2). Paul and his associates make visible (φανερωθῇ) the life of Jesus through their suffering (2 Cor 4:10, 11). Mark Seifrid argues Paul's use of τῇ φανερώσει τῆς ἀληθείας "implies the setting of eschatological judgment" and links it to 2 Cor 5:10—"For all of us must appear (φανερωθῆναι) before the judgement seat of Christ" (cf. 1 Cor 3:13; 4:5; 14:25).[178] However, rather than thinking strictly about eschatological judgment, Paul has in mind the divine revelation and divine presence that believers experience as part of the eschatological new creation people of God.

When 2 Cor 4:2b is read in correlation with the Exodus narrative, which Paul intentionally reengages in 2 Cor 4:3–4, the concept of revelation and divine presence gains further credence. It is Christ who removes the veil by way of the Spirit and thus enables the believer to join the singular unveiled face of the believing community. It is from this new eschatological sphere of being that they see the glory of the Lord and are transformed into this same image, an image which can then manifest Christ to others via this same Spirit. The manifestation of the Spirit is the removing of the veil (2 Cor 3:16), which allows the Corinthians to witness internally the truth of Paul's gospel message and his faithful witness. The unveiling is simultaneously a union with Christ and his body and it takes place ἐνώπιον τοῦ θεοῦ (cf. 2 Cor

---

178. Seifrid, *Second Corinthians*, 193.

7:12). It is not Paul's proclamation of the gospel that removes the veil,[179] at least not directly. The Spirit must first remove the veil, thus enabling this gospel to be heard and received.

Paul sets a clear division between those who are part of the eschatological people of God and those who are not. This contrast is solidified in 2 Cor 4:3–4 with the distinction between veiled and unveiled. The veil is repositioned a third time, from Moses's face (2 Cor 3:13) to Israel's heart (2 Cor 3:15) and now over "our gospel," i.e., "the gospel of Christ" (2 Cor 2:12; 9:13; 10:14; cf. 11:7).[180] This veil is extended to the gospel as it represents Christ and the new covenant. In reality, it sits over the hearts and minds of unbelievers, as is made clear in 2 Cor 4:4 (cf. 2 Cor 3:14; Exod 33:5); it is a metonymy for hard-heartedness.[181] Paul's use of ἀπόλλυμι to refer to those who are veiled points back to 2 Cor 2:15–16 and solidifies the dichotomy between two very different groups: those perishing versus those being saved; those veiled versus those unveiled; and those blinded by the god of this world versus those seeing the image of the one true God. Paul's words are not so much meant to indict the Corinthians as to include them. Together, Paul, his associates, and the Corinthians form the "we all" who have seen the glory of the Lord and who are being transformed by the Spirit (2 Cor 3:18). The antithesis between these two groups provides Paul another outlet for shaping the Corinthians' eschatological identity as the people of God. Paul extends grace and forgiveness to the Corinthians while simultaneously providing a clear impetus for being on the "right" side of the eschatological divide.

In 2 Cor 4:5, Paul also reminds the Corinthians of his commitment to them, which goes hand in hand with his commitment to Christ. Just as the gospel Paul preaches is intrinsically bound to Christ, so too are all ministers of this gospel bound to the body of Christ; they are slaves to the body for Christ's sake. Paul's continued references to his suffering and now to his subjection (δοῦλος) to the Corinthians serves multiple purposes. It stands as a reminder to the Corinthians of the commitment Paul and his associates have for them (cf. 2 Cor 1:24; 12:15) and provides an example of what true commitment to Christ means. It evidences unity and invites recommitment, participation, and imitation (cf. Phil 2:7). Paul's words may also recollect his previous statements in 1 Corinthians—all the work of Paul and his cohort is done under compulsion (1 Cor 9:16–17) and on account of Christ and the gospel in order to become fellow-partakers (1 Cor 9:23) who are not

---

179. *Pace*, Furnish, *Second Corinthians*, 248–49; cf. Thrall, *Second Corinthians*, 319.

180. Matera, *Second Corinthians*, 101.

181. Hafemann, *Second Corinthians*, 177.

disqualified (1 Cor 9:27). Likewise, the Corinthians must recognize the potential for disqualification and the role Paul and his associates play in seeking to build them up rather than tear them down (2 Cor 13:5–10).

Paul concludes this pericope (2 Cor 4:1–6) as well as the whole of this section (2 Cor 3:1—4:6) with an allusion either to Gen 1:3–4 or Isa 9:1 LXX.[182] Either way, his intention is to remind the Corinthians of the creative power of God who is able to "let light shine out of darkness." That is, God has done a new creative work in the midst of the current old creation (cf. 2 Cor 5:17) and is doing a new creative work in the heart and mind of believers as they become part of the unveiled community of Christ. The dichotomy is not between Paul and the Corinthians, nor between ministers of the gospel and all others. Rather, the eschatological dichotomy between old and new is extended to include the authoritative powers behind these spheres of existence. On the one side is the "god of this age" who prevents unbelievers from "seeing the light of the glory of Christ" (2 Cor 4:4) and on the other side is the God who has "shone in our hearts to give the light of the knowledge of the glory of God in the face of Jesus Christ" (2 Cor 4:6).

This contrasting parallel between 2 Cor 4:4 and 4:6 may also shed light on Paul's use of the *fpp* in 4:6, which contrasts unbelievers and believers.[183] This conclusion is strengthened when the parallel between 2 Cor 4:6 and 3:18 is taken into account. The latter focuses on continued transformation (μεταμορφούμεθα) of all believers whereas the former pinpoints the decisive moment of faith (ἔλαμψεν). In both, the emphasis lies on God's action through Christ and the Spirit, both past and present, in the life of Paul, his associates, and all believers.

The connection between 2 Cor 4:5 and 4:6 (ὅτι[184]) could lead to the conclusion that the *fpp* in 4:6 refers to We-Ministers/We-Apostles/We-I. However, the intention behind these words is *not* to defend, to evidence authority, or to divide. Paul and his cohort are examples of the eschatological people of God who demonstrate the Spirit's transformation. At the heart of this transformation is union with the body of Christ and unity within this body. This *fpp* is a We-Community statement intended to remind the Corinthians of God's faithfulness in the past and to invite them to fully embrace the unveiled-face community in Christ.

---

182. For a defense of the former see: Thrall, *Second Corinthians*, 315–16. For a defense of the latter see Aernie, *Is Paul also among the Prophets?*, 204–14.

183. So Meier, *Mystik bei Paulus*, 63.

184. See Harris, *Second Corinthians*, 333.

Confirmation of Christophanic Reference

As noted in the Prolegomena, 2 Cor 3:1—4:6 meets both criteria for being deemed a Christophanic reference. Furthermore, analysis carried out in this chapter shows how Paul employs the Exodus narrative to invite the Corinthians to covenant renewal with Christ, Paul and his associates, and one another. In this way, he appears to invite them to renew their conversion and calling experience, which included a manifestation of the divine. Through allusions to Isaiah, Paul helps them to understand Christ as the singular Servant and Paul and his associates as servants of the Servant. Through his use of the *fpp*, he invites them to embrace a shared calling. The various references to conversion and call and the multiple references to some type of divine manifestation as part of this process suggest this secondary Christophanic reference is most likely intentional.

This conclusion fits the aim of 2 Cor 3:1—4:6. Paul's goal has been to provide a paradigm for believer conversion, call, and transformation, which would unite them together as the eschatological people of God. One way for Paul to achieve this aim is to lessen the gap between himself and the Corinthians. Rather than elevating his unique experience, Paul intentionally extrapolates the universal elements of his Christophany and re-particularizes the particulars for the benefit of his audience.[185] All believers, like Paul, experience Christ. However, in a surprising twist, Paul emphasizes the connection between Christ and the Spirit (2 Cor 3:17-18). Rather than a Christophany, believers experience Christ through a manifestation of the Holy Spirit, a Pneuma-Christophany (cf. Gal 3:1–5; and possibly Phil 3:15).[186] The Spirit enables an internal, *then* external transformation (cf. 2 Cor 4:16) by way of an external, *then* internal mediator, namely, Christ. This experience unites all believes as the singular community of the unveiled face, a new creation people of God who are continually being transformed into Christ's image, by God's glory, through the Spirit.

Conclusion

The uncertainty of a Christophanic reference in Second Corinthians called for a rigorous evaluation of 2 Cor 3:1—4:6 in its literary and socio-historical context. Because this proposed reference was embedded in a confluence of OT allusions, it required significant intertextual analysis. It was argued that Paul used Isa 40–66 to frame the whole of his discussion in 2 Cor 2:14—7:4,

185. Cf. Dunn, *Jesus, Paul and the Law*, 95.
186. See Dunn, *Jesus and Spirit*, 98–99.

showing how Christ's actions had led to an eschatological shift, resulting in deliverance, restoration, and forgiveness of sin. Through reference to Isaiah, Paul also established Christ as the singular Isaianic Servant and showed how he and his associates were the eschatological offspring of the Servant. It was also argued that Paul's extensive use of Exod 32–34 in 2 Cor 3:1—4:6 was designed to help the Corinthians see the folly of their ways and to invite them to covenant renewal with Christ, Paul and his associates, and one another. Furthermore, when the Exodus narrative was read in correlation with Isaiah, it became apparent that Paul was not comparing Moses and himself or their ministries, but Moses and Christ. Christ was put forth as a second Moses figure who surpassed Moses in his ability to extent God's transforming glory to all who turned to him. In this way, Paul's invitation to covenant renewal was simultaneously an invitation to embrace their eschatological identity and calling as servants of the Servant Christ.

Furthermore, the a priori judgment of 2 Cor 3:1—4:6 as a secondary Christophanic reference was confirmed. Paul alluded to this experience as a way of helping the Corinthians understand their own conversion and calling as well as their continued transformation in Christ. Paul's Christophanic reference deliberately stood in the background because he was neither the focus nor trying to establish his authority. Paul moved the focus from his experience and authority and centered it firmly on what God had done and was doing in and through Paul and his associates, and what God could and would do in and through all believers as they joined the covenant people through their faith in the faithfulness of Christ.

Paul's Christophanic reference functioned both didactically and paradigmatically. Didactically, it was designed to teach the Corinthians about who Christ was, what he had done, and what he was continuing to do. It was also intended to teach them about who they were as believers and to inform them about their eschatological identity and calling to be servants of the Servant. Paradigmatically, Paul's Christophanic reference evidenced a pattern for the Corinthians to emulate if they were to embrace this identity and calling. They needed to accept the invitation for reconciliation and follow the example of Paul and his associates in allowing Christ through the Holy Spirit to transform them continually, both internally and externally. Furthermore, the Corinthians needed to embrace certain elements of the ministry of the Spirit, ministry of justification, and ministry of reconciliation in the world.

The most radical element of Paul's Christophanic reference was how his own Christophanic experience was presented through the Exodus narrative as the norm for all believers. Rather than setting his own experience as an unattainable anomaly, Paul removed the particulars of his own

Christophanic experience and re-particularized these elements to fit his audience's situation. They did not have the benefit of the same revelation from Christ, so instead, they experienced Christ through a revelation of the Spirit. They did not have a specific call to apostolic ministry, but they shared with Paul and all believers in an invitation to embrace an eschatological calling to be servants of the Servant. These things moved beyond paradigm as Paul showed that he himself shared in these general elements. Paul, through his Christophanic reference, invited them to recognize the analogous parts of their conversion/call experiences. This, more than anything else, showed the corporate understanding Paul had about his own Christophanic experience and the corporate purpose for which he utilized this narrative.

7

Conclusion

MANY HAVE UNDERTAKEN A study of Paul's Christophany with the aim
of reconstructing the event and/or its impact on Paul's life, theology, and
mission. These objectives have tended toward a removal of the Christophanic references from their literary and socio-historical contexts and toward an amalgamation of the various Pauline references and often also the
Acts references. This study uniquely analyzed why Paul employed these
Christophanic references in their particular contexts, which gave each
reference its own voice. As a result, its significant contribution has been
a rediscovery of how each reference functions within the whole of Paul's
particular epistolary argument. A further contribution is the synthesis of
the study's findings in order to show the shared functionalities of Paul's
various Christophanic references. This can effectively be done now that
the individual evaluations are completed. Additionally, the overall findings of this work allow for some measured assertions concerning Paul's
understanding of the event itself and its impact. This too is made possible
because of the individual evaluations carried out in the body of this book.
While these assertions move beyond the individual literary and socio-
historical contexts, these contexts have provided the foundations.

Synthesis of the Findings

This study began by developing criteria for establishing what constitutes
a Christophanic reference and then categorizing confirmed references as
being either primary or secondary. This, in itself, has been a contribution
to Pauline studies. Five references were confirmed—Gal 1:11–17; 1 Cor
9:1–2, 16–17; 1 Cor 15:1–11; Phil 3:4–14; 2 Cor 3:1—4:6. Of these five, the
first three were classified as primary references, sitting in the forefront, and

the last two were classified as secondary, sitting in the background. Each of these confirmed Christophanic references was extensively evaluated in its literary and socio-historical settings with special attention given to relevant intertextual issues. Based on the conclusions reached in chapters 3–6, a synthesis of the findings can now be carried out, which reveals important shared elements regarding purpose.

It has been shown that each Christophanic reference functions as part of a larger argument fitting the overall theme and focus of the particular epistle in which it is found. These Christophanic references are interpreted by their contexts as well as helping interpret overall themes of their particular epistles. These references cannot be divorced from their contexts without forfeiting at least some of their meaning and functionality and without weakening Paul's overall argument.

Additionally, against much of the scholarly discussion it has been shown that Paul did not primarily utilize these Christophanic references to assert his apostolic authority or to validate or defend his apostleship. This is noteworthy since most apostolic apologia readings of these epistles rely heavily on the argumentation that Paul's Christophanic references serve this purpose. This puts a significant burden upon these scholars to evidence apostolic apologia in other areas of the epistle/s apart from Paul's Christophanic references.

Instead, this study has contributed to scholarship by showing that Paul's Christophanic references always function didactically and paradigmatically. Didactically, Paul utilizes these references to teach the various churches deeper theological truths about Christ, the apostolic ministry, and ultimately about their identity as the eschatological ἐκκλησία of God. These teaching points are intricately connected since what is posited about Christ is exemplified in the apostolic ministry and becomes a defining element in believers' eschatological identity. Within this didactic function, Paul is willing to exhibit his own past weaknesses or failings in order to evidence a divine–human dichotomy and a differentiation between the two ages. This is especially apparent in Paul's multiple references to having persecuted the church (Gal 1:13; 1 Cor 15:9; Phil 3:6).

Paradigmatically, Paul uses his Christophanic references to provide a tangible example for his churches to emulate. This "example" takes on different nuances based on the particular situation, the particular audience, and the particular theological truth Paul is trying to express. Nevertheless, Paul's model emulates Christ's sacrificial actions and missional mindset and provides a pathway for his audiences to embrace their eschatological identity and their transformation into Christ's likeness, which involves a greater recognition of and accountability to the body of Christ and the gospel mission. Paul is even willing to reference his Christophanic experience ironically as part of a negative example of worldly attitudes of power and freedom (1 Cor 9:1–2), only to model the eschatological reversal of these erroneous understandings in the continuation of this Christophanic reference (1 Cor 9:16–17).

Additionally, at least two of Paul's Christophanic references function analogously, which comprises one of the most significant contributions of this study. In Galatians and 2 Corinthians (and possibly also Philippians), Paul intentionally strips his Christophany of its particulars and shapes his argument in such a way as to show the analogous elements of his experience with all believers. Paul speaks of all believers sharing in the same revelation of Christ that Paul experienced. Whereas Paul's revelation appears to be more directly connected to Christ (cf. 1 Cor 15:8), he speaks of believers' experience of the revelation of Christ as taking place through the Holy Spirit and usually by way of the proclaimed gospel. Since Paul's various audiences already appear to know about his unique Christophanic experience, this Pneuma-Christology is not meant to differentiate the two experiences but to align them.

Paul also speaks of all believers sharing in the same calling as his to be servants of the suffering Savior Servant Christ, by uniting with Christ, taking on Christ's righteousness, and participating in the *missio Dei*. This twofold phenomenon, of a shared experience and shared calling, moves beyond mere paradigm. Since Paul's audiences have already experienced conversion/call, he is not here inviting them to emulate his identity, attitude, or actions. Paul is reminding these believers of their initial conversion/call, and doing so in such a way as to move them toward a deeper and more profound understanding of their shared eschatological identity and shared calling in Christ. It is this knowledge that should move them toward greater Christ-likeness.

Each of these purposes highlight the corporate direction of Paul's Christophanic references. Paul's references invite participation in his own experience on multiple levels. Through the didactic elements, Paul invites his audiences to participate through learning; through the paradigmatic elements, Paul invites them to participate through following; and through the analogous elements, Paul invites them to participate through sharing.

Assertions Concerning Paul's Christophanic Experience

Three measured assertions can now be posited with respect to Paul's Christophanic experience and its impact. These are based on the individual contextual evaluations as well as the above synthesis and emphasize the likely impetuses behind why Paul utilizes his Christophanic references for didactic, paradigmatic, and analogous purposes.

First, as has been shown, the book of Isaiah (esp. Isa 40–66) played a strategic role as the basis for various points that Paul was attempting to argue within his Christophanic references, not least with regard to his own experience. It would appear that Paul's understanding of his Christophanic experience was either greatly influenced by his rereading of Isaiah or that Isaiah was the most fitting text for Paul to express information gained from his revelatory experience. Either way, the fact that Paul utilized this text to hold Christ up as the fulfillment of the Isaianic Servant and to argue the call upon all believers to become servants of the Servant shows the importance of Isaiah for Paul and for his communities.

Second, the fact that Paul highlights analogous elements between his Christophanic experience and believers' experience in terms of both the revelatory event and the calling says something about Paul's understanding of his own conversion/call. Paul's Christophany was ultimately an act of being in Christ and part of the body of Christ; it was ontological. The Christophanic experience did not *just* shape him or his reading of the old covenant and the place of the Gentiles in the eschatological kingdom. Paul's experience shaped the way he viewed conversion and call as a whole. For Paul, conversion can only take place through a revelation of Christ, whether directly or through the Holy Spirit, which removes the veil from one's heart and mind and makes that one a part of the eschatological community of believers. Additionally, conversion always comes with a call to share in the mission of the Servant. Whether this understanding comes directly from Paul's Christophany or through his subsequent rereading of the OT illuminated by the Spirit cannot be determined with any certainty. Nevertheless, the Christophany is the controlling factor in Paul's understanding of the ontology of God's eschatological conversion/call.

Third, and closely related to Paul's ontological understanding of conversion/call, is Paul's corporate understanding of conversion/call. This moves beyond saying Paul's conversion/call was purposed for others and beyond saying Paul purposes his Christophanic references for the sake of building up the body of Christ. While these things are true, they are a result of Paul's corporate understanding of conversion/call. In other words, these references are corporate because Paul's theological understanding about conversion/call is ultimately corporate. Paul may have understood his own Christophanic experience as corporate in that through this experience he joined all believers past, present, and future in participating in the mission of God through his participation in Christ. This explains why Paul's

Christophanic references are ultimately a means of solidarity and unification rather than distinction and division. Although personal, at its core, it is a corporate Christophany that shapes Paul's mission and message.

Suggestions for Further Study

This study has significantly advanced the discussion concerning the purpose of Paul's Christophanic references and made measured assertions concerning the Christophanic experience. The conclusions reached in this work provide an opportunity for further research, which, while beyond the scope of this study, may provide additional evidence to strengthen its findings.

First, further research remains to be done on Paul's multiple references to "call" and "grace," as they relate to Paul's Christophanic experience. Paul's "call" language (κλητός, κλῆσις, καλέω) is employed to speak of his own call (Rom 1:1; 1 Cor 1:1) and to believers' call (e.g., Rom 1:6, 7; 1 Cor 1:2, 24; Gal 5:13; 1 Thess 4:7; cf. Phil 3:14). Therefore, Paul's references to himself could function similarly to Gal 1:11–17 and 2 Cor 3:4—4:6, as a way of typifying his own calling or as a way of elevating believers' calling.

Likewise, on five occasions (Rom 1:5; 12:3; 15:15; 1 Cor 3:10; Gal 2:9), Paul closely connects God's "grace" with his own apostolic position and/or work. In four of these reference, there is a formulaic use of the articular aorist passive participle τὴν δοθεῖσάν followed by μοι. The focus is on a past "giving" of grace by God to Paul for a particular purpose. Paul uses a very similar formula to speak of the grace given to believers (Rom 12:6; 1 Cor 1:4; 2 Cor 8:1; cf. the *fpp* in Rom 1:5), which may have an important parallel in speaking about the Holy Spirit given to all believers (1 Cor 12:7–8; 2 Cor 1:22; 5:5; 1 Thess 4:8).[1] This may provide parallels to Paul's Pneuma-Christophany phenomenon in Gal 3:1–5 and 2 Cor 3:17–18 (cf. Phil 3:15).

Finally, an additional study needs to be undertaken on the proposed Christophanic references in the disputed Pauline epistles and most notably Eph 3:1–13. An evaluation of this pericope in correlation with the present study may provide an additional voice into the ongoing discussion of its Pauline authenticity.

---

1. Barclay, *Paul & Gift*, briefly highlights the connection between call and grace as it relates to both Paul and all believers (pp. 332, 354, 358–60). Still, further work needs to be done on this intersection.

Appendix

Chiastic Structure of 1 Corinthians 15:1–11 (NRSV)

A ¹ Now I should remind you, brothers and sisters, of the good news that I proclaimed to you, which you in turn received,

  B in which also you stand, ² through which also you are being saved, if you hold firmly to the message that I proclaimed to you—unless you have come to believe in vain.

   C ³ For I handed on to you as of first importance what I in turn had received: that Christ died for our sins in accordance with the scriptures, ⁴ and that he was buried, and that he was raised on the third day in accordance with the scriptures, ⁵and that he appeared to Cephas,

    D then to the twelve.

     E ⁶Then he appeared to more than five hundred brothers and sisters at one time,

      F most of whom are still alive,

      F¹ though some have died.

     E¹ ⁷ Then he appeared to James,

    D¹ then to all the apostles.

   C¹ ⁸ Last of all, as to someone untimely born, he appeared also to me. ⁹ For I am the least of the apostles, unfit to be called an apostle, because I persecuted the church of God. ¹⁰ But by the grace of God I am what I am,

  B¹ and his grace towards me has not been in vain. On the contrary, I worked harder than any of them—though it was not I, but the grace of God that is with me.

A¹ ¹¹ Whether then it was I or they, so we proclaim and so you have come to believe.

Chiastic Structure of 1 Corinthians 15:1–11 (Greek)

A ¹ Γνωρίζω δὲ ὑμῖν, ἀδελφοί, τὸ εὐαγγέλιον ὃ εὐηγγελισάμην ὑμῖν, ὃ καὶ παρελάβετε,

B ἐν ᾧ καὶ ἑστήκατε, ² δι᾽ οὗ καὶ σῴζεσθε, τίνι λόγῳ εὐηγγελισάμην ὑμῖν εἰ κατέχετε, ἐκτὸς εἰ μὴ εἰκῇ ἐπιστεύσατε.

C ³ παρέδωκα γὰρ ὑμῖν ἐν πρώτοις, ὃ καὶ παρέλαβον, ὅτι Χριστὸς ἀπέθανεν ὑπὲρ τῶν ἁμαρτιῶν ἡμῶν κατὰ τὰς γραφὰς ⁴ καὶ ὅτι ἐτάφη καὶ ὅτι ἐγήγερται τῇ ἡμέρᾳ τῇ τρίτῃ κατὰ τὰς γραφὰς ⁵ καὶ ὅτι ὤφθη Κηφᾷ

D εἶτα τοῖς δώδεκα·

E ⁶ ἔπειτα ὤφθη ἐπάνω πεντακοσίοις ἀδελφοῖς ἐφάπαξ,

F ἐξ ὧν οἱ πλείονες μένουσιν ἕως ἄρτι,

F¹ τινὲς δὲ ἐκοιμήθησαν·

E¹ ⁷ ἔπειτα ὤφθη Ἰακώβῳ

D¹ εἶτα τοῖς ἀποστόλοις πᾶσιν·

C¹ ⁸ ἔσχατον δὲ πάντων ὡσπερεὶ τῷ ἐκτρώματι ὤφθη κἀμοί. ⁹ Ἐγὼ γάρ εἰμι ὁ ἐλάχιστος τῶν ἀποστόλων ὃς οὐκ εἰμὶ ἱκανὸς καλεῖσθαι ἀπόστολος, διότι ἐδίωξα τὴν ἐκκλησίαν τοῦ θεοῦ· ¹⁰ χάριτι δὲ θεοῦ εἰμι ὅ εἰμι,

B¹ καὶ ἡ χάρις αὐτοῦ ἡ εἰς ἐμὲ οὐ κενὴ ἐγενήθη, ἀλλὰ περισσότερον αὐτῶν πάντων ἐκοπίασα, οὐκ ἐγὼ δὲ ἀλλὰ ἡ χάρις τοῦ θεοῦ [ἡ] σὺν ἐμοί.

A¹ ¹¹ εἴτε οὖν ἐγὼ εἴτε ἐκεῖνοι, οὕτως κηρύσσομεν καὶ οὕτως ἐπιστεύσατε.

Bibliography

Adewuya, J. Ayodeji. *Holiness and Community in 2 Cor 6:14—7:1: Paul's View of Communal Holiness in the Corinthian Correspondence.* StBL 40. 2003. Reprint, Eugene: Wipf & Stock, 2011.

Aernie, Jeffrey W. *Is Paul also among the Prophets? An Examination of the Relationship between Paul and the Old Testament Prophetic Tradition in 2 Corinthians.* LNTS 467. London: Bloomsbury, 2012.

Aland, Kurt, et al. *Novum Testamentum Graece.* 28th ed. Stuttgart: Deutsche Bibelgesellschaft, 2012.

Alexander, Loveday. "Hellenistic Letter-Forms and the Structure of Philippians." *JSNT* 37 (1989) 87–101.

Allison, Dale C., Jr. *The New Moses: A Matthean Typology.* Minneapolis: Fortress, 1993.

Anderson, Bernhard W. "Exodus Typology in Second Isaiah." In *Israel's Prophetic Heritage: Essays in Honor of James Muilenburg,* edited by Bernard W. Anderson and Walter Harrelson, 177–95. New York: Harper, 1962.

Arnold, Bradley. "Re-envisioning the Olympic Games: Paul's Use of Athletic Imagery in Philippians." *Theology* 115.4 (2012) 243–52.

Ascough, Richard. *Paul's Macedonian Association.* WUNT 2/161. Tübingen: Mohr/Siebeck, 2003.

Ashton, John. *The Religion of Paul the Apostle.* New Haven: Yale University Press, 2000.

Baasland, Ernst. "Persecution: A Neglected Feature in the Letter to the Galatians." *ST* 38 (1984) 135–50.

Bailey, Kenneth E. *Paul through Mediterranean Eyes: Cultural Studies in 1 Corinthians.* Downers Grove, IL: InterVarsity, 2011.

Baird, William. "Visions, Revelation, and Ministry: Reflections on 2 Cor 12:1–5 and Gal 1:11–17." *JBL* 104 (1985) 651–62.

Baker, William. "Did the Glory of Moses' Face Fade? A Reexamination of καταργέω in 2 Corinthians 3:7–18." *BBR* 10/1 (2000) 1–15

Bakhtin, Mikhail. *The Dialogic Imagination: Four Essays.* Trans. by Caryl Emerson and Michael Holquist. Austin: University of Texas Press, 1981.

Baltzer, Klaus. *Deutero-Isaiah: A Commentary on Isaiah 40–55.* Translated by Margaret Kohl. Hermeneia. Minneapolis: Fortress, 2001.

Balz, Horst Robert, and Gerhard Schneider, eds. *Exegetical Dictionary of the New Testament.* 3 vols. Grand Rapids: Eerdmans, 1990.

Banks, Robert. "The Eschatological Role of Law in Pre- and Post-Christian Jewish Thought." In *Reconciliation and Hope, New Testament Essays on Atonement and*

Eschatology Presented to L. L. Morris on His 60th Birthday, edited by Robert Banks, 173–85. Grand Rapids: Eerdmans, 1974.

Barclay, John M. G. *Obeying the Truth: Paul's Ethics in Galatians*. Minneapolis: Fortress, 1988.

———. *Paul & the Gift*. Grand Rapids: Eerdmans, 2015.

Barnett, Paul. *The Second Epistle to the Corinthians*. NICNT. Grand Rapids: Eerdmans, 1997.

Barrett, C. K. *The Acts of the Apostle, Volume I: Preliminary Introduction and Commentary on Acts I–XIV*. ICC. Edinburgh: T. & T. Clark, 1994.

———. *A Commentary on the First Epistle to the Corinthians*. HNTC. New York: Harper & Row, 1968.

———. *Freedom and Obligation: A Study of the Epistle to the Galatians*. Philadelphia: Westminster, 1985.

———. *The Second Epistle to the Corinthians*. BNTC. London: A & C Black, 1973.

Barth, Karl. *The Resurrection of the Dead*. Translated by H. J. Stenning. 1933. Reprint, Eugene, OR: Wipf & Stock, 2003.

Bateman, Herbert W. IV. "Were the Opponents at Philippi Necessarily Jewish?" *BSac* 155 (1998) 39–61.

Bauckham, Richard. *Jesus and the God of Israel: God Crucified and Other Studies on the New Testament's Christology of Divine Identity*. Grand Rapids: Eerdmans, 2009.

———. "Moses as 'God' in Philo of Alexandria: A Precedent for Christology?" In *The Spirit and Christ in the New Testament and Christian Theology: Essays in Honor of Max Turner*, edited by I. Howard Marshall et al., 246–65. Grand Rapids: Eerdmans, 2012.

Baumert, Norbert. *Täglich Sterben und Auferstehen: Der Literalsinn von 2 Kor 4,12—5,10*. SANT 34. Munich: Kösel, 1973.

Beale, G. K. *The Erosion of Inerrancy in Evangelicalism: Responding to New Challenges to Biblical Authority*. Wheaton, IL: Crossway, 2008.

———. "The Old Testament Background of Reconciliation in 2 Corinthians 5–7 and its Bearing on the Literary Problem of 2 Corinthians 6:14—7:1." *NTS* 35 (1989) 550–81.

Beaulieu, Stephane A. "Egypt as God's People: Isaiah 19:19–25 and Its Allusion to the Exodus." *PRSt* 40/3 (2013) 207–18.

Becker, Eve-Marie. *Schreiben und Verstehen: Paulinische Briefhermeneutik im Zweiten Korintherbrief*. NEzT 4. Tübingen: Francke, 2002.

Beker, J. Christiaan. *Paul the Apostle: The Triumph of God in Life and Thought*. Philadelphia: Fortress, 1980.

Belleville, Linda. "A Letter of Apologetic Self-Commendation: 2 Cor. 1:8—7:16." *NovT* 31 (1989) 142–63.

———. *Reflections of Glory: Paul's Polemical Use of the Moses-Doxa Tradition in 2 Corinthians 3:1–18*. JSNTSup 52. Sheffield: JSOT Press, 1991.

Betz, Hans Dieter. *Galatians: A Commentary on Paul's Letter to the Churches in Galatia*. Hermeneia. Philadelphia: Fortress, 1979.

Beuken, W. A. M. "The Main Theme of Trito-Isaiah: 'The Servants of YHWH.'" *JSOT* 47 (1990) 67–87.

Bickerman, Elias. "The Date of IV Maccabees." In *Studies in Jewish and Christian History: Part 1*, edited by Elias Bickerman, 275–81. AGJU 9/1. Leiden: Brill, 1976.

Bird, Michael F. *Crossing Over Sea and Land: Jewish Missionary Activity in the Second Temple Period.* Peabody, MA: Hendrickson, 2010.

Bird, Michael F., and Preston M. Sprinkle, eds. *The Faith of Jesus Christ: Exegetical, Biblical, and Theological Studies.* Milton Keynes, UK: Paternoster, 2009.

Blenkinsopp, Joseph. *A History of Prophecy in Israel: Revised and Enlarged.* Louisville: Westminster John Knox, 1996.

Blomberg, Craig. *1 Corinthians.* NIVAC. Grand Rapids: Zondervan, 1994.

Bloomquist, L. Gregory. *The Function of Suffering in Philippians.* JSNTSup 78. Sheffield: JSOT Press, 1993.

Bockmuehl, Markus. *The Epistle to the Philippians.* 4th ed. BNTC. London: A. & C. Black, 1997.

———. "'The Form of God' (Phil 2:6) Variations on a Theme of Jewish Mysticism." *JTS* 48 (1997) 1–23.

———. *The Remembered Peter: In Ancient Reception and Modern Debate.* WUNT 262. Tübingen: Mohr/Siebeck, 2010.

———. *Revelation and Mystery in Ancient Judaism and Pauline Christianity.* Grand Rapids: Eerdmans, 1990.

Borgen, Peder, et al. *The Works of Philo: Greek Text with Morphology.* Bellingham: Logos Bible Software, 2005.

Bornkamm, Günther. *Paul.* Translated by D. M. G. Stalker. New York: Harper & Row, 1971.

———. "Die Vorgeschichte des sogennanten Zweiten Korintherbriefes." In *Gesammelte Aufsätze,* IV, 162–94. BEvT 53. Munich: Kaiser, 1971.

Bovon, François. "Une formule prépaulinienne dans l'Épître aux Galates (Ga 1, 4–5)." In *Paganisme Judaïsme, Christianisme: influences et affrontements dans le monde antique: mélanges offerts à Marcel Simon,* edited by A. Benoit, et al., 91–107. Paris: Boccard, 1978.

Brawley, Robert L. "From Reflex to Reflection? Identity in Philippians 2:6–11 and Its Context." In *Reading Paul in Context: Explorations in Identity Formation, Essays in Honour of William S. Campbell,* edited by Kathie Ehrensperger and J. Brian Tucker, 128–46. LNTS 428. London: T. & T. Clark, 2010.

Brower, Kent. *Living as God's Holy People: Holiness and Community in Paul.* Milton Keynes, UK: Paternoster, 2010.

Brown, Colin, ed. *New International Dictionary of New Testament Theology.* 4 vols. Grand Rapids: Zondervan, 1975–1985.

Brown, Jeannine K. *Scripture as Communication: Introducing Biblical Hermeneutics.* Grand Rapids: Baker Academic, 2007.

Brown, Rupert. *Group Processes: Dynamics within and between Groups.* 2nd ed. Oxford: Blackwell, 2000.

Bruce, F. F. *1 and 2 Corinthians.* NCB. London: Oliphants, 1971.

———. *The Epistle of Paul to the Romans.* TNTC 6. Grand Rapids: Eerdmans, 1963.

———. *The Epistle to the Galatians.* NIGTC. Grand Rapids: Eerdmans, 1982.

———. "Galatians Problems: 1. Autobiographical Data." *BJRL* 51 (1966) 292–309.

———. *Philippians.* NIBCNT 11. Peabody: Hendrickson, 1989.

———. *Tradition: Old and New.* Grand Rapids: Zondervan, 1970.

Bryant, Robert A. *The Risen Crucified Christ in Galatians.* SBLDS 185. Atlanta: SBL, 2001.

Buck, Charles, and Greer Taylor. *Saint Paul: A Study of the Development of His Thought*. New York: Scribner, 1969.

Buitenwerf, Rieuwerd. *Book III of the Sibylline Oracles and Its Social Setting: With an Introduction, Translation, and Commentary*. Studia in Veteris Testamenti Pseudepigrapha 17. Leiden: Brill, 2003.

Burk, Denny. "On the Articular Infinitive in Philippians 2:6: A Grammatical Note with Christological Implications." *TynBul* 55 (2004) 253–73.

Burton, Ernest de Witt. *A Critical and Exegetical Commentary on the Epistle to the Galatians*. ICC. Edinburgh: T. & T. Clark, 1921.

Byrskog, Samuel. "Co-Senders, Co-Authors and Paul's Use of the First Person Plural." *ZNW* 87 (1996) 230–50.

Caird, G. B. *Paul's Letters from Prison in the Revised Standard Version*. NCB. Oxford: Oxford University Press, 1976.

Campbell, Constantine R. *Paul and Union with Christ: An Exegetical and Theological Study*. Grand Rapids: Zondervan, 2012.

Campbell, Douglas A. *Framing Paul: An Epistolary Biography*. Grand Rapids: Eerdmans, 2014.

———. *The Rhetoric of Righteousness in Romans 3:21–26*. JSNTSup 65. Sheffield: Sheffield Academic, 1992.

Campbell, William S. "'I Rate All Things as Loss': Paul's Puzzling Accounting System. Judaism as Loss or the Re-evaluation of All Things in Christ?" In *Celebrating Paul: Festschrift in Honor of Jerome Murphy-O'Connor, O.P., and Joseph A. Fitzmyer, S.J*, edited by Peter Spitaler, 39–61. CBQMS 48. Washington: Catholic Biblical Association of America, 2011.

———. *Paul and the Creation of Christian Identity*. LNTS 322. London: T. & T. Clark, 2008.

Carrez, Maurice. "Le 'nous' en 2 Corinthiens: Paul parle-t-il au nom de toute la communauté, du groupe apostolique, de l'équipe ministérielle ou en son nom personnel? Contribution à l'étude de l'apostolicité dans 2 Corinthiens." *NTS* 26 (1980) 474–86.

Carver, Frank G. *2 Corinthians: A Commentary in the Wesleyan Tradition*. NBBC. Kansas City: Beacon Hill, 2009.

Casey, Maurice. *From Jewish Prophet to Gentile God: The Origins and Development of New Testament Christology*. Cambridge: James Clarke, 1991.

Castelli, Elizabeth A. *Imitating Paul: A Discussion of Power*. Louisville: Westminster John Knox, 1991.

Cerfaux, Lucien. "L'hymne au Christ—sérviteur de Dieu (Phil. 2.6–1 = Is. 52.13–53.12)." In *Recueil Lucien Cerfaux* Vol 2, 425–37. BETL 6–7. Gembloux: Duculot, 1954.

Chamblin, Knox. "Revelation and Tradition in the Pauline *Euangelion*." *WTJ* 48 (1986) 1–16.

Chapman, David W. *Ancient Jewish and Christian Perceptions of Crucifixion*. WUNT 2/244. Tübingen: Mohr/Siebeck, 2008.

Charlesworth, James H., ed. *The Messiah: Developments in Earliest Judaism and Christianity*. Minneapolis: Fortress, 1992.

———. *The Old Testament Pseudepigrapha*. 2 vols. New Haven: Yale University Press, 1983–85.

Chester, Andrew. *Messiah and Exaltation: Jewish Messianic and Visionary Traditions and New Testament Christology.* WUNT 207. Tübingen: Mohr/Siebeck, 2007.

Chester, Stephen. *Conversion at Corinth: Perspectives on Conversion in Paul's Theology and the Corinthian Church.* SNTW. London: T. & T. Clark, 2003.

Childs, Brevard S. *The Book of Exodus: A Critical, Theological Commentary.* OTL. Louisville: Westminster John Knox, 1974.

———. *Isaiah.* OTL. Louisville: Westminster John Knox, 2001.

———. "Retrospective Reading of the Old Testament Prophets." *ZAW* 108 (1996) 362–77.

Chisholm, Robert B., Jr. "The Christological Fulfillment of Isaiah's Servant Songs." *BSac* 163 (2006) 387–404.

Chow, John K. *Patronage and Power: A Study of Social Networks in Corinth.* JSNTSup 75. Sheffield: Sheffield Academic, 1992.

Churchill, Timothy W. R. *Divine Initiative and the Christology of the Damascus Road Encounter.* Eugene, OR: Pickwick, 2010.

Ciampa, Roy E. *The Presence and Function of Scripture in Galatians 1 and 2.* WUNT 2.102. Tübingen: Mohr/Siebeck, 1998.

———. "Scriptural Language and Ideas." In *As It Is Written: Studying Paul's Use of Scripture*, edited by Stanley E. Porter and Christopher D. Stanley, 41–57. SBLSymS 50. Atlanta: SBL, 2008.

Ciampa, Roy E., and Brian S. Rosner. *The First Letter to the Corinthians.* PNTC. Grand Rapids: Eerdmans, 2010.

Clarke, Andrew D. *A Pauline Theology of Church Leadership.* LNTS 362. London: T. & T. Clark, 2008.

Clements, Ronald E. "Jeremiah 1–25 and the Deuteronomistic History." In *Understanding Poets and Prophets*, edited by A. G. Auld, 94–113. JSOTSup 152. Sheffield: JSOT, 1993.

Clifford, Richard J. "Narrative and Lament in Isaiah 63.7—64.11." In *To Touch the Text: Biblical and Rhetorical Studies in Honour of Joseph A. Fitzmyer*, edited by Maurya P. Horgan and Paul J. Kobelski, 93–102. New York: Crossroad, 1989.

Cline, David J. A. *I, He, We, and They—A Literary Approach to Isaiah 53.* JSOTSup 1. Sheffield: JSOT, 1976.

Coats, George W. *Moses: Heroic Man, Man of God.* JSOTSup 57. Sheffield: JSOT, 1988.

Cole, R. Alan. *Galatians.* TNTC. 2nd ed. Grand Rapids: Eerdmans, 1989.

Collins, J. J. *The Apocalyptic Imagination: An Introduction to the Jewish Matrix of Christianity.* New York: Crossroads, 1987.

———. *Apocalypticism in the Dead Sea Scrolls.* London: Routledge, 1997.

Collins, Raymond F. *First Corinthians.* SacPag 7. Collegeville, MN: Liturgical, 1999.

———. *Second Corinthians.* PCNT. Grand Rapids: Baker Academic, 2013.

Cook, David. "The Prescript as Programme in Galatians." *JTS* 43 (1992) 511–19.

Conzelmann, Hans. *1 Corinthians: A Commentary on the First Epistle to the Corinthians.* Translated by James W. Leitch. Hermeneia. Philadelphia: Fortress, 1975.

Crafton, Jeffrey A. *The Agency of the Apostle: A Dramatistic Analysis of Paul's Response to Conflict in 2 Corinthians.* JSNTSup 51. Sheffield: JSOT, 1991.

Cranfield, C. E. B. "Changes of Person and Number in Paul's Epistles." In *Paul and Paulinism: Essays in Honour of C. K. Barrett*, edited by M. D. Hooker and S. G. Wilson, 280–289. London: SPCK, 1982.

————. "St. Paul and the Law." In *New Testament Issues*, edited by R. Batey, 149–72. London: SCM, 1970.

Cummins, Stephen A. *Paul and the Crucified Christ in Antioch: Maccabean Martyrdom and Galatians 1 and 2*. SNTSMS 114. Cambridge: Cambridge University Press, 2001.

Dahl, Nils A. "Paul and the Church at Corinth according to 1 Corinthians 1:10–4:21." In *Christian History and Interpretation: Studies Presented to John Knox*, edited by W. R. Farmer et al., 313–35. Cambridge: Cambridge University Press, 1967.

————. "Paul and the Church at Corinth according to 1 Corinthians 1:10–4:21." In *Studies in Paul: Theology for the Early Christian Mission*, edited by Nils Dahl and Paul Donahue, 40–61. Minneapolis: Augsburg, 1977.

Damgaard, Finn. *Recasting Moses: The Memory of Moses in Biographical and Auto-biographical Narratives in Ancient Judaism and 4th-Century Christianity*. ECCA 13. Frankfurt: Lang, 2013.

Danker, Frederick W. *II Corinthians*. ACNT. Minneapolis: Augsburg, 1989.

Davies, W. D. Review of *Galatians: A Commentary of Paul's Letter to the Churches of Galatia*, by H. D. Betz. *RSR* 7 (1981) 310–17.

Dearman, J. Andrew. *Jeremiah and Lamentations*. NIVAC. Grand Rapids: Zondervan, 2002.

De Boer, Martinus C. "The Composition of 1 Corinthians." *NTS* 40 (1994) 229–45.

————. *Galatians*. NTL. Louisville: Westminster John Knox, 2011.

DeSilva, David A. *4 Maccabees*. Guides to Apocrypha and Pseudepigrapha. Sheffield: Sheffield Academic, 1998.

————. *Galatians: A Handbook on the Greek Text*. BHGNT. Waco: Baylor University Press, 2014.

————. "No Confidence in the Flesh: The Meaning and Function of Philippians 3:2–21." *TJ* 15 (1994) 27–54.

————. "The *Testaments of the Twelve Patriarchs* as Witnesses to Pre-Christian Judaism: A Re-Assessment." *JSP* 22/4 (2013) 21–68.

Dibelius, Martin. *An die Thessalonicher I, II. An die Philipper*. HNT 11. Tübingen: Mohr/Siebeck, 1937.

Dickson, John P. *Mission-Commitment in Ancient Judaism and in the Pauline Communities*. WUNT 2/159. Tübingen: Mohr/Siebeck, 2003.

Dietzfelbinger, Christian. *Die Berufung des Paulus als Ursprung seiner Theologie*. WMANT 58. Neukirchen-Vluyn: Neukirchener, 1985.

Dinter, Paul E. "Paul and the Prophet Isaiah." *BTB* (1983) 48–52.

Dodd, Brian J. *Pau's Paradigmatic 'I': Personal Example as Literary Strategy*. JSNTSup 177. Sheffield: Sheffield Academic, 1999.

Donaldson, Terence L. "The 'Curse of the Law' and the Inclusion of the Gentiles: Galatians 3:13–14." *NTS* 32 (1986) 94–112.

————. *Paul and the Gentiles: Remapping the Apostle's Convictional World*. Minneapolis: Fortress, 1997.

Doty, William G. *Letters in Primitive Christianity*. GBS. 1973. Reprint, Eugene, OR: Wipf & Stock, 2014.

Duff, Paul B. "Glory in the Ministry of Death: Gentile Condemnation and Letters of Recommendation in 2 Cor. 3:6–18." *NovT* 46 (2004) 313–37.

Duhm, Bernhard. *Das Buch Jesaia*. GHAT 3.1. Göttingen: Vandenhoeck & Ruprecht, 1892.

Dumbrell, William J. "Paul's Use of Exodus 34 in 2 Corinthians 3." In *God Who Is Rich in Mercy: Essays Presented to Dr. D. B. Knox*, edited by Peter T. O'Brien and David G. Peterson, 179–94. Homebush West, NSW: Lancer, 1986.

Duncan, George S. *The Epistle of Paul to the Galatians*. New York: Harper, 1934.

Dunn, James D. G. "4QMMT and Galatians." *NTS* 43 (1997) 147–153.

————. *Baptism in the Holy Spirit: A Re-examination of the New Testament Teaching of the Gift of the Spirit in Relation to Pentecostalism Today*. London: SCM, 1970.

————. *The Christ and the Spirit: Volume 1 Christology*. Grand Rapids: Eerdmans, 1998.

————. *Christology in the Making: A New Testament Inquiry into the Origins of the Doctrine of the Incarnation*. 2nd ed. Grand Rapids: Eerdmans, 1989.

————. *The Epistle to the Galatians*. BNTC IX. Peabody, MA: Hendrickson, 1993.

————. "How Are the Dead Raised? With What Body Do They Come? Reflections on 1 Corinthians 15." *SwJT* 45 (2002) 4–18.

————. *Jesus and the Spirit*. London: SCM, 1975.

————. *Jesus, Paul and the Law: Studies in Mark and Galatians*. Louisville: Westminster John Knox, 1990.

————. *The New Perspective on Paul*. 2nd ed. Grand Rapids: Eerdmans, 2008.

————. "Once More, ΠΙΣΤΙΣ ΧΡΙΣΤΟΥ." In *Pauline Theology: Volume IV Looking Back, Pressing On*, edited by E. Elizabeth Johnson and David M. Hay, 61–81. Atlanta: Scholars, 1997.

————. "Paul and Justification by Faith." In *The Road from Damascus: The Impact of Paul's Conversion on His Life, Thought, and Ministry*, edited by Richard N. Longenecker, 85–101. Grand Rapids: Eerdmans, 1997.

————. *Romans 1–8*. WBC 38A. Waco, TX: Word, 1988.

————. *Romans 9–16*. WBC 38B. Waco, TX: Word, 1988.

————. *The Theology of Paul the Apostle*. Grand Rapids: Eerdmans, 1998.

Durham, John I. *Exodus*. WBC 3. Waco, TX: Word, 1987.

Ebeling, Gerhard. *Die Wahrheit des Evangeliums: Eine Lesehilfe zum Galaterbrief*. Tübingen: Mohr/Siebeck, 1981.

Ehorn, Seth M. "Galatians 1:8 and Paul's Reading of Abraham's Story." *JTS* 64 (2013) 439–44.

Ehrensperger, Kathy. *Paul and the Dynamic of Power: Communication and Interaction in the Early Christ-Movement*. New York: T. & T. Clark, 2009.

Ellis, E. Earle. *Paul's Use of the Old Testament*. Grand Rapids: Baker, 1981.

————. "Tradition in 1 Corinthians." *NTS* 32 (1986) 481–502.

Enslin, Morton S. *Reapproaching Paul*. Philadelphia: Westminster, 1972.

Eriksson, Anders. *Traditions as Rhetorical Proof: Pauline Argumentation in 1 Corinthians*. ConBNT 29. Stockholm: Almqvist & Wiksell, 1998.

Esler, Philip F. *Conflict and Identity in Romans: The Social Setting of Paul's Letter*. Minneapolis: Fortress, 2003.

Fabry, Heinz-Josef. "Mose, der 'Gesalbte JHWHs': Messianische Aspekte der Mose-Interpretation in Qumran." In *Moses in Biblical and Extra Biblical Traditions*, edited by Axel Graupner and Michael Wolter, 129–42. BZAW 372. Berlin: de Gruyter, 2007.

Fatehi, Mehrdad. *The Spirit's Relation to the Risen Lord in Paul: An Examination of Its Christological Implications*. WUNT 128. Tübingen: Mohr/Siebeck, 2000.

Fee, Gordon D. *The First Epistle to the Corinthians*. NICNT. Grand Rapids: Eerdmans, 1987.

———. *Galatians*. PCS. Dorset, UK: Deo, 2011.

———. *God's Empowering Presence: The Holy Spirit in the Letters of Paul*. Grand Rapids: Baker Academic, 1994.

———. *Pauline Christology: An Exegetical-Theological Study*. Peabody, MA: Hendrickson, 2007.

———. *Paul's Letter to the Philippians*. NICNT. Grand Rapids: Eerdmans, 1995.

Fitzgerald, John T. *Cracks in an Earthen Vessel: An Examination of the Catalogues of Hardships in the Corinthian Correspondence*. SBLDS 99. Atlanta: Scholars, 1988.

Fitzmyer, Joseph A. *First Corinthians: A New Translation with Introduction and Commentary*. AYB 32. New Haven: Yale University Press, 2008.

———. "Qumrân and the Interpolated Paragraph in 2 Cor 6,14—7,1." *CBQ* 23 (1961) 271–80.

———. *To Advance the Gospel: New Testament Studies*. 2nd ed. Grand Rapids: Eerdmans, 1998.

Flemming, Dean. *Philippians: A Commentary in the Wesleyan Tradition*. NBBC. Kansas City: Beacon Hill, 2009.

Fletcher-Louis, Crispin. "4Q374: A Discourse on the Sinai Tradition: The Deification of Moses and Early Christology." *DSD* 3 (1996) 236–52.

Fortna, Robert T. "Philippians: Paul's Most Egocentric Letter." In *The Conversation Continues, Studies in Paul and John in Honor of J. Louis Martyn*, edited by Robert T. Fortna and Beverly R. Gaventa, 220–34. Nashville: Abingdon, 1990.

Foster, Christopher G. "Communal Participation in the Spirit: The Corinthian Correspondence in Light of Early Jewish Mysticism in the Dead Sea Scrolls." Ph.D. diss., University of Manchester, 2013.

Foster, Paul. "Πίστις Χριστοῦ Terminology in Philippians and Ephesians." In *The Faith of Jesus Christ: Exegetical, Biblical, and Theological Studies*, edited by Michael F. Bird and Preston M. Sprinkle, 91–110. Milton Keynes, UK: Paternoster, 2009.

———. "Who Wrote 2 Thessalonians? A Fresh Look at an Old Problem." *JSNT* 35 (2012) 150–75.

Fotopoulos, John. "Arguments Concerning Food Offered to Idols: Corinthian Quotations and Pauline Refutations in a Rhetorical *Partitio*." *CBQ* 67 (2005) 611–31.

Fowl, Stephen E. *Philippians*. THNTC. Grand Rapids: Eerdmans, 2005.

———. *The Story of Christ in the Ethics of Paul: An Analysis of the Function of the Hymnic Material in the Pauline Corpus*. JSNTSup 36. Sheffield: JSOT, 1990.

Fredriksen, Paula. "The Birth of Christianity and the Origins of Christian Anti-Judaism." In *Jesus, Judaism, and Christian Anti-Judaism: Reading the New Testament after the Holocaust*, edited by Paula Fredriksen and Adele Reinhartz, 8–30. Louisville: Westminster John Knox, 2002.

———. *From Jesus to Christ: The Origin of the New Testament Images of Jesus*. 2nd ed. New Haven: Yale University Press, 2000.

———. "Judaism, the Circumcision of Gentiles, and Apocalyptic Hope: Another Look at Galatians 1 and 2." *JTS* 42 (1991) 533–64.

———. "Paul and Augustine: Conversion Narratives, Orthodox Traditions, and the Retrospective Self." *JTS* 37 (1986) 3–34.

———. "What 'Parting of the Ways'? Jews, Gentiles, and the Ancient Mediterranean City." In *The Ways that Never Parted: Jews and Christians in Late Antiquity and the Early Middle Ages*, edited by Adam H. Becker and Annette Yoshiko Reed, 35–63. TSAJ 95. Tübingen: Mohr/Siebeck, 2003.

Fretheim, Terence E. *Exodus*. IBC. Louisville: Westminster John Knox, 1988.

Fringer, Rob A. "The Antithetical Identity of the Philippian Opponents and Paul's Shaping of Eschatological Identity." *AP* 11 (2015) 112–24.

———. "Dying to Be the Church: 1 Corinthians 15 and Paul's Shocking Revelation about Death and Resurrection." *CTaM* 6.2 (2015) 1–10.

Fung, Ronald Y. K. *The Epistle to the Galatians*. NICNT. Grand Rapids: Eerdmans, 1988.

Furnish, Victor Paul. *II Corinthians: A New Translation with Introduction and Commentary*. AB 32A. Garden City: Doubleday, 1984.

———. *The Theology of the First Letter to the Corinthians*. NTT. Cambridge: Cambridge University Press, 1999.

Gager, John G. *Reinventing Paul*. New York: Oxford University Press, 2000.

Gammie, John G. "Spatial and Ethical Dualism in Jewish Wisdom and Apocalyptic Literature." *JBL* 93 (1974) 356–85.

Garland, David E. *2 Corinthians*. NAC 29. Nashville: Broadman & Holman, 1999.

———. "The Composition and Unity of Philippians: Some Neglected Literary Factors." *NovT* 27.2 (1985) 141–73.

———. *First Corinthians*. BECNT. Grand Rapids: Baker, 2003.

Garrett, Duane A. "Veiled Hearts: The Translation and Interpretation of 2 Corinthians 3." *JETS* 53 (2010) 729–72.

Gaston, Lloyd. *Paul and the Torah*. Vancouver: University of British Columbia Press, 1990.

Gaventa, Beverly Roberts. *From Darkness to Light: Aspects of Conversion in the New Testament*. Philadelphia: Fortress, 1986.

———. "Galatians 1 and 2: Autobiography as Paradigm." *NovT* 28.4 (1986) 309–26.

———. *Our Mother Saint Paul*. Louisville: Westminster John Knox, 2007.

———. "Paul's Conversion: A Critical Sifting of the Epistolary Evidence." Ph.D. diss., Duke University, 1978.

———. "The Singularity of the Gospel: A Reading of Galatians." In *Pauline Theology*. Vol. 1, *Thessalonians, Philippians, Galatians, Philemon*, edited by Jouette Bassler, 147–59. Minneapolis: Fortress, 1991.

———. "The Singularity of the Gospel Revisited." In *Galatians and Christian Theology: Justification, the Gospel, and Ethics in Paul's Letter*, edited by Mark W. Elliott et al., 187–99. Grand Rapids: Baker Academic, 2014.

Georgi, Dieter. *The Opponents of Paul in Second Corinthians*. Translated by Harold W. Attridge et al. Philadelphia: Fortress, 1986.

Gerhardsson, Birger. "Evidence for Christ's Resurrection According to Paul: 1 Cor 15:1–11." In *Neotestamentica et Philonica: Studies in Honor of Peder Borgen*, edited by D. E. Aune et al., 73–91. NovTSup 106. Leiden: Brill, 2003.

Gignilliat, Mark S. *Paul and Isaiah's Servants: Paul's Theological Reading of Isaiah 40–66 in 2 Corinthians 5:14—6:10*. LNTS 330. London: T. & T. Clark, 2007.

———. "Who is Isaiah's Servant? Narrative Identity and Theological Potentiality." *SJT* 61 (2008) 125–36.

Goldingay, John. "The Arrangement of Isaiah XLI–XLV." *VT* 29 (1979) 289–99.

———. *Isaiah*. NIBCOT. Peabody, MA: Hendrickson, 2001.

Gorman, Michael J. *Apostle of the Crucified Lord: A Theological Introduction to Paul and His Letters*. Grand Rapids: Eerdmans, 2004.

———. *Cruciformity: Paul's Narrative Spirituality of the Cross*. Grand Rapids: Eerdmans, 2001.

————. *Inhabiting the Cruciform God: Kenosis, Justification, and Theosis in Paul's Narrative Soteriology*. Grand Raids: Eerdmans, 2009.

Goulder, Michael D. "The Visionaries of Laodicea." *JSNT* 43 (1991) 15–39.

Grayston, Kenneth. "The Opponents in Philippians 3." *ExpTim* 97 (1986) 170–72.

Greathouse, William M., and George Lyons. *Romans 9–16: A Commentary in the Wesleyan Tradition*. NBBC. Kansas City: Beacon Hill, 2008.

Gundry, Robert H. "Style and Substance in 'the Myth of God Incarnate' according to Philippians 2:6–11." In *Crossing the Boundaries: Essays in Biblical Interpretation in Honour of Michael D. Goulder*, edited by Stanley E. Porter et al., 271–93. BIS 8. Leiden: Brill, 1994.

Gupta, Nijay K. *Worship that Makes Sense to Paul: A New Approach to the Theology and Ethics of Paul's Cultic Metaphors*. BZNW 175. Berlin: de Gruyter, 2010.

Guyette, Fred. "The Genre of the Call Narrative: Beyond Habel's Model." *JBQ* 43.1 (2015) 54–58.

Habel, Norm. "The Form and Significance of the Call Narratives." *ZAW* 77 (1965) 297–323.

Habermann, Jürgen. *Präexistenzaussagen im Neuen Testament*. Europäische Hochschulschriften 23/362. Frankfurt: Lang, 1990.

Hafemann, Scott J. *2 Corinthians*. NIVAC. Grand Rapids: Zondervan, 2000.

————. "Moses in the Apocrypha and Pseudepigrapha: A Survey." *JSP* 7 (1990) 79–104.

————. *Paul, Moses, and the History of Israel: The Letter/Spirit Contrast and the Argument from Scripture in 2 Corinthians 3*. Peabody, MA: Hendrickson, 1996.

————. *Suffering and Ministry in the Spirit: Paul's Defence of His Ministry in II Corinthians: 2:14—3:3*. PBTM. Carlisle: Paternoster, 2000.

Hansen, G. Walter. *Abraham in Galatians: Epistolary and Rhetorical Contexts*. JSNTSup 29. Sheffield: Sheffield Academic, 1989.

————. *The Letter to the Philippians*. PNTC. Nottingham: Apollos, 2009.

————. "A Paradigm of the Apocalypse: The Gospel in the Light of Epistolary Analysis." In *The Galatians Debate: Contemporary Issues in Rhetorical and Historical Interpretation*, edited by Mark D. Nanos, 143–154. Peabody, MA: Hendrickson, 2003.

Hanson, Paul D. *The People Called: The Growth of Community in the Bible: With a New Introduction*. Louisville: Westminster John Knox, 2001.

Harmon, Matthew S. *She Must and Shall Go Free: Paul's Isaianic Gospel in Galatians*. BZNW 168. Berlin: de Gruyter, 2010.

Harris, Murray J. *The Second Epistle to the Corinthians*. NIGTC. Grand Rapids: Eerdmans, 2005.

————. *Slave of Christ: A New Testament Metaphor for Total Devotion to Christ*. NSBT 8. Leicester: Apollos, 1999.

Harvey, A. E. *Renewal through Suffering: A Study of 2 Corinthians*. SNTW. Edinburgh: T. & T. Clark, 1996.

Hatina, Thomas R. "Intertextuality and Historical Criticism in New Testament Studies: Is There a Relationship?" *BibInt* 7 (1999) 28–43.

Hawthorne, Gerald F. *Philippians*. WBC 43. Nashville: Nelson, 1983.

Hawthorne, Gerald F., and Ralph P. Martin. *Philippians: Revised*. WBC 43. Nashville: Nelson, 2004.

Hays, Richard B. "Christology and Ethics in Galatians: The Law of Christ." *CBQ* 49 (1987) 268–90.

―――. *The Conversion of the Imagination: Paul as Interpreter of Israel's Scripture.* Grand Rapids: Eerdmans, 2005.

―――. *Echoes of Scripture in the Letters of Paul.* New Haven: Yale University Press, 1989.

―――. *The Faith of Jesus Christ: The Narrative Substructure of Galatians 3:1―4:11.* 2nd ed. BRS. Grand Rapids: Eerdmans, 2002.

―――. *First Corinthians.* IBC. Louisville: John Knox, 1997.

―――. "Galatians." In *New Interpreter's Bible*, edited by Leander E. Keck, vol. 11, 181–348. Nashville, Abingdon, 2000.

―――. "ΠΙΣΤΙΣ and Pauline Christology: What Is at Stake?" In *Pauline Theology.* Vol. 4, *Looking Back, Pressing On*, edited by E. Elizabeth Johnson and David M. Hay, 35–60. Atlanta: Scholars, 1997.

Heard, Warren Joel, Jr. "Maccabean Martyr Theology: Its Genesis, Antecedents and Significance for the Earliest Soteriological Interpretation of the Death of Jesus." Ph.D. thesis, University of Aberdeen, 1987.

Heil, John Paul. *The Rhetorical Role of Scripture in 1 Corinthians.* SBLMS 15. Atlanta: SBL, 2005.

Hellerman, Joseph H. "ΜΟΡΦΗ ΘΕΟΥ as a Signifier of Social Status in Philippians 2:6." *JETS* 52 (2009) 779–97.

―――. *Reconstructing Honor in Roman Philippi: Carmen Christi as Cursus Pudorum.* SNTSMS 132. Cambridge: Cambridge University Press, 2005.

Hengel, Martin. *Between Jesus and Paul: Studies in the Earliest History of Christianity.* Translated by John Bowden. London: SCM, 1983.

―――. *Crucifixion in the Ancient World and the Folly of the Message of the Cross.* Translated by John Bowden. London: SCM, 1977.

Hengel, Martin, and Anna Maria Schwemer. *Paul Between Damascus and Antioch: The Unknown Years.* Translated by John Bowden. London: SCM, 1997.

Hengel, Martin, with Daniel P. Bailey. "The Effective History of Isaiah 53 in the Pre-Christian Period." In *The Suffering Servant: Isaiah 53 in Jewish and Christian Sources*, edited by Bernd Janowski and Peter Stuhlmacher, translated by Daniel P. Bailey, 75–146. Grand Rapids: Eerdmans, 2004.

Hodge, Caroline Johnson. *If Sons, Then Heirs: A Study of Kinship and Ethnicity in the Letters of Paul.* Oxford: Oxford University Press, 2007.

Hofius, Otfried. "Erwägungen zur Gestalt und Herkunft des paulinischen Versöhnungsgedankens." *ZTK* 77 (1980) 186–99.

―――. "The Forth Servant Song in the New Testament Letters." In *The Suffering Servant: Isaiah 53 in Jewish and Christian Sources*, edited by Bernd Janowski and Peter Stuhlmacher, translated by Daniel P. Bailey, 163–88. Grand Rapids: Eerdmans, 2004.

Hogeterp, Albert L. A. *Expectations of the End: A Comparative Traditio-Historical Study of Eschatological, Apocalyptic and Messianic Ideas in the Dead Sea Scrolls and the New Testament.* STDJ 33. Leiden: Brill, 2009.

Hollander, H. W., and G. E. Van der Hout. "The Apostle Paul Calling Himself an Abortion: 1 Cor. 15:8 within the Context of 1 Cor. 15:8–10." *NovT* 38 (1996) 224–36.

Holloway, Paul A. *Consolation in Philippians: Philosophical Sources and Rhetorical Strategy.* SNTSMS 112. Cambridge: Cambridge University Press, 2001.

Hooker, Morna D. "'Beyond the Things Which Are Written': An Examination of 1 Cor. IV.6." *NTS* 10 (1963) 127–32.

———. *Jesus and the Servant: The Influence of the Servant Concept of Deutero-Isaiah in the New Testament.* London: SPCK, 1959.

———. "The Letter to the Philippians: Introduction, Commentary, and Reflections." In *New Interpreter's Bible*, edited by Leander E. Keck, vol. 11, 467–549. Nashville: Abingdon, 2000.

Hoover, Roy. "The HARPAGMOS Enigma: A Philological Solution." *HTR* 64 (1971) 95–119.

Horsley, Richard A. *1 Corinthians.* ANTC. Nashville: Abingdon, 1998.

Hughes, Philip E. *Paul's Second Epistle to the Corinthians.* NICNT. Grand Rapids: Eerdmans, 1962.

Hurd, John C. "Reflections Concerning Paul's 'Opponents' in Galatia." In *Paul and His Opponents*, edited by Stanley E. Porter, 129–48. Pauline Studies 2. Leiden: Brill, 2005.

Hurd, John C., Jr. *The Origin of 1 Corinthians.* London: SPCK, 1965.

Isocrates. Translated by George Norlin. 3 vols. LCL. Cambridge: Harvard University Press, 1928–1929.

Jasper, David. "Literary Reading of the Bible." In *The Cambridge Companion to Biblical Interpretation*, edited by John Barton, 21–34. Cambridge Companions to Religion. Cambridge: Cambridge University Press, 1998.

Jeremias, Joachim. "Zu Phil ii 7: ΕΑΥΤΟΝ ΕΚΕΝΩΣΕΝ." *NovT* 6 (1963) 182–88.

Jervell, Jacob. *The Unknown Paul: Essays on Luke-Acts and Early Christian History.* Minneapolis: Augsburg, 1984.

Jervis, L. Ann. *Galatians.* NIBCNT. Peabody, MA: Hendrickson, 1999.

Jewett, Robert. "The Agitators and the Galatian Congregation." *NTS* 17 (1971) 198–212.

Jokiranta, Jutta. *Social Identity and Sectarianism in the Qumran Movement.* STDJ 105. Leiden: Brill, 2013.

Jones, F. Stanley. *"Freiheit" in den Briefen des Apostels Paulus: Eine historische, exegetische und religionsgeschichtliche Studie.* GTA 34. Göttingen: Vandenhoeck & Ruprecht, 1987.

Jones, Peter R. "The Apostle Paul: Second Moses to the New Covenant Community, A Study in Pauline Apostolic Authority." In *God's Inerrant Word: An International Symposium on the Trustworthiness of Scripture*, edited by J. W. Montgomery, 219–41. Minneapolis: Bethany Fellowship, 1974.

Jonge, Marinus de. "Christian Influence in the Testaments of the Twelve Patriarchs." In *Studies on the Testaments of the Twelve Patriarchs*, edited by Marinus de Jonge, 193–246. VTP 3. Leiden: Brill, 1975.

———. "The Earliest Christian Use of *Christos*: Some Suggestions." *NTS* 32 (1986) 321–43.

———. "Jesus' Death for Others and the Death of the Maccabean Martyrs." In *Text and Testimony: Essays on the New Testament and Apocryphal Literature in Honour of A. F. J. Klijn*, edited by Tijitze Baarda, 142–51. Kampen: Kok Pharos, 1988.

Josephus, Flavius. *The Works of Josephus: New Updated Edition.* Translated by William Whiston. Peabody, MA: Hendrickson, 1995.

Jowers, Dennis. "The Meaning of ΜΟΡΦΗ in Philippians 2:6–7." *JETS* 49 (2006) 739–66.

Kaiser, Walter C., Jr. "The Old Promise and the New Covenant: Jeremiah 31:31–34." *JETS* 12 (1969) 11–23.

Keener, Craig. *Acts: An Exegetical Commentary.* Vol. 2, 3:1—14:28. Grand Rapids: Baker, 2013.

Kennedy, George A. *New Testament Interpretation through Rhetorical Criticism.* Chapel Hill: University of North Carolina Press, 1984.

Keown, Mark J. *Congregational Evangelism in Philippians: The Centrality of an Appeal for Gospel Proclamation to the Fabric of Philippians.* PBM. Milton Keynes, UK: Paternoster, 2008.

Khobnya, Svetlana. *The Father Who Redeems and the Son Who Obeys: Consideration of Paul's Teaching in Romans.* Eugene, OR: Pickwick Publications, 2013.

Kim, Seyoon. *The Origin of Paul's Gospel.* WUNT 4. 1981. Reprint. Eugene, OR: Wipf & Stock, 2007.

———. *Paul and the New Perspective: Second Thoughts on the Origin of Paul's Gospel.* Grand Rapids: Eerdmans, 2002.

Kittel, Gerhard, and Gerhard Friedrich, eds. *Theological Dictionary of the New Testament.* 10 vols. Translated by Geoffrey W. Bromiley. Grand Rapids: Eerdmans, 1964–1976.

Kittel, Rudolph, et al. *Biblia Hebraica Stuttgartensia.* Stuttgart: Deutsche Bibelstiftung, 1997.

Koch, Dietrich-Alex. *Die Schrift als Zeuge des Evangeliums: Untersuchungen zur Verwendung und zum Verständnis der Schrift bei Paulus.* BHT 69. Tübingen: Mohr/Siebeck, 1986.

Koch, Klaus. *The Rediscovery of Apocalyptic: A Polemical Work on a Neglected Area of Biblical Studies and Its Damaging Effects on Theology and Philosophy.* SBT 2/22. London: SCM, 1972.

Koester, Helmut. "'The Purpose of the Polemic of a Pauline Fragment (Philippians III)." *NTS* 8 (1961/2) 317–32.

Koole, Jan L. *Isaiah III.* HCOT. Kampen: Kok Pharos, 1997.

Kooten, George H. van. "Why Did Paul Include an Exegesis of Moses' Shining Face (Exodus 34) in 2 Cor 3? Moses' Strength, Well-being and (Transitory) Glory, according to Philo, Josephus, Paul, and the Corinthian Sophists." In *The Significance of Sinai: Traditions about Sinai and Divine Revelation in Judaism and Christianity,* edited by George J. Brooke et al., 149–81. TBNJCT 12. Leiden: Brill, 2008.

Koperski, Veronica. *The Knowledge of Christ Jesus My Lord: The High Christology of Philippians 3:7–11.* CBET 16. Kampen: Kok Pharos, 1996.

Kreitzer, Larry. "'When He at Last Is First!': Philippians 2:9–11 and the Exaltation of the Lord." In *Where Christology Began: Essays on Philippians 2,* edited by Ralph P. Martin and Brian J. Dodd, 111–27. Louisville: Westminster John Knox, 1998.

Kristeva, Julia. *Desire in Language: A Semiotic Approach to Literature and Art.* Edited by Leon S. Roudiez. New York: Columbia University Press, 1980.

Kuck, David W. *Judgment and Community Conflict: Paul's Use of Apocalyptic Judgment Language in 1 Corinthians 3:5—4:5.* NovTSup 66. Leiden: Brill, 1992.

Ladd, George E. *A Theology of the New Testament.* 2nd ed. Grand Rapids: Eerdmans, 1993.

Lambrecht, Jan. *Second Corinthians.* SacPag 8. Collegeville: Liturgical, 1999.

———. "Transformation in 2 Corinthians 3,18." *Bib* 64 (1983) 243–54.

Lane, William L. "Covenant: The Key to Paul's Conflict with Corinth." *TynBul* 33 (1982) 3–29.

Lategan, Bernard. "Is Paul Defending His Apostleship in Galatians? The Function of Galatians 1:11–12 and 2:19–20 in the Development of Paul's Argument." *NTS* 34 (1988) 411–30.

Lierman, John. *The New Testament Moses.* WUNT 2/173. Tübingen: Mohr/Siebeck, 2004.

Lietzmann, Hans. *An die Galater.* 2nd ed. HNT 10. Tübingen: Mohr/Siebeck, 1923.

Lightfoot, J. B. *Saint Paul's Epistles to the Colossians and to Philemon.* London: Macmillan, 1897.

———. *Saint Paul's Epistle to the Galatians.* London: Macmillan, 1865.

Lindemann, Andreas. *Der erste Korintherbrief.* HNT 9.1. Tübingen: Mohr/Siebeck, 2000.

Lim, Kar Yong. *'The Sufferings of Christ Are Abundant in Us' (2 Corinthians 1:5): A Narrative-dynamics Investigation of Paul's Sufferings in 2 Corinthians.* LNTS 399. London: T. & T. Clark, 2009.

Lindars, Barnabas. *New Testament Apologetics: The Doctrinal Significance of the Old Testament Quotations.* London: SCM, 1961.

Litwa, M. David. *We Are Being Transformed: Deification in Paul's Soteriology.* BZNW 187. Berlin: de Gruyter, 2012.

Lohmeyer, Ernst. *Die Briefe an die Philipper.* KEK 9/1. Göttingen: Vandenhoeck & Ruprecht, 1964.

Long, Fredrick J. *Ancient Rhetoric and Paul's Apology: The Compositional Unity of 2 Corinthians.* SNTSMS 131. Cambridge: Cambridge University Press, 2004.

Longenecker, Bruce W. *The Triumph of Abraham's God: The Transformation of Identity in Galatians.* Nashville: Abingdon, 1988.

Longenecker, Richard. *Galatians.* WBC 41. Dallas: Word, 1990.

———. "A Realized Hope, a New Commitment, and a Developed Proclamation: Paul and Jesus." In *The Road from Damascus: The Impact of Paul's Conversion on His Life, Thought, and Ministry,* edited by Richard N. Longenecker, 18–42. Grand Rapids: Eerdmans, 1997.

Lull, David J. *The Spirit in Galatia: Paul's Interpretation of Pneuma as Divine Power.* SBLDS 49. 1980. Reprint, Eugene, OR: Wipf & Stock, 2006.

Lyons, George. *Galatians: A Commentary in the Wesleyan Tradition.* NBBC. Kansas City, MO: Beacon Hill, 2012.

———. *Pauline Autobiography: Toward a New Understanding.* SBLDS 73. Atlanta: Scholars, 1985.

Malcolm, Matthew R. *Paul and the Rhetoric of Reversal in 1 Corinthians: The Impact of Paul's Gospel on His Macro-Rhetoric.* SNTSMS 155. New York: Cambridge University Press, 2013.

Malina, Bruce J., and John J. Pilch. *Social-Science Commentary on the Letters of Paul.* Minneapolis: Fortress, 2006.

Marshall, I. Howard. *The Acts of the Apostle: An Introduction and Commentary.* TNTC. Grand Rapids: Eerdmans, 1980.

———. "The Meaning of 'Reconciliation.'" In *Unity and Diversity in New Testament Theology: Essays in Honor of George E. Ladd,* edited by Robert A. Guelich, 117–32. Grand Rapids: Eerdmans, 1978.

———. *New Testament Theology.* Downers Grove, IL: InterVarsity, 2004.

Marshall, Peter. *Enmity in Corinth: Social Conventions in Paul's Relations with the Corinthians.* WUNT 2/23. Tübingen: Mohr/Siebeck, 1987.

Martin, Dale B. *The Corinthian Body.* New Haven: Yale University Press, 1995.

———. *Slavery as Salvation: The Metaphor of Slavery in Pauline Christianity.* New Haven: Yale University Press, 1990.

Martin, Ralph P. *2 Corinthians.* WBC 40. Waco, TX: Word, 1986.

———. *Philippians.* Revised Edition. NCBC. London: Marshall, Morgan & Scott, 1980.

Martin, Ralph P., and Brian J. Dodd, eds. *Where Christology Began: Essays on Philippians 2.* Louisville: Westminster John Knox, 1998.

Martínez, Florentino García, and Eibert J. C. Tigchelaar. *The Dead Sea Scrolls: Study Edition.* 2 vols. 2nd ed. Leiden: Brill, 1997–1998.

Martyn, J. Louis. *Galatians: A New Translation with Introduction and Commentary.* AB 33A. New York: Doubleday, 1997.

Matera, Frank J. *II Corinthians: A Commentary.* NTL. Louisville: Westminster John Knox, 2003.

———. *God's Saving Grace: A Pauline Theology.* Grand Rapids: Eerdmans, 2012.

Mauser, Ulrich, *The Gospel of Peace: A Scriptural Message for Today's World.* Louisville: Westminster John Knox, 1992.

McCant, Jerry W. *2 Corinthians.* RNBC. Sheffield: Sheffield Academic, 1999.

———. "Paul's Periodic Apologia." In *Rhetorics and Hermeneutics: Wilhelm Wuellner and His Influence,* edited by J. D. Hester, 175–92. ESEC 9. New York: T. & T. Clark, 2004.

McGrath, James F. *The Only True God: Early Christian Monotheism in Its Jewish Context.* Urbana: University of Illinois Press, 2009.

McKeating, Henry. "Ezekiel the 'Prophet Like Moses'?" *JSOT* 61 (1994) 97–109.

McKenzie, John L. *Second Isaiah: A New Translation with Introduction and Commentary.* AB 20. Garden City, NY: Doubleday, 1968.

McKnight, Scot. *Galatians.* NIVAC. Grand Rapids: Zondervan, 1995.

———. *A Light among the Gentiles: Jewish Missionary Activity in the Second Temple Period.* Minneapolis: Fortress, 1991.

Meier, Hans-Christoph. *Mystik bei Paulus: zur Phänomenologie religiöser Erfahrung im Newuem Testament.* TANZ 26. Tübingen: Francke, 1998.

Meyers, Carol. *Exodus.* NCBC. Cambridge: Cambridge University Press, 2005.

Miller, James C. "Paul and His Ethnicity: Reframing the Categories." In *Paul as Missionary: Identity, Activity, Theology, and Practice,* edited by Trevor J. Burke and Brian S. Rosner, LNTS 420, 37–50. London: T. & T. Clark, 2011.

Miller, Geoffrey D. "Intertextuality in Old Testament Research." *CBR* 9 (2010) 283–309.

Mitchell, Margaret. *Paul and the Rhetoric of Reconciliation: An Exegetical Investigation of the Language and Composition of 1 Corinthians.* Louisville: Westminster John Knox, 1993.

———. "Rhetorical Shorthand in Pauline Argumentation: The Function of 'the Gospel' in the Corinthian Correspondence." In *Gospel in Paul: Studies on Corinthians, Galatians and Romans for Richard N. Longenecker,* edited by L. Ann Jervis and Peter Richardson, 63–88. JSNTSup 108. Sheffield: Sheffield Academic, 1994.

Moo, Douglas J. *Galatians.* BECNT. Grand Rapids: Baker Academic, 2013.

Morgan, Robert. "Incarnation, Myth, and Theology." In *Where Christology Began: Essays on Philippians 2,* edited by Ralph P. Martin and Brian J. Dodd, 43–73. Louisville: Westminster John Knox, 1998.

Morland, Kjell Arne. *The Rhetoric of Curse in Galatians: Paul Confronts Another Gospel.* ESEC 5. Atlanta: Scholars, 1995.

Morse, Holly. "What's in a Name? Analysing the Appellation 'Reception History' within Biblical Studies." *BibRec* 3 (2014) 243–64.

Moule, C. F. D. "Once More, Who Where the Hellenists?" *ExpTim* 70/4 (1959) 100–02.

Moyise, Steve. "Intertextuality and Biblical Studies: A Review." *VEE* 23 (2002) 418–31.

———. "Intertextuality and the Study of the Old Testament in the New Testament." In *The Old Testament in the New Testament,* edited by Steve Moyise, 14–41. JSNTSup 189. Sheffield: Sheffield Academic, 2000.

———. *Paul and Scripture.* Grand Rapids, Baker Academic, 2010.

Moyise, Steve, and Maarten J. J. Menken, eds. *Isaiah in the New Testament.* NTSI. New York: T. & T. Clark, 2005.

Munck, Johannes. *Paul: The Salvation of Mankind.* London: SCM, 1959.

Murphy-O'Connor, Jerome. "Co-Authorship in the Corinthian Correspondence." *RB* 100 (1993) 562–79.

———. *Paul: A Critical Life.* Oxford: Clarendon, 1996.

———. *Paul the Letter-Writer: His World, His Options, His Skills.* GNS 41. Collegeville, MN: Liturgical, 1995.

———. "Philo and 2 Cor 6:14–7:1." *RB* 95 (1988) 55–69.

———. *The Theology of the Second Letter to the Corinthians.* NTT. Cambridge: Cambridge University Press, 1991.

———. "Tradition and Redaction in 1 Cor 15:3–7." *CBQ* 43 (1981) 582–98.

Nanos, Mark D., ed. *The Galatians Debate: Contemporary Issues in Rhetorical and Historical Interpretation.* Peabody, MA: Hendrickson, 2002.

———. *The Irony of Galatians: Paul's Letter in First-Century Context.* Minneapolis: Fortress, 2002.

———. "Paul's Reversal of Jews Calling Gentiles 'Dogs' (Philippians 3:2): 1600 Years of an Ideological Tale Wagging an Exegetical Dog?" *BibInt* 17 (2009) 448–82.

———. "What Was at Stake in Peter's 'Eating with Gentiles' at Antioch?" In *The Galatians Debate: Contemporary Issues in Rhetorical and Historical Interpretation,* edited by Mark D. Nanos, 282–318. Peabody, MA: Hendrickson, 2003.

Nash, Robert S. *1 Corinthians.* SHBC. Macon, GA; Smyth & Helwys, 2009.

Nasuti, Harry P. "The Woes of the Prophets and the Rights of the Apostle: The Internal Dynamics of 1 Corinthians 9." *CBQ* 50 (1988) 246–64.

Neusner, Jacob et al., eds. *Judaisms and Their Messiahs at the Turn of the Christian Era.* Cambridge: Cambridge University Press, 1987.

Newman, Carey C. *Paul's Glory-Christology: Tradition and Rhetoric.* NovTSup 69. 1992. Reprint, Library of Early Christology. Waco, TX: Baylor University Press, 2017.

Novenson, Matthew V. *Christ Among the Messiahs: Christ Language in Paul and Messiah Language in Ancient Judaism.* Oxford: Oxford University Press, 2012.

———. "The Jewish Messiahs, the Pauline Christ, and the Gentile Question." *JBL* 128 (2009) 357–73.

Oakes, Peter. *Galatians.* PCNT. Grand Rapids: Baker Academic, 2015.

———. *Philippians: From People to Letter.* SNTSMS 110. Cambridge: Cambridge University Press, 2007.

O'Brien, Peter T. *The Epistle to the Philippians.* NIGTC. Grand Rapids: Eerdmans, 1991.

———. *Introductory Thanksgivings in the Letters of Paul.* NovTSup 49. Leiden: Brill, 1977.

O'Kane, Martin. "Isaiah a Prophet in the Footsteps of Moses." *JSOT* 69 (1996) 29–51.

Ortlund, Dane C. *Zeal without Knowledge: The Concept of Zeal in Romans 10, Galatians 1, and Philippians 3.* LNTS 472. London: T. & T. Clark, 2012.

Oswalt, John N. *The Book of Isaiah: Chapters 1–39.* NICOT. Grand Rapids: Eerdmans, 1986.

————. *The Book of Isaiah: Chapters 40–66.* NICOT. Grand Rapids: Eerdmans, 1998.

————. *Isaiah.* NIVAC. Grand Rapids: Zondervan, 2003.

Park, M. Sydney. *Submission within the Godhead and the Church in the Epistle to the Philippians: An Exegetical and Theological Examination of the Concept of Submission in Philippians 2 and 3.* LNTS 361. London: T. & T. Clark, 2007.

Park, Young-Ho. *Paul's Ekklesia as a Civic Assembly: Understanding the People of God in Their Politico-Social World.* WUNT 393. Tübingen: Mohr/Siebeck, 2015.

Patte, Daniel. *Paul's Faith and the Power of the Gospel: A Structural Introduction to the Pauline Letters.* 1983. Reprint, Eugene, OR: Wipf & Stock, 2016.

Perkins, Pheme. *First Corinthians.* PCNT. Grand Rapids, Baker, 2012.

Perriman, Andrew. "The Pattern of Christ's Sufferings: Colossians 1:23 and Philippians 3:10–11." *TynBul* 42 (1991) 62–79.

Peterlin, Davorin. *Paul's Letter to the Philippians in the Light of Disunity in the Church.* NovTSup 79. Leiden: Brill, 1995.

Peterman, G. W. *Paul's Gift from Philippi: Conventions of Gift-Exchange and Christian Giving.* SNTSMS 92. Cambridge: Cambridge University Press, 1997.

Petersen, David L. "Eschatology (Old Testament)." In *ABD* 2:575–79.

Pfitzner, Victor C. *Paul and the Agon Motif: Traditional Athletic Imagery in the Pauline Literature.* NovTSup 16. Leiden: Brill, 1967.

Philip, Finny. *The Origins of Pauline Pneumatology: The Eschatological Bestowal of the Spirit upon Gentiles in Judaism and in the Early Development of Paul's Theology.* WUNT 2/194. Tübingen: Mohr/Siebeck, 2005.

Phillips, Thomas E. *Paul, His Letters, and Acts.* LPS. Edited by Stanley E. Porter. Peabody, MA: Hendrickson, 2009.

Philo. *The Works of Philo: New Updated Edition.* Translated by C. D. Yonge. Peabody, MA: Hendrickson, 1993.

Pilhofer, Peter. *Philippi, Band 1: Die erste christliche Gemeinde Europas.* WUNT 1/87. Tübingen: Mohr/Siebeck, 1995.

Plummer, Robert L. *Paul's Understanding of the Church's Mission: Did the Apostle Paul Expect the Early Church Christian Communities to Evangelise?* PBM. Milton Keynes, UK: Paternoster, 2006.

Plutarch. *Moralia.* Translated by Frank C. Babbitt et al. 15 vols. LCL. London: Heinemann, 1927–1976.

Polaski, Sandra Hack. *Paul and the Discourse of Power.* GCT 8. Sheffield: Sheffield Academic, 1999.

Polycarp. *To the Philippians.* Translated by Kirsopp Lake. LCL. Cambridge: Harvard University Press, 1912.

Porter, James. "Intertextuality and the Discourse Community." *RRev* 5 (1986) 34–47.

Porter, Stanley E. *Idioms of the Greek New Testament.* 2nd ed. Sheffield: Sheffield Academic, 1994.

————. Καταλλάσσω *in Ancient Greek Literature, with Reference to the Pauline Writings.* Cordoba: El Almendro, 1994.

————. *Paul in Acts.* LPS. Peabody, MA: Hendrickson, 2001.

————. *When Paul Met Jesus: How an Idea Got Lost in History*. New York: Cambridge University Press, 2016.

Price, Robert M. "Apocryphal Apparitions: 1 Corinthians 15:3–11 as a Post-Pauline Interpolation." In *The Empty Tomb: Jesus beyond the Grave*, edited by Robert M. Price and Jeffery Jay Lowder, 69–104. Amherst, NY: Prometheus, 2005.

Prior, Michael. *Paul the Letter-Writer and the Second Letter to Timothy*. JSNTSup 23. Sheffield: JSOT, 1989.

Pyne, Robert A. "The 'Seed,' the Spirit, and the Blessing of Abraham." *BSac* 152 (1995) 211–22.

Quintilian. *Intitutio Oratoria*. Translated by H. E. Butler. 4 vols. LCL. Cambridge: Harvard University Press, 1920–1922.

Rabens, Volker. "*Pneuma* and the Beholding of God: Reading Paul in the Context of Philonic Mystical Traditions." In *The Holy Spirit, Inspiration and the Cultures of Antiquity: Multidisciplinary Perspectives*, edited by Jörg Frey and John R. Levison, 293–329. Ekstasis 5. Berlin: de Gruyter, 2014.

Radl, Walter. "Der Sinn von *gnōrizō* in 1 Kor 15,1." *BZ* 28 (1984) 243–45.

Rahlfs, Alfred, and Robert Hanhart, eds. *Septuaginta*. Peabody, MA: Hendrickson, 2006.

Räisänen, Heikki. "Paul's Conversion and the Development of His View of the Law." *NTS* 33 (1987) 404–19.

Rendtorff, Rolf. "The Composition of the Book of Isaiah." In *Canon and Theology: Overtures to an Old Testament Theology*, edited by Rolf Rendtorff, 146–69. Minneapolis: Fortress, 1993.

Reumann, John. *Philippians: A New Translation with Introduction and Commentary*. AYB 33B. New Haven: Yale University Press, 2008.

Richards, E. Randolph. *Paul and First-Century Letter Writing: Secretaries, Composition, and Collection*. Downers Grove, IL: InterVarsity, 2004.

Riddle, Donald W. *Paul: Man of Conflict*. Nashville: Cokesbury, 1940.

Rohde, Joachim. *Der Brief des Paulus an die Galater*. THKNT 9. Berlin: Evangelische, 1989.

Rosner, Brian S. *Paul, Scripture, & Ethics: A Study of 1 Corinthians 5–7*. Grand Rapids: Baker, 1994.

Routledge, Robin L. "Is There a Narrative Substructure Underlying the Book of Isaiah?" *TynBul* 55 (2004) 183–204.

Rowland, Christopher. *The Open Heaven: A Study of Apocalyptic in Judaism and Early Christianity*. New York: Crossroad, 1982.

Saldarini, Anthony J. "Delegitimation of Leaders in Matthew 23." *CBQ* 54 (1992) 659–80.

Sampley, J. Paul. "'Before God, I do not lie' (Gal. 1.20): Paul's Self-Defence in the Light of Roman Legal Praxis." *NTS* 23 (1977) 477–82.

————. *Pauline Partnership in Christ: Christian Community and Commitment in Light of Roman Law*. Philadelphia: Fortress, 1980.

Sanders, E. P. *Paul, the Law, and the Jewish People*. Minneapolis: Fortress, 1983.

Sandnes, Karl Olav. *Paul—One of the Prophets? A Contribution to the Apostle's Self-Understanding*. WUNT 2/43. Tübingen: Mohr/Siebeck, 1991.

Saw, Insawn. *Paul's Rhetoric in 1 Corinthians 15: An Analysis Utilizing the Theories of Classical Rhetoric*. Lewiston, NY: Mellen Biblical, 1994.

Scharbert, Josef. "Stellvertretendes Sühneleiden in den Ebed-Jahwe-Liedern und in altorientalischen Ritualtexten." *BZ* 2 (1958) 190–213.

Schenk, Wolfgang. *Die Philipperbriefe des Paulus: Kommentar.* Stuttgart: Kohlhammer, 1984.

Schlier, Heinrich. *Der Brief an die Galater.* KEK 7. Göttingen: Vandenhoeck & Ruprecht, 1962.

Schmithals, Walter. *Die Briefe des Paulus in ihrer Ursprünglichen Form.* ZWB. Zurich: Theologischer, 1984.

———. *Gnosticism in Corinth: An Investigation of the Letter to the Corinthians.* Translated by John E. Steely. Nashville: Abingdon, 1971.

———. *Paul and James.* SBT 1/46. London: SCM, 1965.

———. *Paul and the Gnostics.* Translated by John E. Steely. Nashville: Abingdon, 1972.

Schüssler Fiorenza, E. "Rhetorical Situation and Historical Reconstruction in 1 Corinthians." *NTS* 33 (1987) 386–403.

Schreiner, Thomas R. *Galatians.* ZECNT. Grand Rapids: Zondervan, 2010.

Schubert, Paul. *Form and Function of the Pauline Thanksgiving.* BZNW 20. Berlin: Töpelmann, 1939.

Schultz, Richard. "The King in the Book of Isaiah." In *The Lord's Anointed: Interpretation of Old Testament Messianic Texts,* edited by Philip E. Satterthwaite et al., 141–63. Grand Rapids: Baker, 1995.

Schütz, John H. *Paul and the Anatomy of Apostolic Authority.* SNTSMS 26. Cambridge: Cambridge University Press, 1975.

Schweitzer, Albert. *The Mysticism of Paul the Apostle.* 3rd ed. Translated by William Montgomery. Baltimore: John Hopkins University Press, 1998.

Scott, James M. *2 Corinthians.* NIBCNT 8. Peabody: Hendrickson, 1998.

———. *Adoption as Sons of God: An Exegetical Investigation into the Background of* ΥΙΟΘΕΣΙΑ *in the Pauline Corpus.* WUNT 2/48. Tübingen: Mohr/Siebeck, 1992.

Seeley, David. "The Background of the Philippians Hymn (2:6–11)." *JHC* 1 (1994) 49–72.

Segal, Alan F. *Life after Death: A History of the Afterlife in the Religions of the West.* New York: Doubleday, 2004.

———. *Paul the Convert: The Apostolate and Apostasy of Saul the Pharisee.* New Haven: Yale, 1990.

Seifrid, Mark A. *The Second Letter to the Corinthians.* PNTC. Grand Rapids: Eerdmans, 2014.

Seitz, Christopher R. "The Book of Isaiah 40–66: Introduction, Commentary, and Reflections." In *New Interpreter's Bible,* edited by Leander E. Keck, 4:309–552. Nashville: Abingdon, 2001.

———. "How is the Prophet Isaiah Present in the Latter Half of the Book? The Logic of Chapters 40–66 within the Book of Isaiah." *JBL* 115 (1996) 219–40.

———. "Isaiah, Book of (First Isaiah), (Third Isaiah)." In *ABD,* 3:472–88, 501–7.

Shum, Shiu-Lun. *Paul's Use of Isaiah in Romans: A Comparative Study of Paul's Letter to the Romans and the Sybilline and Qumran Sectarian Texts.* WUNT 2/156. Tübingen: Mohr/Siebeck, 2002.

Sider, Ronald. "St. Paul's Understanding of the Nature and Significance of the Resurrection in 1 Corinthians XV 1–19." *NovT* 19 (1977) 124–41.

Silva, Moisés. *Interpreting Galatians: Explorations in Exegetical Method.* Grand Rapids: Baker Academic, 2001.

————. "Old Testament in Paul." In *Dictionary of Paul and His Letters*, edited by Gerald F. Hawthorne et al., 630–42. Downers Grove, IL: InterVarsity, 1993.

————. *Philippians*. 2nd ed. BECNT. Grand Rapids: Baker Academic, 2005.

————. "Philippians." In *Commentary on the New Testament Use of the Old Testament*, edited by G. K. Beale and D. A. Carson, 835–40. Grand Rapids: Baker, 2007.

Sim, Margaret. *A Relevant Way to Read: A New Approach to Exegesis and Communication*. Eugene, OR: Pickwick, 2016.

Smit, Joop. "The Letter of Paul to the Galatians: A Deliberative Speech." *NTS* 35 (1989) 1–26.

Smith, Morton. "On the History of ΑΠΟΚΑΛΥΠΤΩ and ΑΠΟΚΑΛΥΨΙΣ." In *Apocalypticism in the Mediterranean World and the Near East: Proceedings of the International Colloquium on Apocalypticism, Uppsala, August 12–17, 1979*, edited by David Hellholm, 9–20. Tübingen: Mohr/Siebeck, 1989.

Spieckermann, Hermann. "The Conception and Prehistory of the Idea of Vicarious Suffering in the Old Testament." In *The Suffering Servant: Isaiah 53 in Jewish and Christian Sources*, edited by Bernd Janowski and Peter Stuhlmacher, 1–15. Translated by Daniel P. Bailey. Grand Rapids: Eerdmans, 2004.

Stanley, Christopher D. *Arguing with Scripture: The Rhetoric of Quotations in the Letters of Paul*. New York: T. & T. Clark, 2004.

————. *Paul and the Language of Scripture: Citation Technique in the Pauline Epistles and Contemporary Literature*. SNTSMS 74. Cambridge: Cambridge University Press, 1992.

Stanley, David M. "The Theme of the Servant of Yahweh in Primitive Christian Soteriology, and its Transposition by St. Paul." *CBQ* 16 (1954) 385–425.

Strecker, Georg. "Das Evangelium Jesus Christi." In *Jesus Christus in Historie und Theologie: Neutestamentliche Festschrift für Hans Conzelmann zum 60. Geburtstag*, edited by Georg Strecker, 503–48. Tübingen: Mohr/Siebeck, 1975.

Stendahl, Krister. *Paul among Jews and Gentiles*. London: SCM, 1977.

Stockhausen, Carol K. *Moses' Veil and the Glory of the New Covenant: The Exegetical Substructure of II Cor. 3,1—4,6*. AnBib 116. Roma: Editrice Pontificio Istituto Biblico, 1989.

Stone, Michael E. "Apocalyptic Literature." In *Jewish Writings of the Second Temple Period: Apocrypha, Pseudepigrapha, Qumran, Sectarian Writings, Philo, Josephus*, 383–441. CRINT 2/2. Assen: Van Gorcum, 1984.

Stowers, Stanley K. *Letter Writing in Greco Roman Antiquity*. LEC 5. Philadelphia: Westminster, 1986.

Sturff, Richard E. "Defining the Word 'Apocalyptic': A Problem in Biblical Criticism." In *Apocalyptic and the New Testament: Essays in Honor of J. Louis Martyn*, edited by Joel Marcus and Marion L. Soards, 17–48. JSNTSup 24. Sheffield: Sheffield Academic, 1989.

Sturm, Ricard E. "An Exegetical Study of the Apostle Paul's Use of the Words *Apokalyptō/Apokalypsis*: The Gospel as God's Apocalypse." PhD thesis, Union Theological Seminary, 1983.

Stuhlmacher, Peter. *Das paulinische Evangelium*. FRLANT 95. Göttingen: Vandenhoeck & Ruprecht, 1968.

————. "Isaiah 53 in the Gospels and Acts." In *The Suffering Servant: Isaiah 53 in Jewish and Christian Sources*, edited by Bernd Janowski and Peter Stuhlmacher, 147–62. Translated by Daniel P. Bailey. Grand Rapids: Eerdmans, 2004.

————. "The Pauline Gospel." In *The Gospel and the Gospels*, edited by Peter Stuhl-macher, 149–72. Grand Rapids: Eerdmans, 1991.

————. *Paul's Letter to the Romans: A Commentary*. Translated by Scott J. Hafemann. Louisville: Westminster John Knox, 1994.

Swanson, Dwight. "The Text of Isaiah at Qumran." In *Interpreting Isaiah: Issues and Approaches*, edited by David G. Firth and H. G. M. Williamson, 191–212. Downers Grove, IL: InterVarsity, 2009.

Talbert, Charles H. *Reading Corinthians: A Literary and Theological Commentary*. Rev. ed. RTNT. Macon, GA: Smyth & Helwys, 2002.

Theissen, Gerd. *Psychological Aspects of Pauline Theology*. Philadelphia: Fortress, 1987.

————. *The Social Setting of Pauline Christianity: Essays on Corinth*. Translated by John H. Schütz. 1982. Reprint, Eugene, OR: Wipf & Stock, 2004.

Thiselton, Anthony C. *The First Epistle to the Corinthians: A Commentary on the Greek Text*. NIGTC. Grand Rapids: Eerdmans, 2000.

————. *New Horizons in Hermeneutics*. Grand Rapids: Zondervan, 1992.

Thompson, J. A. *The Book of Jeremiah*. NICOT. Grand Rapids: Eerdmans, 1980.

Thompson, Michael B. *Clothed with Christ: The Example and Teaching of Jesus in Romans 12.1—15.13*. JSNTSup 59. Sheffield: JSOT, 1991.

————. "Paul in the Book of Acts: Differences and Distance." *ExpTim* 122.9 (2011) 425–36.

Thrall, Margaret. *A Critical and Exegetical Commentary on the Second Epistle to the Corinthians*. Vol. 1. ICC. Edinburgh: T. & T. Clark, 1994.

Tilling, Chris. *Paul's Divine Christology*. Grand Rapids: Eerdmans, 2015.

Travis, Stephen H. "Paul's Boasting in 2 Corinthians 10–12." In *Studia Evangelica*, Vol. 6, *Papers Presented to the 4th International Congress on New Testament Studies Held at Oxford, 1969*, edited by E. A. Livingstone, 527–32. Berlin: Akademie, 1973.

Tuckett, Christopher M. "The Corinthians Who Say 'There is No Resurrection of the Dead' (1 Cor 15.12)." In *The Corinthian Correspondence*, edited by R. Bieringer, 245–75. BETL 125. Leuven: Leuven University Press, 1996.

Van Henten, J. W. "Datierung und Herkunft des Vierten Makkabäerbuches." In *Tradition and Re-Interpretation in Early Christian Literature: Essays in Honour of Jürgen C. H. Lebram*, edited by J. W. van Henten, 136–49. Leiden: Brill, 1986.

Vanhoozer, Kevin J. *Is There a Meaning in This Text? The Bible, the Reader, and the Morality of Literary Knowledge*. Grand Rapids: Zondervan, 1998.

Van Voorst, Robert E. "Why is There No Thanksgiving Period in Galatians? An Assessment of an Exegetical Commonplace." *JBL* 129 (2010) 153–72.

Verhoef, E. "The Senders of the Letters to the Corinthians and the Use of 'I' and 'We'." In *The Corinthian Correspondence*, edited by R. Bieringer, 417–25. BETL 125. Leuven: Leuven University Press, 1996.

Verseput, D. J. "Paul's Gentile Mission and the Jewish Christian Community: A Study of the Narrative in Galatians 1 and 2." *NTS* 39 (1993) 36–58.

Vielhauer, Philipp. "On the 'Paulinism' of Acts." In *Studies in Luke-Acts*, edited by Leander E. Keck and J. Louis Martyn, 33–50. Nashville: Abingdon, 1966.

Vincent, Marvin R. *The Epistles to the Philippians and to Philemon*. ICC. Edinburgh: T. & T. Clark, 1985.

Wagner, J. Ross. *Heralds of the Good News: Isaiah and Paul "in Concert" in the Letter to the Romans*. NovTSup 101. Leiden: Brill, 2003.

———. "Isaiah in Romans and Galatians." In *Isaiah in the New Testament*, edited by Steve Moyise and Maarten J. J. Menken, 117–32. NTSI. New York: T. & T. Clark, 2005.

———. "'Not beyond the Things Which are Written': A Call to Boast Only in the Lord (1 Cor. 4:6)." *NTS* 44 (1998) 279–87.

Wallace, Daniel B. *Greek Grammar Beyond the Basics: An Exegetical Syntax of the New Testament.* Grand Rapids: Zondervan, 1996.

Wallace, James. *Snatched into Paradise (2 Cor 12:1–10) Paul's Heavenly Journey in the Context of Early Christian Experience.* BZNW 179. Berlin: de Gruyter, 2011.

Ware, James P. *Paul and the Mission of the Church: Philippians in Ancient Jewish Context.* Grand Rapids: Baker Academic, 2011.

Watson, Duane F. "Paul's Boasting in 2 Corinthians 10–13 as Defense of His Honor: A Social-Rhetorical Analysis." In *Rhetorical Argumentation in Biblical Texts: Essays from the Lund 2000 Conference*, edited by Anders Eriksson et al., 260–75. ESEC 8. Harrisburg, PA: Trinity, 2002.

Watson, Francis. *Paul and the Hermeneutics of Faith.* London: T. & T. Clark, 2004.

Watts, John D. W. *Isaiah 1–33.* WBC 24. Waco, TX: Word, 1985.

———. *Isaiah 34–66.* WBC 25. Waco, TX: Word, 1987.

Webb, William J. *Returning Home: New Covenant and Second Exodus as the Context for 2 Corinthians 6:14—7:1.* JSNTSup 85. Sheffield: JSOT, 1993.

Westerholm, Stephen. "'Letter' and 'Spirit': The Foundation of Pauline Ethics." *NTS* 30 (1984) 229–48.

Westermann, Claus. *Isaiah 40–66: A Commentary.* David M. G. Stalker. OTL. Philadelphia: Westminster, 1969.

White, L. Michael. "Paul and *Pater Familias*." In *Paul in the Greco-Roman World: A Handbook*, edited by J. Paul Sampley, 457–87. Harrisburg, PA: Trinity, 2003.

Whittle, Sarah. *Covenant Renewal and the Consecration of the Gentiles in Romans.* SNTSMS 161. New York: Cambridge University Press, 2015.

Wilckens, Ulrich. "Die Bekehrung des Paulus als religionsgeschichtliches Problem." In *Rechtfertigung als Freiheit: Paulusstudien*, 11–32. Neukirchen-Vluyn: Neukirchener, 1974.

Wilcox, Peter, and David Paton-Williams. "The Servant Songs in Deutero-Isaiah." *JSOT* 42 (1988) 79–102.

Wilk, Florian. *Die Bedeutung des Jesajabuches für Paulus.* FRLANT 179. Göttingen: Vandenhoeck & Ruprecht, 1998.

———. "Isaiah in 1 and 2 Corinthians." In *Isaiah in the New Testament*, edited by Steve Moyise and Maarten J. J. Menken, 133–58. NTSI. London: T. & T. Clark, 2005.

Williams, Demetrius K. *Enemies of the Cross of Christ: The Terminology of the Cross and Conflict in Philippians.* JSNTSup 223. Sheffield: Sheffield Academic, 2002.

Williams, Jarvis J. *Maccabean Martyr Traditions in Paul's Theology of Atonement: Did Martyr Theology Shape Paul's Conception of Jesus's Death?* Eugene, OR: Wipf & Stock, 2010.

Williamson, H. G. M. "Recent Issues in the Study of Isaiah." In *Interpreting Isaiah: Issues and Approaches*, edited by David G. Firth and H. G. M. Williamson, 21–39. Downers Grove, IL: InterVarsity, 2009.

———. *Variations on a Theme: King, Messiah and Servant in the Book of Isaiah.* Didsbury Lectures, 1997. Carlisle, UK: Paternoster, 1998.

Willis, Wendell. "An Apostolic Apologia? The Form and Function of 1 Corinthians 9." *JSNT* 24 (1985) 33–48.

Winger, Michael. "Tradition, Revelation and Gospel: A Study in Galatians." *JSNT* 53 (1994) 65–86.

Winter, Bruce W. "Carnal Conduct and Sanctification in 1 Corinthians: *Simul sanctus et peccator?*" In *Holiness and Ecclesiology in the New Testament*, edited by Kent E. Brower and Andy Johnson, 184–200. Grand Rapids: Eerdmans, 2007.

———. *Philo and Paul among the Sophists*. SNTSMS 96. Cambridge: Cambridge University Press, 1997.

———. *Seek the Welfare of the City: Christians as Benefactors and Citizens*. Carlisle, UK: Paternoster, 1994.

Wiseman, Timothy P. *Remus: A Roman Myth*. Cambridge: Cambridge University Press, 1995.

Witherington, Ben III. *Conflict and Community in Corinth: A Socio-Rhetorical Commentary on 1 and 2 Corinthians*. Grand Rapids: Eerdmans, 1995.

———. *Grace in Galatia: A Commentary on St Paul's Letter to the Galatians*. Edinburgh: T. & T. Clark, 1998.

———. *The Paul Quest: The Renewed Search for the Jew of Tarsus*. Downers Grove, IL: InterVarsity, 1998.

———. *Paul's Letter to the Philippians: A Socio-Rhetorical Commentary*. Grand Rapids: Eerdmans, 2011.

Wong, Emily. "The Lord is the Spirit (2 Cor 3,17a)." *ETL* 61 (1985) 48–72.

Wortham, Robert A. "Christology and Community Identity in the Philippians Hymn: The Philippians Hymn as Social Drama (Philippians 2:5–11)." *PRSt* 23 (1996) 268–87.

Wright, N. T. *The Climax of the Covenant: Christ and the Law in Pauline Theology*. Minneapolis: Fortress, 1991.

———. *Jesus and the Victory of God*. COQG 2. Minneapolis: Fortress, 1996.

———. *The New Testament and the People of God*. COQG 1. Minneapolis: Fortress, 1992.

———. *Paul and the Faithfulness of God: Parts III and IV*. COQG 4. London: SPCK, 2013.

———. "Paul's Gospel and Caesar's Empire." In *Paul and Politics: Ekklesia, Israel Imperium Interpretations. Essays in Honor of Kristen Stendahl*, edited by Richard A. Horsley, 160–83. Harrisburg, PA: Trinity, 2000.

———. *The Resurrection of the Son of God*. COQG 3. London: SPCK, 2003.

———. *What Saint Paul Really Said: Was Paul of Tarsus the Real Founder of Christianity?* Grand Rapids: Eerdmans, 1997.

Wuellner, Wilhelm. "Greek Rhetoric and Pauline Argumentation." In *Early Christian Literature and the Classical Intellectual Tradition*, edited by William R. Schoedel and Robert L. Wilken, 177–88. Théologie historique 54. Paris: Beauchesne, 1979.

———. "Rhetorical Criticism." In *The Postmodern Bible: The Bible and Culture Collective*, edited by Elizabeth A. Castelli et al., 149–86. New Haven: Yale University Press, 1995.

Yates, John W. *The Spirit and Creation in Paul*. WUNT 2/251. Tübingen: Mohr/Siebeck, 2008.

Yoon, David I. "The Ideological Inception of Intertextuality and its Dissonance in Current Biblical Studies." *CBR* 12 (2013) 58–76.

Ancient Document Index

Galatians *(continued)*

4:14	57
4:19	71
4:21—5:1	159
4:21–31	49
4:27	41, 49n77
4:28	59
4:29	68
4:30	49n77
4:31	59
5:1	98, 168
5:4	71, 81
5:5	64
5:7–8	69
5:8	71
5:11	59, 68
5:13	58n129, 59, 71, 184
5:14	49n77
5:24	64
6:1	59
6:2	77
6:11–13	78
6:11	141
6:12	68, 78
6:14	64
6:18	59

Ephesians

1:1	24, 85n7
1:17	25n6, 61n146
3:1–13	24, 184
3:3	25n6, 61n146
3:5	25n7, 61n147
5:2	44
5:25	44

Philippians

1:1	28, 42, 58, 98, 134, 141, 158
1:5	130
1:6	125, 136, 166n139
1:7	30n42, 95n61, 115, 130
1:9–10	30
1:10	166n139
1:11	123, 135
1:14	125
1:15–18	63
1:16	95n61
1:19	65, 109, 115, 130, 169
1:20–23	131
1:20	123, 164n130
1:21	127
1:27	60, 117
1:28	117–18
1:29–30	127
1:29	123, 134
2	97
2:1–5	120
2:1–4	119
2:1	134
2:2	30, 30n42
2:3–4	120
2:3	120
2:4	120
2:5–11	146, 169
2:5	30, 30n42, 119–20, 127, 131, 134–35
2:6–11	45, 116–24, 116n7, 117n19, 129–30, 132, 136, 162
2:6–8	96, 127
2:6	131
2:7–9	44, 134
2:7–8	122, 132
2:7	121, 134, 175
2:8–9	130n84
2:9–11	121, 132
2:9	51, 122
2:10–11	122
2:11	121, 167n148
2:12–16	134
2:12	131
2:13	131
2:14–15	118
2:15–16	118
2:15	117
2:16	166n139
2:17	131, 133